Java Data Science Cookbook

Explore the power of MLlib, DL4j, Weka, and more

Rushdi Shams

BIRMINGHAM - MUMBAI

Java Data Science Cookbook

First published: March 2017

Production reference: 1240317

Published by Packt Publishing Ltd.
Livery Place
35 Livery Street
Birmingham
B3 2PB, UK.
ISBN 978-1-78712-253-6

www.packtpub.com

Credits

Author

Rushdi Shams

Reviewer

Prashant Verma

Commissioning Editor

Veena Pagare

Acquisition Editor

Ajith Menon

Content Development Editor

Cheryl Dsa

Technical Editor

Dharmendra Yadav

Copy Editors

Vikrant Phadke

Manisha Sinha

Project Coordinator

Nidhi Joshi

Proofreader

Safis Editing

Indexer

Aishwarya Gangawane

Graphics

Tania Dutta

Production Coordinator

Arvindkumar Gupta

About the Author

Rushdi Shams has a PhD on application of machine learning in Natural Language Processing (NLP) problem areas from Western University, Canada. Before starting work as a machine learning and NLP specialist in industry, he was engaged in teaching undergrad and grad courses. He has been successfully maintaining his YouTube channel named "Learn with Rushdi" for learning computer technologies.

I would like to acknowledge the Almighty Allah for giving me the strength, support, and knowledge to finish the book.

I extend my thanks to my family members, friends, and colleagues for continuous support, encouragement, and constructive criticism.

I would also like to thank Ajith and Cheryl from Packt for their continuous and spontaneous collaboration with me.

About the Reviewer

Prashant Verma started his IT career in 2011 as a Java developer at Ericsson, working in the telecom domain. After a couple of years of Java EE experience, he moved into the big data domain, and has worked on almost all the popular big data technologies such as Hadoop, Spark, Kafka, Flume, Mongo, Cassandra, and so on. He has also worked in Scala and Python. Currently, he works with QA Infotech as Lead Data Engineer, working on solving e-learning domain problems using data analytics and machine learning.

Prashant has also worked on *Apache Spark for Java Developers*, Packt as a Technical Reviewer.

I want to thank Packt Publishing for giving me the chance to review the book, as well as my employer and my family for their patience while I was busy working on this book.

www.PacktPub.com

For support files and downloads related to your book, please visit www.PacktPub.com.

Did you know that Packt offers eBook versions of every book published, with PDF and ePub files available? You can upgrade to the eBook version at www.PacktPub.com and as a print book customer, you are entitled to a discount on the eBook copy. Get in touch with us at service@packtpub.com for more details.

At www.PacktPub.com, you can also read a collection of free technical articles, sign up for a range of free newsletters and receive exclusive discounts and offers on Packt books and eBooks.

https://www.packtpub.com/mapt

Get the most in-demand software skills with Mapt. Mapt gives you full access to all Packt books and video courses, as well as industry-leading tools to help you plan your personal development and advance your career.

Why subscribe?

- Fully searchable across every book published by Packt
- Copy and paste, print, and bookmark content
- On demand and accessible via a web browser

Customer Feedback

Thanks for purchasing this Packt book. At Packt, quality is at the heart of our editorial process. To help us improve, please leave us an honest review on this book's Amazon page at https://www.amazon.com/dp/1787122530.

If you'd like to join our team of regular reviewers, you can e-mail us at customerreviews@packtpub.com. We award our regular reviewers with free eBooks and videos in exchange for their valuable feedback. Help us be relentless in improving our products!

To my lovely wife, Mah-Zereen, and adorable daughter, Ruayda.

Table of Contents

Preface

Data science is a popular field for specialization nowadays and covers the broad spectrum of artificial intelligence, such as data processing, information retrieval, machine learning, natural language processing, big data, deep neural networks, and data visualization. In this book, we will understand the techniques that are both modern and smart and presented as easy-to-follow recipes for over 70 problems.

Keeping in mind the high demand for quality data scientists, we have compiled recipes using core Java as well as well-known, classic, and state-of-the-art data science libraries written in Java. We start with the data collection and cleaning process. Then we see how the obtained data can be indexed and searched. Afterwards, we cover statistics both descriptive and inferential and their application to data. Then, we have two back-to-back chapters on the application of machine learning on data that can be foundation for building any smart system. Modern information retrieval and natural language processing techniques are also covered. Big data is an emerging field, and a few aspects of this popular field are also covered. We also cover the very basics of deep learning using deep neural networks. Finally, we learn how to represent data and information obtained from data using meaningful visuals or graphs.

The book is aimed at anyone who has an interest in data science and plans to apply data science using Java to understand underlying data better.

What this book covers

Chapter 1, *Obtaining and Cleaning Data*, covers different ways to read and write data as well as to clean it to get rid of noise. It also familiarizes the readers with different data file types, such as PDF, ASCII, CSV, TSV, XML, and JSON. The chapter also covers recipes for extracting web data.

Chapter 2, *Indexing and Searching Data*, covers how to index data for fast searching using Apache Lucene. The techniques described in this chapter can be seen as the basis for modern-day search techniques.

Chapter 3, *Analyzing Data Statistically*, covers the application of Apache Math API to collect and analyze statistics from data. The chapter also covers higher level concepts such as the statistical significance test, which is the standard tool for researchers when they compare their results with benchmarks.

Chapter 4, *Learning from Data - Part 1*, covers basic classification, clustering, and feature selection exercises using the Weka machine learning Workbench.

Chapter 5, *Learning from Data - Part 2*, is a follow-up chapter that covers data import and export, classification, and feature selection using another Java library named the Java Machine Learning (Java-ML) Library. The chapter also covers basic classification with the Stanford Classifier and Massive Online Access (MOA).

Chapter 6, *Retrieving Information from Text Data*, covers the application of data science to text data for information retrieval. It covers the application of core Java as well as popular libraries such as OpenNLP, Stanford CoreNLP, Mallet, and Weka for the application of machine learning to information extraction and retrieval tasks.

Chapter 7, *Handling Big Data*, covers the application of big data platforms for machine learning, such as Apache Mahout and Spark-MLib.

Chapter 8, *Learn Deeply from Data*, covers the very basics of deep learning using the Deep Learning for Java (DL4j) library. We cover the word2vec algorithm, belief networks, and auto-encoders.

Chapter 9, *Visualizing Data*, covers the GRAL package to generate an appealing and informative display based on data. Among the many functionalities of the package, fundamental and basic plots have been selected.

What you need for this book

We have used Java to solve real-world data science problems. Our focus was to deliver content that can be effective for anyone who wants to know how to solve problems with Java. A minimum knowledge of Java is required, such as classes, objects, methods, arguments and parameters, exceptions, and exporting Java Archive (JAR) files. The code is well supported with narrations, information, and tips to help the readers understand the context and purpose. The theories behind the problems solved in this book, on many occasions, are not thoroughly discussed, but references for interested readers are provided whenever necessary.

Who this book is for

The book is for anyone who wants to know how to solve real-world problems related to data science using Java. The book, as it is very comprehensive in terms of coverage, can also be very useful for practitioners already engaged with data science and looking for solving issues in their projects using Java.

Sections

In this book, you will find several headings that appear frequently (Getting ready, How to do it..., How it works..., There's more..., and See also).

To give clear instructions on how to complete a recipe, we use these sections as follows:

Getting ready

This section tells you what to expect in the recipe, and describes how to set up any software or any preliminary settings required for the recipe.

How to do it...

This section contains the steps required to follow the recipe.

How it works...

This section usually consists of a detailed explanation of what happened in the previous section.

There's more...

This section consists of additional information about the recipe in order to make the reader more knowledgeable about the recipe.

See also

This section provides helpful links to other useful information for the recipe.

Conventions

In this book, you will find a number of text styles that distinguish between different kinds of information. Here are some examples of these styles and an explanation of their meaning.

Code words in text, database table names, folder names, filenames, file extensions, pathnames, dummy URLs, user input, and Twitter handles are shown as follows: "Among them, you will find a folder named `lib`, which is the folder of interest."

A block of code is set as follows:

```
classVals = new ArrayList<String>();
  for (int i = 0; i < 5; i++){
    classVals.add("class" + (i + 1));
}
```

Any command-line input or output is written as follows:

```
@relation MyRelation

@attribute age numeric
@attribute name string
@attribute dob date yyyy-MM-dd
@attribute class {class1,class2,class3,class4,class5}

@data
35,'John Doe',1981-01-20,class3
30,'Harry Potter',1986-07-05,class1
```

New terms and **important words** are shown in bold. Words that you see on the screen, for example, in menus or dialog boxes, appear in the text like this: "Select **System info** from the **Administration** panel."

Warnings or important notes appear in a box like this.

Tips and tricks appear like this.

Reader feedback

Feedback from our readers is always welcome. Let us know what you think about this book-what you liked or disliked. Reader feedback is important for us as it helps us develop titles that you will really get the most out of.

To send us general feedback, simply e-mail feedback@packtpub.com, and mention the book's title in the subject of your message.

If there is a topic that you have expertise in and you are interested in either writing or contributing to a book, see our author guide at www.packtpub.com/authors.

Customer support

Now that you are the proud owner of a Packt book, we have a number of things to help you to get the most from your purchase.

Downloading the example code

You can download the example code files for this book from your account at http://www.packtpub.com. If you purchased this book elsewhere, you can visit http://www.packtpub.com/support and register to have the files e-mailed directly to you.

You can download the code files by following these steps:

1. Log in or register to our website using your e-mail address and password.
2. Hover the mouse pointer on the **SUPPORT** tab at the top.
3. Click on **Code Downloads & Errata**.
4. Enter the name of the book in the **Search** box.
5. Select the book for which you're looking to download the code files.
6. Choose from the drop-down menu where you purchased this book from.
7. Click on **Code Download**.

You can also download the code files by clicking on the **Code Files** button on the book's webpage at the Packt Publishing website. This page can be accessed by entering the book's name in the **Search** box. Please note that you need to be logged in to your Packt account.

Once the file is downloaded, please make sure that you unzip or extract the folder using the latest version of:

- WinRAR / 7-Zip for Windows
- Zipeg / iZip / UnRarX for Mac
- 7-Zip / PeaZip for Linux

The code bundle for the book is also hosted on GitHub at `https://github.com/PacktPublishing/Java-Data-Science-Cookbook`. We also have other code bundles from our rich catalog of books and videos available at `https://github.com/PacktPublishing/`. Check them out!

Downloading the color images of this book

We also provide you with a PDF file that has color images of the screenshots/diagrams used in this book. The color images will help you better understand the changes in the output. You can download this file from `https://www.packtpub.com/sites/default/files/downloads/JavaDataScienceCookbook_ColorImages.pdf`.

Errata

Although we have taken every care to ensure the accuracy of our content, mistakes do happen. If you find a mistake in one of our books-maybe a mistake in the text or the code-we would be grateful if you could report this to us. By doing so, you can save other readers from frustration and help us improve subsequent versions of this book. If you find any errata, please report them by visiting `http://www.packtpub.com/submit-errata`, selecting your book, clicking on the **Errata Submission Form** link, and entering the details of your errata. Once your errata are verified, your submission will be accepted and the errata will be uploaded to our website or added to any list of existing errata under the Errata section of that title.

To view the previously submitted errata, go to `https://www.packtpub.com/books/content/support`and enter the name of the book in the search field. The required information will appear under the **Errata** section.

Piracy

Piracy of copyrighted material on the Internet is an ongoing problem across all media. At Packt, we take the protection of our copyright and licenses very seriously. If you come across any illegal copies of our works in any form on the Internet, please provide us with the location address or website name immediately so that we can pursue a remedy.

Please contact us at copyright@packtpub.com with a link to the suspected pirated material.

We appreciate your help in protecting our authors and our ability to bring you valuable content.

Questions

If you have a problem with any aspect of this book, you can contact us at questions@packtpub.com, and we will do our best to address the problem.

1
Obtaining and Cleaning Data

In this chapter, we will cover the following recipes:

- Retrieving all file names from hierarchical directories using Java
- Retrieving all file names from hierarchical directories using Apache Commons IO
- Reading contents from text files all at once using Java 8
- Reading contents from text files all at once using Apache Commons IO
- Extracting PDF text using Apache Tika
- Cleaning ASCII text files using Regular Expressions
- Parsing Comma Separated Value files using Univocity
- Parsing Tab Separated Value files using Univocity
- Parsing XML files using JDOM
- Writing JSON files using JSON.simple
- Reading JSON files using JSON.simple
- Extracting web data from a URL using JSoup
- Extracting web data from a website using Selenium `Webdriver`
- Reading table data from MySQL database

Introduction

Every data scientist needs to deal with data that is stored on disks in several formats, such as ASCII text, PDF, XML, JSON, and so on. Also, data can be stored in database tables. The first and foremost task for a data scientist before doing any analysis is to obtain data from these data sources and of these formats, and apply data-cleaning techniques to get rid of noises present in them. In this chapter, we will see recipes to accomplish this important task.

We will be using external Java libraries (Java archive files or simply JAR files) not only for this chapter but throughout the book. These libraries are created by developers or organizations to make everybody's life easier. We will be using Eclipse IDE for code development, preferably on the Windows platform, and execution throughout the book. Here is how you can include any external JAR file, and in many recipes, where I instruct you to include external JAR files into your project, this is what you need to do.

You can add a JAR file in a project in Eclipse by right-clicking on the **Project** | **Build Path** | **Configure Build Path**. Under the **Libraries** tab, click on **Add External JARs...**, and select the external JAR file(s) that you are going to use for a particular project:

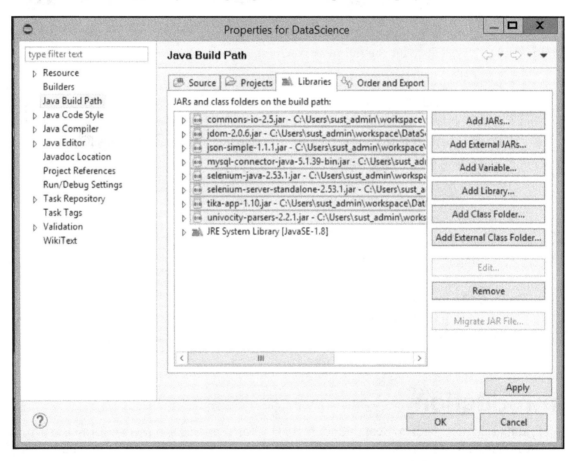

Retrieving all filenames from hierarchical directories using Java

This recipe (and the following) is for the data scientist who wants to retrieve the file paths and names (for some future analysis) from a complex directory structure that contains numerous directories and files inside a root directory.

Getting ready

In order to perform this recipe, we will require the following:

1. Create directories within directories (as many layers as you want).
2. Create text files in some of these directories while leaving some directories empty for more excitement.

How to do it...

1. We are going to create a `static` method that takes a `File` argument, which is eventually the root directory or the directory to start with. The method will return a set of files that are found within this root directory (and in all other subsequent directories):

   ```
   public static Set<File> listFiles(File rootDir) {
   ```

2. First, create a `HashSet` that will contain the file information:

   ```
   Set<File> fileSet = new HashSet<File>();
   ```

3. Once the `HashSet` is created, we need to check whether the root directory or the directories within it are `null`. For such cases, we do not need to proceed further:

   ```
   if (rootDir == null || rootDir.listFiles() == null){
           return fileSet;
   }
   ```

4. We consider one directory (or file) from the root directory at a time and check whether we are dealing with a file or with a directory. In the case of a file, we add that to our `HashSet`. In the case of a directory, we recursively call this method again by sending the path and name of the directory:

```java
for (File fileOrDir : rootDir.listFiles()) {
            if (fileOrDir.isFile()){
               fileSet.add(fileOrDir);
            }
            else{
               fileSet.addAll(listFiles(fileOrDir));
            }
        }
```

5. Finally, we return the `HashSet` to the caller of this method:

```java
        return fileSet;
            }
```

The complete method, with the class and the driver method to run it, is as follows:

```java
import java.io.File;
import java.util.HashSet;
import java.util.Set;

public class TestRecursiveDirectoryTraversal {
    public static void main(String[] args){
        System.out.println(listFiles(new File("Path for root
            directory")).size());
    }
    public static Set<File> listFiles(File rootDir) {
        Set<File> fileSet = new HashSet<File>();
        if(rootDir == null || rootDir.listFiles()==null){
            return fileSet;
        }
        for (File fileOrDir : rootDir.listFiles()) {
            if (fileOrDir.isFile()){
               fileSet.add(fileOrDir);
            }
            else{
               fileSet.addAll(listFiles(fileOrDir));
            }
        }

        return fileSet;
    }
}
```

Note the use of `HashSet` to store the paths and names of the files. This means that we will not have any duplicates since the `Set` data structures in Java do not contain duplicate entries.

Retrieving all filenames from hierarchical directories using Apache Commons IO

Listing of file names in hierarchical directories can be done recursively as demonstrated in the previous recipe. However, this can be done in a much easier and convenient way and with less coding using the Apache Commons IO library.

Getting ready

In order to perform this recipe, we will require the following:

1. In this recipe, we will be using a Java library from Apache named Commons IO. Throughout the book, we will be using version 2.5. Download the JAR file of your choice from here:
   `https://commons.apache.org/proper/commons-io/download_io.cgi`
2. Include the JAR file in your project an external JAR in Eclipse.

How to do it...

1. Create a method that takes the root directory in the hierarchy of directories as input:

   ```
   public void listFiles(String rootDir){
   ```

2. Create a file object with the root directory name:

   ```
   File dir = new File(rootDir);
   ```

3. The `FileUtils` class of the Apache Commons library contains a method named `listFiles()`. Use this method to retrieve all the file names, and put the names in a list variable with `<File>` generics. Use `TrueFileFilter.INSTANCE` to match all directories:

```
List<File> files = (List<File>) FileUtils.listFiles(dir,
    TrueFileFilter.INSTANCE, TrueFileFilter.INSTANCE);
```

4. The file names can be displayed on the standard output as follows. As we now have the names in a list, we have a means to process the data in these files further:

```
for (File file : files) {
    System.out.println("file: " + file.getAbsolutePath());
}
```

5. Close the method:

```
}
```

The method in this recipe, the class for it, and the driver method to run it are as follows:

```java
import java.io.File;
import java.util.List;
import org.apache.commons.io.FileUtils;
import org.apache.commons.io.filefilter.TrueFileFilter;

public class FileListing{
    public static void main (String[] args){
        FileListing fileListing = new FileListing();
        fileListing.listFiles("Path for the root directory here");
    }
    public void listFiles(String rootDir){
        File dir = new File(rootDir);

        List<File> files = (List<File>) FileUtils.listFiles(dir,
            TrueFileFilter.INSTANCE, TrueFileFilter.INSTANCE);
        for (File file : files) {
            System.out.println("file: " + file.getAbsolutePath());
        }
    }
}
```

If you want to list files with some particular extensions, there is a method in Apache Commons library called `listFiles`, too. However, the parameters are different; the method takes three parameters, namely, file directory, `String[]` extensions, boolean recursive. Another interesting method in this library is listFilesAndDirs (File directory, IOFileFilter fileFilter, IOFileFilter dirFilter) if someone is interested in listing not only files but also directories. Detailed information can be found at `https://co mmons.apache.org/proper/commons-io/javadocs/`.

Reading contents from text files all at once using Java 8

On many occasions, data scientists have their data in text format. There are many different ways to read text file contents, and they each have their own pros and cons: some of them consume time and memory, while some are fast and do not require much computer memory; some read the text contents all at once, while some read text files line by line. The choice depends on the task at hand and a data scientist's approach to that task.

This recipe demonstrates how to read text file contents all at once using Java 8.

How to do it...

1. First, create a `String` object to hold the path and name of the text file you are going to read:

   ```
   String file = "C:/dummy.txt";
   ```

2. Using the `get()` method of the `Paths` class, we get to the path of the file we are trying to read. The parameter for this method is the `String` object that points to the name of the file. The output of this method is fed to another method named `lines()`, which is in the `Files` class. This method reads all lines from a file as a `Stream`, and therefore, the output of this method is directed to a `Stream` variable. Because our `dummy.txt` file contains string data, the generics of the `Stream` variable is set to `String`.

The entire process of reading needs a `try...catch` block for attempts such as reading a file that does not exist or damaged and so on.

The following code segment displays the contents of our `dummy.txt` file. The `stream` variable contains the lines of the text file, and therefore, the `forEach()` method of the variable is used to display each line content:

```
try (Stream<String> stream = Files.lines(Paths.get(file))) {
stream.forEach(System.out::println); } catch (IOException e) {
System.out.println("Error reading " + file.getAbsolutePath());
}
```

Reading contents from text files all at once using Apache Commons IO

The same functionality described in the previous recipe can be achieved using Apache Commons IO API.

Getting ready

In order to perform this recipe, we will require the following:

1. In this recipe, we will be using a Java library from Apache named Commons IO. Download the version of your choice from here:
   https://commons.apache.org/proper/commons-io/download_io.cgi
2. Include the JAR file in your project an external JAR in Eclipse.

How to do it...

1. Say, you are trying to read the contents of a file located in your `C:/ drive` named `dummy.txt`. First, you need to create a file object for accessing this file as follows:

```
File file = new File("C:/dummy.txt");
```

2. Next, create a string object to hold the text contents of your file. The method we will be using from Apache Commons IO library is called `readFileToString`, which is a member of the class named `FileUtils`. There are many different ways you can call this method. But for now, just know that we need to send two arguments to this method. First, the `file` object, which is the file we will be reading, and then the encoding of the file, which in this example is `UTF-8`:

```
String text = FileUtils.readFileToString(file, "UTF-8");
```

3. The preceding two lines will be enough to read text file content and put that in a variable. However, you are not only a data scientist, you are a smart data scientist. Therefore, you need to add a few lines before and after the code just to handle exceptions thrown by Java methods if you try to read a file that does not exist, or is corrupted, and so on. The completeness of the preceding code can be achieved by introducing a `try...catch` block as follows:

```
File file = new File("C:/dummy.txt");
try {
String text = FileUtils.readFileToString(file, "UTF-8");
} catch (IOException e) {
System.out.println("Error reading " + file.getAbsolutePath());
}
```

Extracting PDF text using Apache Tika

One of the most difficult file types for parsing and extracting data is PDF. Some PDFs are not even possible to parse because they are password-protected, while some others contain scanned texts and images. This dynamic file type, therefore, sometimes becomes the worst nightmare for data scientists. This recipe demonstrates how to extract text from PDF files using Apache Tika, given that the file is not encrypted or password-protected and contains text that is not scanned.

Getting ready

In order to perform this recipe we will require the following:

1. Download Apache Tika 1.10 JAR file from `http://archive.apache.org/dist/t` `ika/tika-app-1.10.jar`, and include it in your Eclipse project as an external Java library.
2. Have any unlocked PDF file saved as `testPDF.pdf` on your `C: drive`.

How to do it...

1. Create a method named `convertPdf(String)`, which takes the name of the PDF file to be converted as parameter:

   ```
   public void convertPDF(String fileName){
   ```

2. Create an input stream that will contain the PDF data as a stream of bytes:

   ```
   InputStream stream = null;
   ```

3. Create a `try` block as follows:

   ```
   try{
   ```

4. Assign the file to the `stream` you have just created:

   ```
   stream = new FileInputStream(fileName);
   ```

5. There are many different parsers offered in the Apache Tika package. If you do not know which parser you are going to use, or say you have not only PDFs but also other types of documents to get converted, you should use an `AutoDetectParser` as follows:

   ```
   AutoDetectParser parser = new AutoDetectParser();
   ```

6. Create a handler to handle the body content of the file. Note the −1 as the parameter of the constructor. Usually, Apache Tika is limited to handling files with at most 100,000 characters. The −1 value ensures that this limitation is overlooked by the body handler:

   ```
   BodyContentHandler handler = new BodyContentHandler(-1);
   ```

7. Create a metadata object:

```
Metadata metadata = new Metadata();
```

8. Call the `parser()` method of the parser object with all these objects you just created:

```
parser.parse(stream, handler, metadata, new ParseContext());
```

9. Use the `tostring()` method of the handler object to get the body text extracted from the file:

```
System.out.println(handler.toString());
```

10. Close the `try` block and complement it with a `catch` block and `finally` block, and close the method as follows:

```
}catch (Exception e) {
            e.printStackTrace();
        }finally {
            if (stream != null)
                try {
                    stream.close();
                } catch (IOException e) {
                    System.out.println("Error closing stream");
                }
        }
    }
```

The full method with the driver method in a class will be as follows. The method you have just created can be called by sending it the path and the name of the PDF file you need to convert, which is in your C: drive saved as `testPDF.pdf`:

```
import java.io.FileInputStream;
import java.io.IOException;
import java.io.InputStream;
import org.apache.tika.metadata.Metadata;
import org.apache.tika.parser.AutoDetectParser;
import org.apache.tika.parser.ParseContext;
import org.apache.tika.sax.BodyContentHandler;

public class TestTika {
    public static void main(String args[]) throws Exception {
        TestTika tika = new TestTika();
        tika.convertPdf("C:/testPDF.pdf");
    }
    public void convertPdf(String fileName){
```

```
InputStream stream = null;
try {
    stream = new FileInputStream(fileName);
    AutoDetectParser parser = new AutoDetectParser();
    BodyContentHandler handler = new BodyContentHandler(-1);
    Metadata metadata = new Metadata();
    parser.parse(stream, handler, metadata, new
        ParseContext());
    System.out.println(handler.toString());
}catch (Exception e) {
    e.printStackTrace();
}finally {
    if (stream != null)
        try {
            stream.close();
        } catch (IOException e) {
            System.out.println("Error closing stream");
        }
    }
}
}
```

Cleaning ASCII text files using Regular Expressions

ASCII text files can contain unnecessary units of characters that eventually are introduced during a conversion process, such as PDF-to-text conversion or HTML-to-text conversion. These characters are often seen as noise because they are one of the major roadblocks for data processing. This recipe cleans several noises from ASCII text data using Regular Expressions.

How to do it...

1. Create a method named `cleanText(String)` that takes the text to be cleaned in the `String` format:

   ```
   public String cleanText(String text){
   ```

2. Add the following lines in your method, return the cleaned text, and close the method. The first line strips off non-ASCII characters. The line next to it replaces continuous white spaces with a single white space. The third line erases all the ASCII control characters. The fourth line strips off the ASCII non-printable characters. The last line removes non-printable characters from Unicode:

```
text = text.replaceAll("[^p{ASCII}]","");
text = text.replaceAll("s+", " ");
text = text.replaceAll("p{Cntrl}", "");
text = text.replaceAll("[^p{Print}]", "");
text = text.replaceAll("p{C}", "");

return text;
}
```

The full method with the driver method in a class will look as follows:

```
public class CleaningData {
    public static void main(String[] args) throws Exception {
        CleaningData clean = new CleaningData();
        String text = "Your text here you have got from some file";
        String cleanedText = clean.cleanText(text);
        //Process cleanedText
    }
    public String cleanText(String text){
        text = text.replaceAll("[^p{ASCII}]","");
        text = text.replaceAll("s+", " ");
        text = text.replaceAll("p{Cntrl}", "");
        text = text.replaceAll("[^p{Print}]", "");
        text = text.replaceAll("p{C}", "");
        return text;
    }
}
```

Parsing Comma Separated Value (CSV) Files using Univocity

Another very common file type that data scientists handle is **Comma Separated Value (CSV)** files, where data is separated by commas. CSV files are very popular because they can be read by most of the spreadsheet applications, such as MS Excel.

In this recipe, we will see how we can parse CSV files and handle data points retrieved from them.

Getting ready

In order to perform this recipe, we will require the following:

1. Download the Univocity JAR file from `http://oss.sonatype.org/content/repositories/releases/com/univocity/univocity-parsers/2.2.1/univocity-parsers-2.2.1.jar`. Include the JAR file in your project in Eclipse as external library.

2. Create a CSV file from the following data using Notepad. The extension of the file should be `.csv`. You save the file as `C:/testCSV.csv`:

   ```
   Year,Make,Model,Description,Price
   1997,Ford,E350,"ac, abs, moon",3000.00
   1999,Chevy,"Venture ""Extended Edition""","",4900.00
   1996,Jeep,Grand Cherokee,"MUST SELL!
   air, moon roof, loaded",4799.00
   1999,Chevy,"Venture ""Extended Edition, Very Large""",,5000.00
   ,,"Venture ""Extended Edition""","",4900.00
   ```

How to do it…

1. Create a method named `parseCsv(String)` that takes the name of the file as a String argument:

   ```
   public void parseCsv(String fileName){
   ```

2. Then create a settings object. This object provides many configuration settings options:

   ```
   CsvParserSettings parserSettings = new CsvParserSettings();
   ```

3. You can configure the parser to automatically detect what line separator sequence is in the input:

   ```
   parserSettings.setLineSeparatorDetectionEnabled(true);
   ```

4. Create a `RowListProcessor` that stores each parsed row in a list:

   ```
   RowListProcessor rowProcessor = new RowListProcessor();
   ```

5. You can configure the parser to use a `RowProcessor` to process the values of each parsed row. You will find more `RowProcessors` in the `com.univocity.parsers.common.processor` package, but you can also create your own:

   ```
   parserSettings.setRowProcessor(rowProcessor);
   ```

6. If the CSV file that you are going to parse contains headers, you can consider the first parsed row as the headers of each column in the file:

   ```
   parserSettings.setHeaderExtractionEnabled(true);
   ```

7. Now, create a `parser` instance with the given settings:

   ```
   CsvParser parser = new CsvParser(parserSettings);
   ```

8. The `parse()` method will parse the file and delegate each parsed row to the `RowProcessor` you defined:

   ```
   parser.parse(new File(fileName));
   ```

9. If you have parsed the headers, the `headers` can be found as follows:

   ```
   String[] headers = rowProcessor.getHeaders();
   ```

10. You can then easily process this String array to get the header values.

11. On the other hand, the row values can be found in a list. The list can be printed using a for loop as follows:

    ```
    List<String[]> rows = rowProcessor.getRows();
    for (int i = 0; i < rows.size(); i++){
        System.out.println(Arrays.asList(rows.get(i)));
    }
    ```

12. Finally, close the method:

    ```
    }
    ```

The entire method can be written as follows:

```
import java.io.File;
import java.util.Arrays;
import java.util.List;

import com.univocity.parsers.common.processor.RowListProcessor;
import com.univocity.parsers.csv.CsvParser;
import com.univocity.parsers.csv.CsvParserSettings;

public class TestUnivocity {
    public void parseCSV(String fileName){
        CsvParserSettings parserSettings = new CsvParserSettings();
        parserSettings.setLineSeparatorDetectionEnabled(true);
        RowListProcessor rowProcessor = new RowListProcessor();
        parserSettings.setRowProcessor(rowProcessor);
        parserSettings.setHeaderExtractionEnabled(true);
        CsvParser parser = new CsvParser(parserSettings);
        parser.parse(new File(fileName));

        String[] headers = rowProcessor.getHeaders();
        List<String[]> rows = rowProcessor.getRows();
        for (int i = 0; i < rows.size(); i++){
            System.out.println(Arrays.asList(rows.get(i)));
        }
    }
    public static void main(String[] args){
        TestUnivocity test = new TestUnivocity();
        test.parseCSV("C:/testCSV.csv");
    }
}
```

 There are many CSV parsers that are written in Java. However, in a comparison, Univocity is found to be the fastest one. See the detailed comparison results here: https://github.com/uniVocity/csv-parsers-comparison

Parsing Tab Separated Value (TSV) file using Univocity

Unlike CSV files, **Tab Separated Value (TSV)** files contain data that is separated by tab delimiters. This recipe shows you how to retrieve data points from TSV files.

Getting ready

In order to perform this recipe, we will require the following:

1. Download the Univocity JAR file from
   `http://oss.sonatype.org/content/repositories/releases/com/univocity/un`
   `ivocity-parsers/2.2.1/univocity-parsers-2.2.1.jar`. Include the JAR file in
   your project in Eclipse an external library.

2. Create a TSV file from the following data using Notepad. The extension of the file
   should be `.tsv`. You save the file as `C:/testTSV.tsv`:

```
Year    Make    Model    Description Price
1997    Ford    E350     ac, abs, moon    3000.00
1999    Chevy   Venture  "Extended Edition"        4900.00
1996    Jeep    Grand Cherokee  MUST SELL!nair, moon roof, loaded  4799.00
1999    Chevy   Venture  "Extended Edition, Very Large"        5000.00
        Venture "Extended Edition"        4900.00
```

How to do it...

1. Create a method named `parseTsv(String)` that takes the name of the file as a
   String argument:

   ```
   public void parseTsv(String fileName){
   ```

2. The line separator for the TSV file in this recipe is a newline character or `n`. To set
   this character as the line separator, modify the settings:

   ```
   settings.getFormat().setLineSeparator("n");
   ```

3. Using these settings, create a TSV parser:

   ```
   TsvParser parser = new TsvParser(settings);
   ```

4. Parse all rows of the TSV file at once as follows:

   ```
   List<String[]> allRows = parser.parseAll(new File(fileName));
   ```

5. Iterate over the list object to print/process the rows as follows:

```
for (int i = 0; i < allRows.size(); i++){
       System.out.println(Arrays.asList(allRows.get(i)));
    }
```

6. Finally, close the method:

```
    }
```

The full method with the driver method in a class will look like the following:

```
import java.io.File;
import java.util.Arrays;
import java.util.List;

import com.univocity.parsers.tsv.TsvParser;
import com.univocity.parsers.tsv.TsvParserSettings;

public class TestTsv {
   public void parseTsv(String fileName){
       TsvParserSettings settings = new TsvParserSettings();
       settings.getFormat().setLineSeparator("n");
       TsvParser parser = new TsvParser(settings);
       List<String[]> allRows = parser.parseAll(new File(fileName));
       for (int i = 0; i < allRows.size(); i++){
         System.out.println(Arrays.asList(allRows.get(i)));
       }
   }
}
```

Parsing XML files using JDOM

Unlike text data, which is often unstructured, organizing data in XML files is a popular method to prepare, convey, and exploit data in a structured way. There are several ways to parse contents of XML files. In this book, we will limit our recipes to an external Java library for XML parsing named JDOM.

Getting ready

In order to perform this recipe, we will require the following:

1. Download version 2.06 of the JAR file for JDOM from `http://www.jdom.org/dow nloads/index.html`.
2. In Eclipse, create a project and include the JAR file an external JAR.
3. Open up notepad. Create a new file named `xmldummy` with the `.xml` extension. The content of the file will be as simple as follows:

```xml
<?xml version="1.0"?>
<book>
    <author>
        <firstname>Alice</firstname>
        <lastname>Peterson</lastname>
    </author>
    <author>
        <firstname>John</firstname>
        <lastname>Doe</lastname>
    </author>
</book>
```

How to do it...

1. Create a `SAXBuilder` object named `builder`:

```java
SAXBuilder builder = new SAXBuilder();
```

2. Now you need to create a `File` object to point to the XML file that you will be parsing. If you have saved your XML file in the `C:/` drive, then type in the following code segment:

```java
File file = new File("c:/dummyxml.xml");
```

3. In a `try` block, you are going to create a `Document` object, which will be your XML file:

```java
try {
    Document document = (Document) builder.build(file);
```

4. When you are parsing an XML, as it is tree structured, you need to know the root element of the file to start traversing the tree (in other words, to start parsing systematically). So, you are creating a `rootNode` object of type `Element` to hold the root element, which in our example is <book> node:

```
Element rootNode = document.getRootElement();
```

5. Then, you will be retrieving all the children nodes of your root node that have the name `author`. The names come as a list, and therefore, you will be using a list variable to hold them:

```
List list = rootNode.getChildren("author");
```

6. Next, you will be iterating over this list using a `for` loop to get the elements of the entries in this list. Each element will be kept in an `Element` type variable named node. This variable has a method named `getChildText()`, which takes the name of its child as parameter; the method returns the textual content of the named child element, or `null` if there is no such child. This method is convenient because calling `getChild().getText()` can throw a `NullPointerException`:

```
for (int i = 0; i < list.size(); i++) {
    Element node = (Element) list.get(i);
System.out.println("First Name : " +
  node.getChildText("firstname"));
System.out.println("Last Name : " +
  node.getChildText("lastname"));
}
```

7. Finally, you will be closing the `try` block; put the following `catch` blocks to handle exceptions:

```
} catch (IOException io) {
    System.out.println(io.getMessage());
} catch (JDOMException jdomex) {
    System.out.println(jdomex.getMessage());
}
```

The complete code for the recipe is as follows:

```
import java.io.File;
import java.io.IOException;
import java.util.List;

import org.jdom2.Document;
import org.jdom2.Element;
```

```java
import org.jdom2.JDOMException;
import org.jdom2.input.SAXBuilder;

public class TestJdom {

    public static void main(String[] args){
        TestJdom test = new TestJdom();
        test.parseXml("C:/dummyxml.com");

    }
    public void parseXml(String fileName){
        SAXBuilder builder = new SAXBuilder();
        File file = new File(fileName);
        try {
            Document document = (Document) builder.build(file);
            Element rootNode = document.getRootElement();
            List list = rootNode.getChildren("author");
            for (int i = 0; i < list.size(); i++) {
                Element node = (Element) list.get(i);
                System.out.println("First Name : " +
                    node.getChildText("firstname"));
                System.out.println("Last Name : " +
                    node.getChildText("lastname"));
            }
        } catch (IOException io) {
            System.out.println(io.getMessage());
        } catch (JDOMException jdomex) {
            System.out.println(jdomex.getMessage());
        }
    }
}
```

There are many different types of XML parsers, and each has its own benefits **Dom Parser**: These parsers load the complete content of the document in memory and create its complete hierarchical tree in memory. **SAX Parser**: These parsers do not load the complete document into the memory and parse the documents on event-based triggers. **JDOM Parser**: JDOM parsers parse the document in a similar fashion to DOM parser but in a more convenient way. **StAX Parser**: These parsers handle the document in a similar fashion to SAX parser but in a more efficient way. **XPath Parser**: These parsers parse the document based on expressions and are used extensively with XSLT. **DOM4J Parser**: This is a Java library to parse XML, XPath, and XSLT using Java Collections Framework that provides support for DOM, SAX, and JAXP.

Writing JSON files using JSON.simple

Just like XML, JSON is also a human-readable Data Interchange Format that is lightweight. It stands for JavaScript Object Notation. This is becoming a popular format generated and parsed by modern web applications. In this recipe, you will see how you can write JSON files.

Getting ready

In order to perform this recipe, we will require the following:

1. Download `json-simple-1.1.1.jar` from `https://code.google.com/archive/p/json-simple/downloads` and include the JAR file as external library to your Eclipse project.

How to do it...

1. Create a method named `writeJson(String outFileName)` that takes the name of the JSON file we will be generating as output with the JSON information in this recipe.
2. Create a JSON object and use the object's `put()` method to populate a few fields. For instance, say your fields will be books and their authors. The following code will be creating a JSON object and populate a book name from the Harry Potter series and its author's name:

```
JSONObject obj = new JSONObject();
    obj.put("book", "Harry Potter and the Philosopher's Stone");
    obj.put("author", "J. K. Rowling");
```

3. Next, say that we have three reviewer comments for this book. They can be put together in a JSON array. The array can be populated as follows. First, we use `add()` of the array object to add the reviews. When all the reviews are added to the array, we will be putting the array to the JSON object we created in the previous step:

```
JSONArray list = new JSONArray();

list.add("There are characters in this book that will remind us of all the
people we have met. Everybody knows or knew a spoilt, overweight boy like
Dudley or a bossy and interfering (yet kind-hearted) girl like Hermione");
```

```
list.add("Hogwarts is a truly magical place, not only in the most obvious
way but also in all the detail that the author has gone to describe it so
vibrantly.");

list.add("Parents need to know that this thrill-a-minute story, the first
in the Harry Potter series, respects kids' intelligence and motivates them
to tackle its greater length and complexity, play imaginative games, and
try to solve its logic puzzles. ");

obj.put("messages", list);
```

4. We will be writing down the information in the JSON object to an output file because this file will be used to demonstrate how we can read/parse a JSON file. The following `try...catch` code blocks write down the information to a JSON file:

```
try {

        FileWriter file = new FileWriter("c:test.json");
        file.write(obj.toJSONString());
        file.flush();
        file.close();

} catch (IOException e) {
        //your message for exception goes here.
}
```

5. The content of the JSON object can also be displayed on the standard output as follows:

```
System.out.print(obj);
```

6. Finally, close the method:

```
}
```

The entire class, the method described in this recipe, and the driver method to call the method with an output JSON file name are as follows:

```
import java.io.FileWriter;
import java.io.IOException;
import org.json.simple.JSONArray;
import org.json.simple.JSONObject;

public class JsonWriting {

    public static void main(String[] args) {
```

```
        JsonWriting jsonWriting = new JsonWriting();
        jsonWriting.writeJson("C:/testJSON.json");
    }

    public void writeJson(String outFileName){
        JSONObject obj = new JSONObject();
        obj.put("book", "Harry Potter and the Philosopher's Stone");
        obj.put("author", "J. K. Rowling");

        JSONArray list = new JSONArray();
        list.add("There are characters in this book that will remind us
            of all the people we have met. Everybody knows or knew a
                spoilt, overweight boy like Dudley or a bossy and interfering
                    (yet kind-hearted) girl like Hermione");
        list.add("Hogwarts is a truly magical place, not only in the most
            obvious way but also in all the detail that the author has gone
                to describe it so vibrantly.");
        list.add("Parents need to know that this thrill-a-minute story,
            the first in the Harry Potter series, respects kids'
                intelligence and motivates them to tackle its greater length
                    and complexity, play imaginative games, and try to solve
                        its logic puzzles. ");

        obj.put("messages", list);

        try {

            FileWriter file = new FileWriter(outFileName);
            file.write(obj.toJSONString());
            file.flush();
            file.close();

        } catch (IOException e) {
            e.printStackTrace();
        }

        System.out.print(obj);
    }
}
```

The output file will be containing data as follows. Note that the output shown here has been modified to increase readability, and the actual output is one, big, flat piece of text:

```
{
"author":"J. K. Rowling",
"book":"Harry Potter and the Philosopher's Stone",
"messages":[
            "There are characters in this book that will remind us of all the
```

people we have met. Everybody knows or knew a spoilt, overweight boy like
Dudley or a bossy and interfering (yet kind-hearted) girl like Hermione",
        "Hogwarts is a truly magical place, not only in the most obvious
way but also in all the detail that the author has gone to describe it so
vibrantly.",
        "Parents need to know that this thrill-a-minute story, the first
in the Harry Potter series, respects kids' intelligence and motivates them
to tackle its greater length and complexity, play imaginative games, and
try to solve its logic puzzles."
        ]
}

Reading JSON files using JSON.simple

In this recipe, we will see how we can read or parse a JSON file. As our sample input file,
we will be using the JSON file we created in the previous recipe.

Getting ready

In order to perform this recipe, we will require the following:

1. Use the previous recipe to create a JSON file with book, author, and reviewer
   comments information. This file will be used as an input for parsing/reading in
   this recipe.

How to do it ...

1. As we will be reading or parsing a JSON file, first, we will be creating a JSON
   parser:

   ```
   JSONParser parser = new JSONParser();
   ```

2. Then, in a `try` block, we will be retrieving the values in the fields book and
   author. However, to do that, we first use the `parse()` method of the parser to
   read the input JSON file. The `parse()` method returns the content of the file as
   an object. Therefore, we will need an `Object` variable to hold the content. Then,
   the `object` will be assigned to a JSON object for further processing. Notice the
   type cast of the `Object` variable during the assignment:

   ```
   try {
   ```

```
    Object obj = parser.parse(new FileReader("c:test.json"));
    JSONObject jsonObject = (JSONObject) obj;

    String name = (String) jsonObject.get("book");
    System.out.println(name);

    String author = (String) jsonObject.get("author");
    System.out.println(author);
}
```

3. The next field to retrieve from the input JSON file is the review field, which is an array. We iterate over this field as follows:

```
JSONArray reviews = (JSONArray) jsonObject.get("messages");
    Iterator<String> iterator = reviews.iterator();
    while (iterator.hasNext()) {
        System.out.println(iterator.next());
    }
}
```

4. Finally, we create catch blocks to handle three types of exceptions that may occur during the parsing, and then close the method:

```
} catch (FileNotFoundException e) {
        //Your exception handling here
    } catch (IOException e) {
        //Your exception handling here
    } catch (ParseException e) {
        //Your exception handling here
    }
}
```

The entire class, the method described in this recipe, and the driver method to run the method are as follows:

```
import java.io.FileNotFoundException;
import java.io.FileReader;
import java.io.IOException;
import java.util.Iterator;
import org.json.simple.JSONArray;
import org.json.simple.JSONObject;
import org.json.simple.parser.JSONParser;
import org.json.simple.parser.ParseException;

public class JsonReading {
    public static void main(String[] args){
        JsonReading jsonReading = new JsonReading();
```

```
        jsonReading.readJson("C:/testJSON.json");
    }
    public void readJson(String inFileName) {
        JSONParser parser = new JSONParser();
        try {
            Object obj = parser.parse(new FileReader(inFileName));
            JSONObject jsonObject = (JSONObject) obj;

            String name = (String) jsonObject.get("book");
            System.out.println(name);

            String author = (String) jsonObject.get("author");
            System.out.println(author);

            JSONArray reviews = (JSONArray) jsonObject.get("messages");
            Iterator<String> iterator = reviews.iterator();
            while (iterator.hasNext()) {
                System.out.println(iterator.next());
            }
        } catch (FileNotFoundException e) {
            //Your exception handling here
        } catch (IOException e) {
            //Your exception handling here
        } catch (ParseException e) {
            //Your exception handling here
        }
    }
}
```

On successful execution of the code, you will be able to see the contents of the input file on the standard output.

Extracting web data from a URL using JSoup

A large amount of data, nowadays, can be found on the Web. This data is sometimes structured, semi-structured, or even unstructured. Therefore, very different techniques are needed to extract them. There are many different ways to extract web data. One of the easiest and handy ways is to use an external Java library named JSoup. This recipe uses a certain number of methods offered in JSoup to extract web data.

Getting ready

In order to perform this recipe, we will require the following:

1. Go to `https://jsoup.org/download`, and download the `jsoup-1.9.2.jar` file. Add the JAR file to your Eclipse project an external library.
2. If you are a Maven fan, please follow the instructions on the download page to include the JAR file into your Eclipse project.

How to do it...

1. Create a method named `extractDataWithJsoup(String url)`. The parameter is the URL of any webpage that you need to call the method. We will be extracting web data from this URL:

```
public void extractDataWithJsoup(String href){
```

2. Use the `connect()` method by sending the URL where we want to connect (and extract data). Then, we will be chaining a few more methods with it. First, we will chain the `timeout()` method that takes milliseconds as parameters. The methods after that define the user-agent name during this connection and whether attempts will be made to ignore connection errors. The next method to chain with the previous two is the `get()` method that eventually returns a `Document` object. Therefore, we will be holding this returned object in `doc` of the `Document` class:

```
doc =
   Jsoup.connect(href).timeout(10*1000).userAgent
      ("Mozilla").ignoreHttpErrors(true).get();
```

3. As this code throws `IOException`, we will be using a `try...catch` block as follows:

```
Document doc = null;
try {
 doc = Jsoup.connect(href).timeout(10*1000).userAgent
   ("Mozilla").ignoreHttpErrors(true).get();
   } catch (IOException e) {
      //Your exception handling here
}
```

We are not used to seeing times in milliseconds. Therefore, it is a nice practice to write 10*1000 to denote 10 seconds when millisecond is the time unit in a coding. This enhances readability of the code.

4. A large number of methods can be found for a `Document` object. If you want to extract the title of the URL, you can use title method as follows:

```
if(doc != null){
    String title = doc.title();
```

5. To only extract the textual part of the web page, we can chain the `body()` method with the `text()` method of a `Document` object, as follows:

```
String text = doc.body().text();
```

6. If you want to extract all the hyperlinks in a URL, you can use the `select()` method of a `Document` object with the `a[href]` parameter. This gives you all the links at once:

```
Elements links = doc.select("a[href]");
```

7. Perhaps you wanted to process the links in a web page individually? That is easy, too–you need to iterate over all the links to get the individual links:

```
for (Element link : links) {
    String linkHref = link.attr("href");
    String linkText = link.text();
    String linkOuterHtml = link.outerHtml();
    String linkInnerHtml = link.html();
System.out.println(linkHref + "t" + linkText + "t" +
    linkOuterHtml + "t" + linkInnterHtml);
}
```

8. Finally, close the if-condition with a brace. Close the method with a brace:

```
    }
}
```

The complete method, its class, and the driver method are as follows:

```
import java.io.IOException;
import org.jsoup.Jsoup;
import org.jsoup.nodes.Document;
import org.jsoup.nodes.Element;
import org.jsoup.select.Elements;
```

```
public class JsoupTesting {
    public static void main(String[] args){
        JsoupTesting test = new JsoupTesting();
        test.extractDataWithJsoup("Website address preceded by http://");
    }

    public void extractDataWithJsoup(String href){
        Document doc = null;
        try {
            doc = Jsoup.connect(href).timeout(10*1000).userAgent
                ("Mozilla").ignoreHttpErrors(true).get();
        } catch (IOException e) {
            //Your exception handling here
        }
        if(doc != null){
            String title = doc.title();
            String text = doc.body().text();
            Elements links = doc.select("a[href]");
            for (Element link : links) {
                String linkHref = link.attr("href");
                String linkText = link.text();
                String linkOuterHtml = link.outerHtml();
                String linkInnerHtml = link.html();
                System.out.println(linkHref + "t" + linkText + "t"  +
                    linkOuterHtml + "t" + linkInnterHtml);
            }
        }
    }
}
```

Extracting web data from a website using Selenium Webdriver

Selenium is a Java-based tool to help automating software testing or quality assurance. Interestingly enough, Selenium can be used to automatically retrieve and utilize web data. This recipe shows you how.

Getting ready

In order to perform this recipe, we will require the following:

1. Download `selenium-server-standalone-2.53.1.jar` and `selenium-java-2.53.1.zip` from
   `http://selenium-release.storage.googleapis.com/index.html?path=2.53/`.
   From the latter, extract the `selenium-java-2.53.1.jar` file. Include these two
   JAR files in your eclipse project an external Java library.
2. Download and install Firefox 47.0.1 from
   `https://ftp.mozilla.org/pub/firefox/releases/47.0.1/` by selecting the
   version appropriate for your operating system.

> Because of the version conflict issues between Selenium and Firefox, once
> you run code with a particular version, turn off the automatic update
> download and installation option in Firefox.

How to do it...

1. Create a method named `extractDataWithSelenium(String)` that takes a
   `String` as a parameter, which eventually is the URL from where we are going to
   extract data. There can be many different types of data that we can extract from
   URLs, such as the title, the headers, and the values in a selection drop-down box.
   This recipe only concentrates on extracting the text part of the webpage:

   ```
   public String extractDataWithSelenium(String url){
   ```

2. Next, create a Firefox web driver using the following code:

   ```
   WebDriver driver = new FirefoxDriver();
   ```

3. Use the `get()` method of the `WebDriver` object by passing the URL:

   ```
   driver.get("http://cogenglab.csd.uwo.ca/rushdi.htm");
   ```

4. The text of the webpage can be found using `xpath`, where the value of `id` is content:

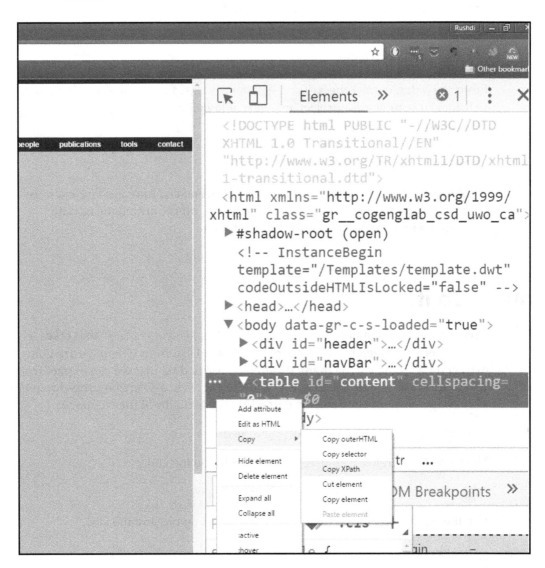

5. Find this particular element with the `findElement()` method. This method returns a `WebElement` object. Create a `WebElement` object named `webElement` to hold the returned value:

```
WebElement webElement = driver.findElement(By.xpath("//*
    [@id='content']"));
```

6. The `WebElement` object has a method named `getText()`. Call this method to retrieve the text of the web page, and put the text into a `String` variable as follows:

```
String text = (webElement.getText());
```

7. Finally, return the String variable and close the method:

```
}
```

The complete code segment with the driver main() method for the recipe looks like the following:

```
import org.openqa.selenium.By;
import org.openqa.selenium.WebDriver;
import org.openqa.selenium.WebElement;
import org.openqa.selenium.firefox.FirefoxDriver;

public class TestSelenium {
    public String extractDataWithSelenium(String url) {
        WebDriver driver = new FirefoxDriver();
        driver.get("http://cogenglab.csd.uwo.ca/rushdi.htm");
        WebElement webElement = driver.findElement(By.xpath("//*
            [@id='content']"));
```

```
        System.out.println(webElement.getText());
        return url;
    }

    public static void main(String[] args){
        TestSelenium test = new TestSelenium();
        String webData = test.extractDataWithSelenium
          ("http://cogenglab.csd.uwo.ca/rushdi.htm");
        //process webData
    }
}
```

Selenium and Firefox have compatibility issues. Some Selenium versions do not work with some Firefox versions. The recipe provided here works fine with the versions mentioned in the recipe. But it does not have any guarantee that it will work with other Selenium or Firefox versions.

Because of the version conflict issues between Selenium and Firefox, once you run a code with a particular version of the both, turn off the automatic update download and installation option in Firefox.

Reading table data from a MySQL database

Data can be stored in database tables also. This recipe demonstrates how we can read data from a table in MySQL.

Getting ready

In order to perform this recipe, we will require the following:

1. Download and install MySQL community server from
   http://dev.mysql.com/downloads/mysql/. The version used in this recipe is
   5.7.15.

2. Create a database named `data_science`. In this database, create a table named `books` that contains data as follows:

id	book_name	author_name	date_created
1	The Hunger Games	Suzanne Collins	2008-09-14 00:00:00
2	Harry Potter and the Sorcerer's Stone	J.K. Rowling	1997-07-30 00:00:00
3	Divergent	Veronica Roth	2011-04-25 00:00:00

The choice of the field types does not matter for this recipe, but the names of the fields need to exactly match those from the exhibit shown here.

3. Download the platform independent MySql JAR file from `http://dev.mysql.co m/downloads/connector/j/`, and add it an external library into your Java project. The version used in this recipe is 5.1.39.

How to do it...

1. Create a method as public void `readTable(String user, String password, String server)` that will take the user name, password, and server name for your MySQL database as parameters:

```
public void readTable(String user, String password, String
    server){
```

2. Create a MySQL data source, and using the data source, set the user name, password, and server name:

```
MysqlDataSource dataSource = new MysqlDataSource();
    dataSource.setUser(user);
    dataSource.setPassword(password);
    dataSource.setServerName(server);
```

3. In a `try` block, create a connection for the database. Using the connection, create a statement that will be used to execute a `SELECT` query to get information from the table. The results of the query will be stored in a result set:

```
try{
    Connection conn = dataSource.getConnection();
    Statement stmt = conn.createStatement();
    ResultSet rs = stmt.executeQuery("SELECT * FROM
        data_science.books");
```

4. Now, iterate over the result set, and retrieve each column data by mentioning the column name. Note the use of the method that gives us the data you need to know the field type before you can use them. For instance, as we know that the ID filed is integer, we are able to use the `getInt()` method:

```
while (rs.next()){
    int id = rs.getInt("id");
    String book = rs.getString("book_name");
    String author = rs.getString("author_name");
    Date dateCreated = rs.getDate("date_created");
    System.out.format("%s, %s, %s, %sn", id, book, author,
        dateCreated);
}
```

5. Close the result set, the statement, and connection after iteration:

```
rs.close();
    stmt.close();
    conn.close();
```

6. Catch some exceptions as you can have during this reading data from the table and close the method:

```
}catch (Exception e){
    //Your exception handling mechanism goes here.
    }
}
```

The complete method, the class, and the driver method to execute the method are as follows:

```
import java.sql.*;
import com.mysql.jdbc.jdbc2.optional.MysqlDataSource;
public class TestDB{
    public static void main(String[] args){
        TestDB test = new TestDB();
```

```
            test.readTable("your user name", "your password", "your MySQL
                server name");
    }
    public void readTable(String user, String password, String server)
        {
        MysqlDataSource dataSource = new MysqlDataSource();
        dataSource.setUser(user);
        dataSource.setPassword(password);
        dataSource.setServerName(server);
        try{
            Connection conn = dataSource.getConnection();
            Statement stmt = conn.createStatement();
            ResultSet rs = stmt.executeQuery("SELECT * FROM
                data_science.books");
            while (rs.next()){
                int id = rs.getInt("id");
                String book = rs.getString("book_name");
                String author = rs.getString("author_name");
                Date dateCreated = rs.getDate("date_created");
                System.out.format("%s, %s, %s, %sn", id, book,
                    author, dateCreated);
            }
            rs.close();
            stmt.close();
            conn.close();
        }catch (Exception e){
            //Your exception handling mechanism goes here.
        }
    }
}
```

This code displays the data in the table that you created.

2
Indexing and Searching Data

In this chapter, we will cover the following recipes:

- Indexing data with Apache Lucene
- Searching indexed data with Apache Lucene

Introduction

In this chapter, you will learn two very important recipes. The first recipe demonstrates how you can index your data, and the second recipe, which is very closely connected to the first recipe, demonstrates how you can search through your indexed data.

For both indexing and searching, we will be using Apache Lucene. Apache Lucene is a free, opensource Java software library used heavily for information retrieval. It is supported by the Apache Software Foundation and is released under the Apache Software License.

Many different modern search platforms, such as Apache Solr and ElasticSearch, or crawling platforms, such as Apache Nutch, use Apache Lucene in the backend for data indexing and searching. Therefore, any data scientist who learns those search platforms will benefit from the two basic recipes in this chapter.

Indexing data with Apache Lucene

In this recipe, we will demonstrate how to index a large amount of data with Apache Lucene. Indexing is the first step for searching data fast. In action, Lucene uses an inverted full-text index. In other words, it considers all documents, splits them into words or tokens, and then builds an index for each token so that it knows in advance exactly which document to look for if a term is searched.

Getting ready

The following are the steps to be implemented:

1. To download Apache Lucene, go to `http://lucene.apache.org/core/downloads.html`, and click on the Download button. At the time of writing, the latest version of Lucene was 6.4.1. Once you click on the Download button, it will take you to the mirror websites that host the distribution:

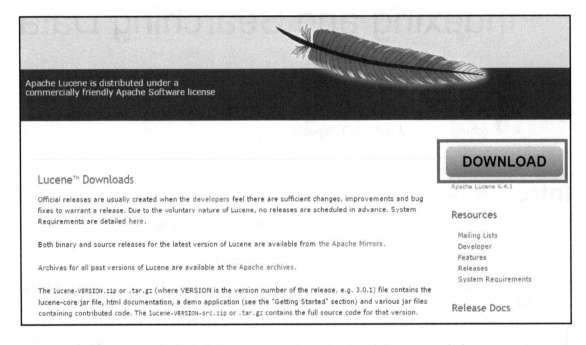

Apache Lucene is distributed under a commercially friendly Apache Software license

DOWNLOAD
Apache Lucene 6.4.1

Lucene™ Downloads

Official releases are usually created when the developers feel there are sufficient changes, improvements and bug fixes to warrant a release. Due to the voluntary nature of Lucene, no releases are scheduled in advance. System Requirements are detailed here.

Both binary and source releases for the latest version of Lucene are available from the Apache Mirrors.

Archives for all past versions of Lucene are available at the Apache archives.

The lucene-VERSION.zip or .tar.gz (where VERSION is the version number of the release, e.g. 3.0.1) file contains the lucene-core jar file, html documentation, a demo application (see the "Getting Started" section) and various jar files containing contributed code. The lucene-VERSION-src.zip or .tar.gz contains the full source code for that version.

Resources

Mailing Lists
Developer
Features
Releases
System Requirements

Release Docs

2. Choose any appropriate mirror for downloading. Once you click a mirror website, it will take you to a directory of distribution. Download the `lucene-6.4.1.zip` file onto your system:

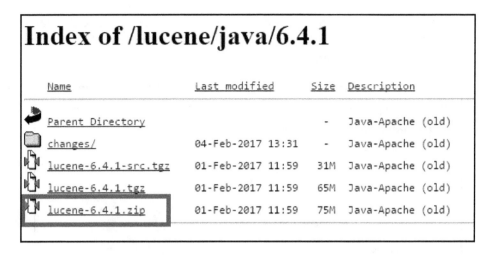

3. Once you download it, unzip the distribution. You will see a nicely organized folder distribution, as follows:

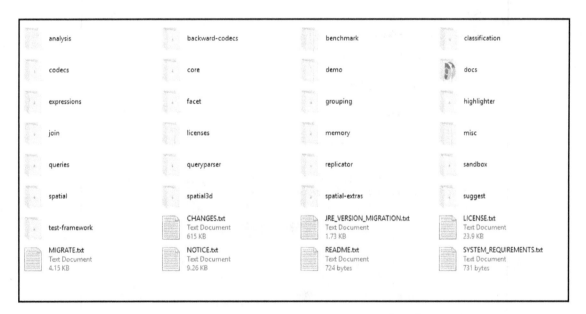

4. Open Eclipse, and create a project named `LuceneTutorial`. To do that, open Eclipse and go to File. Then go to **New...** and Java Project. Take the name of the project and click on **Finish**:

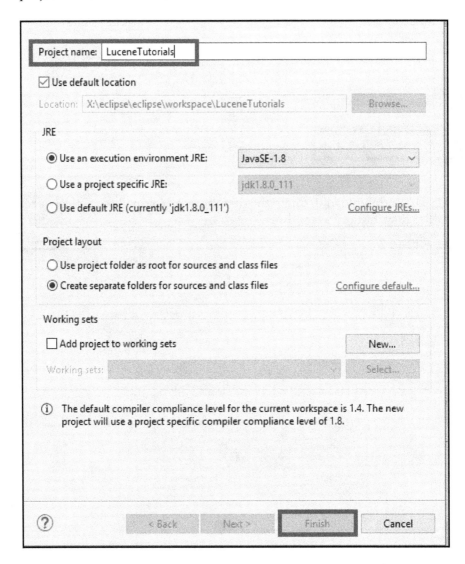

5. Now you will be inserting JAR files necessary for this recipe as external libraries into your project. Right-click on your project name in the **Package Explorer**. Select **Build Path** and then **Configure Build Path...** This will open properties for your project:

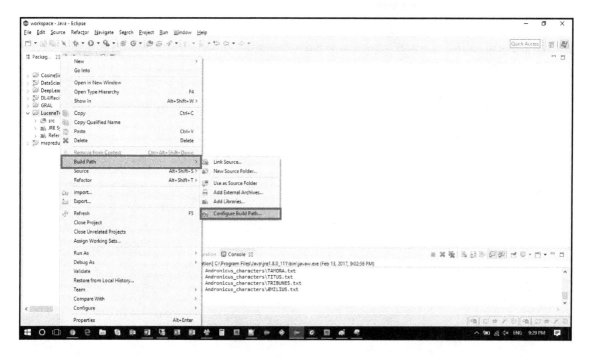

6. Click on the Add External Jars button, and then add the following JAR files from Lucene 6.4.1 distributions:
    - `lucene-core-6.4.1.jar`, which can be found in `lucene-6.4.1\core` of your unzipped Lucene distribution
    - `lucene-queryparser-6.4.1.jar`, which can be found in `lucene-6.4.1\queryparser` of your unzipped Lucene distribution
    - `Lucene-analyzers-common-6.4.1.jar`, which can be found in `lucene-6.4.1\analysis\common` of your unzipped Lucene distribution

After adding the JAR files, click on **OK**:

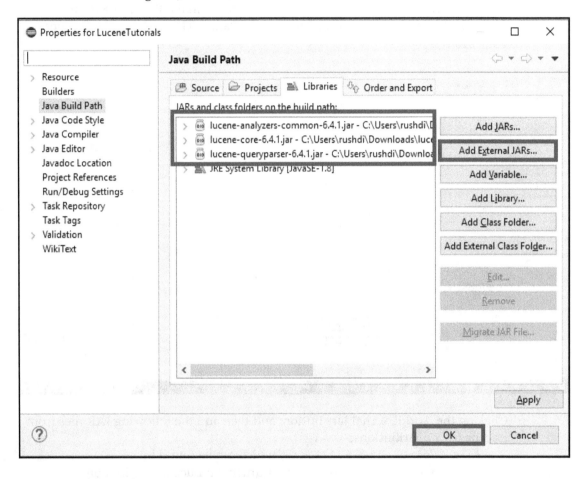

7. For indexing, you will be using the writings of William Shakespeare in text format. Open a browser, and go to http://norvig.com/ngrams/. This will open a page named Natural Language Corpus Data: Beautiful Data. In the files in the Download section, you will find a .txt file named shakespeare. Download this file anywhere in your system.

8. Unzip the files and you will see that the distribution contains three folders, `comedies`, `historical`, and `tragedies`:

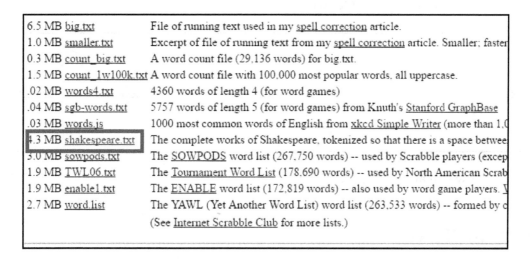

6.5 MB	big.txt	File of running text used in my spell correction article.
1.0 MB	smaller.txt	Excerpt of file of running text from my spell correction article. Smaller; faster
0.3 MB	count_big.txt	A word count file (29,136 words) for big.txt.
1.5 MB	count_1w100k.txt	A word count file with 100,000 most popular words, all uppercase.
.02 MB	words4.txt	4360 words of length 4 (for word games)
.04 MB	sgb-words.txt	5757 words of length 5 (for word games) from Knuth's Stanford GraphBase
.03 MB	words.js	1000 most common words of English from xkcd Simple Writer (more than 1,0
4.3 MB	shakespeare.txt	The complete works of Shakespeare, tokenized so that there is a space betwee
3.0 MB	sowpods.txt	The SOWPODS word list (267,750 words) -- used by Scrabble players (excep
1.9 MB	TWL06.txt	The Tournament Word List (178,690 words) -- used by North American Scrab
1.9 MB	enable1.txt	The ENABLE word list (172,819 words) -- also used by word game players. \
2.7 MB	word.list	The YAWL (Yet Another Word List) word list (263,533 words) -- formed by c
		(See Internet Scrabble Club for more lists.)

9. Create a folder in your project directory. Right-click on your project in Eclipse and go to **New**, and then click **Folder**. As the folder name, type in input and click on **Finish**:

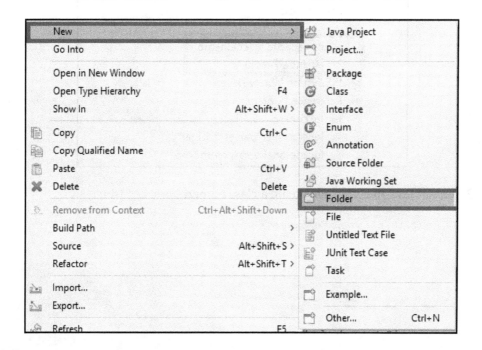

10. Copy the `shakespeare.txt` in step 8 into the folder you created in step 9.

11. Follow the instructions in step 9 to create another folder named index. At this stage, your project folder will look like this:

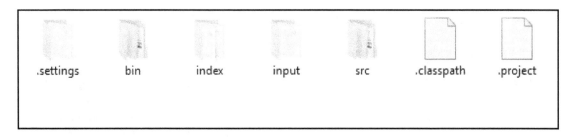

Now you are ready for coding.

How to do it...

1. Create a package in your project named `org.apache.lucene.demo`, and create a Java file in the package named `IndexFiles.java`:

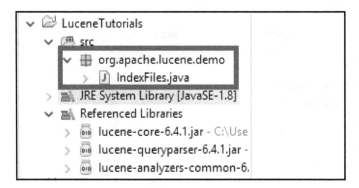

2. In that Java file, you will create a class named `IndexFiles`:

```
public class IndexFiles {
```

3. The first method you will write is called `indexDocs`. The method indexes any given file using the given index writer. If a directory is provided as argument, the method recursively iterates over files and directories found under the given directory. This method indexes one document per input file:

> This method is relatively slow, and therefore for better performances, put multiple documents into your input file(s).

```
static void indexDocs(final IndexWriter writer, Path path)
    throws IOException {
```

- writer is the index writer that writes index where the given file or directory information will be stored
- path is the file to index, or the directory containing the files for which index will be created

4. If a directory is provided, the directory will be iterated or traversed recursively:

```
if (Files.isDirectory(path)) {
    Files.walkFileTree(path, new SimpleFileVisitor<Path>() {
```

5. You will then be overriding a method named `visitFile` to visit the file or directory based on the given path and basic file attributes:

```
@Override
    public FileVisitResult visitFile(Path file,
        BasicFileAttributes attrs) throws IOException {
```

6. Next, you will be calling a static method that you will create later, named `indexDoc`. We have deliberately left the catch block empty as we have let you decide what to do if a file cannot be indexed:

```
try {
    indexDoc(writer, file,
        attrs.lastModifiedTime().toMillis());
    } catch (IOException ignore) {
}
```

7. Return from the `visitFile` method:

```
return FileVisitResult.CONTINUE;
    }
```

8. Close the blocks:

```
}
        );
    }
```

9. In the else block, call the `indexDoc` method. Remember that in the `else` block, you are dealing with files, not directories:

```
else {
  indexDoc(writer, path,
    Files.getLastModifiedTime(path).toMillis());
}
```

10. Close the `indexDocs()` method:

```
}
```

11. Now create a method to deal with indexing of a single document:

```
static void indexDoc(IndexWriter writer, Path file, long
    lastModified) throws IOException {
```

12. First, create a `try` block to create a new empty document:

```
try (InputStream stream = Files.newInputStream(file)) {
    Document doc = new Document();
```

13. Next, add the path of the file as a field. As a field name, type "path". The field will be searchable or indexed. However, note that you do not tokenize the field and do not index term frequency or positional information:

```
Field pathField = new StringField("path", file.toString(),
    Field.Store.YES);
doc.add(pathField);
```

14. Add the last modified date of the file, a field named `"modified"`:

```
doc.add(new LongPoint("modified", lastModified));
```

15. Add the contents of the file to a field named `"contents"`. The reader that you specify will make sure that the text of the file is tokenized and indexed, but not stored:

```
doc.add(new TextField("contents", new BufferedReader(new
    InputStreamReader(stream, StandardCharsets.UTF_8))));
```

 If the file is not in `UTF-8` encoding, then searching for special characters will fail.

16. Create an index for the file:

```
if (writer.getConfig().getOpenMode() == OpenMode.CREATE) {
    System.out.println("adding " + file);
    writer.addDocument(doc);
}
```

17. There is a chance that the document might have been indexed already. Your `else` block will handle those cases. You will use `updateDocument` instead of replacing the old one matching the exact path, if present:

```
else {
    System.out.println("updating " + file);
    writer.updateDocument(new Term("path", file.toString()),
        doc);
}
```

18. Close the try block and the method:

```
    }
}
```

19. Now let's create the main method for the class.

```
public static void main(String[] args) {
```

20. You will be providing three options from the console when you run your program:
    - The first option is index, and the parameter will be the folder that contains indexes
    - The second option is docs, and the parameter will be the folder that contains your text files
    - And the last option is update, and the parameter will denote whether you want to create new indexes or update old indexes

    To hold the values of these three parameters, create and initialize three variables:

    ```
    String indexPath = "index";
    String docsPath = null;
    boolean create = true;
    ```

21. Set the values of the three options:

    ```
    for(int i=0;i<args.length;i++) {
      if ("-index".equals(args[i])) {
          indexPath = args[i+1];
          i++;
      } else if ("-docs".equals(args[i])) {
          docsPath = args[i+1];
          i++;
      } else if ("-update".equals(args[i])) {
          create = false;
      }
    }
    ```

22. Set the document directory:

    ```
    final Path docDir = Paths.get(docsPath);
    ```

23. Now you will start indexing the files in your directory. First, set the timer, as you will be timing the indexing latency:

    ```
    Date start = new Date();
    ```

24. For indexing, Create a directory and create an analyzer (in this case, you will be using a basic, standard analyzer and an index writer configurer):

```
try {

    Directory dir = FSDirectory.open(Paths.get(indexPath));
    Analyzer analyzer = new StandardAnalyzer();
    IndexWriterConfig iwc = new IndexWriterConfig(analyzer);
```

25. With the index writer configured and based on the input regarding the creation or update of the index, set the open modes for the indexing. If you choose to create a new index, the open mode will be set to CREATE. Otherwise, it will be CREATE_OR_APPEND:

```
if (create) {
    iwc.setOpenMode(OpenMode.CREATE);
} else {
    iwc.setOpenMode(OpenMode.CREATE_OR_APPEND);
}
```

26. Create an index writer:

```
IndexWriter writer = new IndexWriter(dir, iwc);
indexDocs(writer, docDir);
```

27. Close the `writer`:

```
writer.close();
```

28. At this point, you are almost done with the coding. Just complete the tracking of time for indexing:

```
Date end = new Date();
System.out.println(end.getTime() - start.getTime() + " total
    milliseconds");
```

29. Close the `try` block. We intentionally left the `catch` block blank so that you can decide what you do in the case of an exception during indexing:

```
} catch (IOException e) {
}
```

30. Close the main method and close the class:

```
}
}
```

31. Right-click on your project in Eclipse, select **Run As,** and click on **Run Configurations...**:

32. Go to the **Arguments** tab in the Run Configurations window. In the Program Arguments option, put `-docs input\ -index index\`. Click on **Run**:

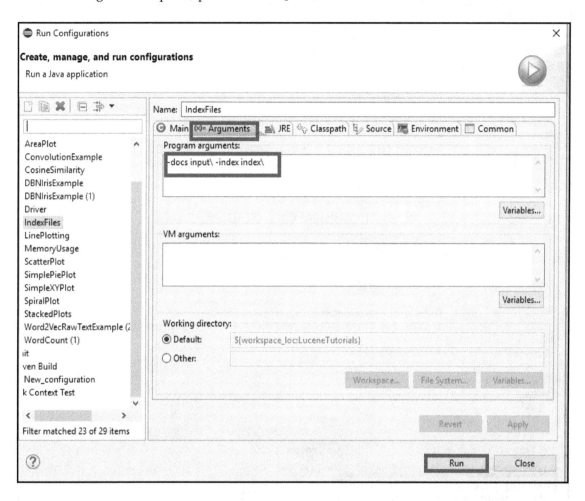

33. The output of the code is as follows:

```java
          final Path docDir = Paths.get(docsPath);

          Date start = new Date();
          try {
              System.out.println("Indexing to directory '" + indexPath + "'...");

              Directory dir = FSDirectory.open(Paths.get(indexPath));
              Analyzer analyzer = new StandardAnalyzer();
              IndexWriterConfig iwc = new IndexWriterConfig(analyzer);

              if (create) {
                  iwc.setOpenMode(OpenMode.CREATE);
              } else {
                  iwc.setOpenMode(OpenMode.CREATE_OR_APPEND);
              }
              IndexWriter writer = new IndexWriter(dir, iwc);
              indexDocs(writer, docDir);

              writer.close();

              Date end = new Date();
              System.out.println(end.getTime() - start.getTime() + " total millise

          } catch (IOException e) {
          }
      }
  }
```

```
Problems  @ Javadoc  Declaration  Console ␡
<terminated> IndexFiles [Java Application] C:\Program Files\Java\jre1.8.0_111\bin\javaw.exe (Feb 16, 2017, 11:19:36
Indexing to directory 'index'...
adding input\shakespeare.txt
1383 total milliseconds
```

How it works...

The complete code for the recipe is as follows:

```
package org.apache.lucene.demo;

import org.apache.lucene.analysis.Analyzer;
import org.apache.lucene.analysis.standard.StandardAnalyzer;
import org.apache.lucene.document.Document;
import org.apache.lucene.document.Field;
import org.apache.lucene.document.LongPoint;
import org.apache.lucene.document.StringField;
import org.apache.lucene.document.TextField;
import org.apache.lucene.index.IndexWriter;
import org.apache.lucene.index.IndexWriterConfig.OpenMode;
import org.apache.lucene.index.IndexWriterConfig;
import org.apache.lucene.index.Term;
import org.apache.lucene.store.Directory;
import org.apache.lucene.store.FSDirectory;
import java.io.BufferedReader;
import java.io.IOException;
import java.io.InputStream;
import java.io.InputStreamReader;
import java.nio.charset.StandardCharsets;
import java.nio.file.FileVisitResult;
import java.nio.file.Files;
import java.nio.file.Path;
import java.nio.file.Paths;
import java.nio.file.SimpleFileVisitor;
import java.nio.file.attribute.BasicFileAttributes;
import java.util.Date;

public class IndexFiles {
    static void indexDocs(final IndexWriter writer, Path path) throws
      IOException {
        if (Files.isDirectory(path)) {
            Files.walkFileTree(path, new SimpleFileVisitor<Path>() {
                @Override
                public FileVisitResult visitFile(Path file,
                  BasicFileAttributes attrs) throws IOException {
                    try {
                        indexDoc(writer, file,
                          attrs.lastModifiedTime().toMillis());
                    } catch (IOException ignore) {
                    }
                    return FileVisitResult.CONTINUE;
                }
            }
        }
```

```
                      );
            } else {
              indexDoc(writer, path,
                Files.getLastModifiedTime(path).toMillis());
            }
        }

        static void indexDoc(IndexWriter writer, Path file, long
            lastModified) throws IOException {
            try (InputStream stream = Files.newInputStream(file)) {
                Document doc = new Document();
                Field pathField = new StringField("path", file.toString(),
                  Field.Store.YES);
                doc.add(pathField);
                doc.add(new LongPoint("modified", lastModified));
                doc.add(new TextField("contents", new BufferedReader(new
                    InputStreamReader(stream, StandardCharsets.UTF_8))));

                if (writer.getConfig().getOpenMode() == OpenMode.CREATE) {
                    System.out.println("adding " + file);
                    writer.addDocument(doc);
                } else {
                    System.out.println("updating " + file);
                    writer.updateDocument(new Term("path", file.toString()),
                      doc);
                }
            }
        }
    }
    public static void main(String[] args) {
        String indexPath = "index";
        String docsPath = null;
        boolean create = true;
        for(int i=0;i<args.length;i++) {
            if ("-index".equals(args[i])) {
                indexPath = args[i+1];
                i++;
            } else if ("-docs".equals(args[i])) {
                docsPath = args[i+1];
                i++;
            } else if ("-update".equals(args[i])) {
                create = false;
            }
        }

        final Path docDir = Paths.get(docsPath);

        Date start = new Date();
        try {
```

```
    System.out.println("Indexing to directory '" + indexPath +
       "'...");

    Directory dir = FSDirectory.open(Paths.get(indexPath));
    Analyzer analyzer = new StandardAnalyzer();
    IndexWriterConfig iwc = new IndexWriterConfig(analyzer);

    if (create) {
       iwc.setOpenMode(OpenMode.CREATE);
    } else {
       iwc.setOpenMode(OpenMode.CREATE_OR_APPEND);
    }
    IndexWriter writer = new IndexWriter(dir, iwc);
    indexDocs(writer, docDir);

    writer.close();

    Date end = new Date();
    System.out.println(end.getTime() - start.getTime() + " total
       milliseconds");

  } catch (IOException e) {
  }
 }
}
```

Searching indexed data with Apache Lucene

Now that you have indexed your data, you will be searching the data using Apache Lucene in this recipe. The code for searching in this recipe depends on the index that you created in the previous recipe, and therefore, it will only successfully execute if you followed the instructions in the previous recipe.

Getting ready

1. Complete the previous recipe. After completing the previous recipe, go to the index directory in your project that you created in step 11 of that recipe. Make sure that you see some indexing files there:

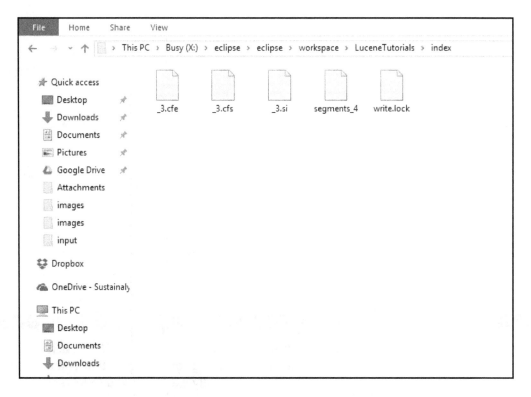

2. Create a Java file named `SearchFiles` in the `org.apache.lucene.demo` package you created in the previous recipe:

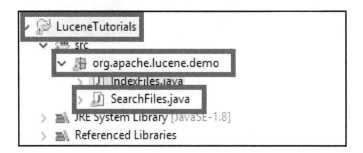

3. Now you are ready to type in some code in the `SearchFiles.java` file.

How to do it...

1. Open `SearchFiles.java` in the editor of Eclipse and create the following class:

```
public class SearchFiles {
```

2. You need to create two constant String variables. The first variable will contain the path of your `index` that you created in the previous recipe. The second variable will contain the field contents where you will be searching. In our case, we will be searching in the `contents` field of the `index`:

```
public static final String INDEX_DIRECTORY = "index";
public static final String FIELD_CONTENTS = "contents";
```

3. Start creating your main method:

```
public static void main(String[] args) throws Exception {
```

4. Create an `indexreader` by opening the indexes in your `index` directory:

```
IndexReader reader =
  DirectoryReader.open(FSDirectory.open
    (Paths.get(INDEX_DIRECTORY)));
```

5. The next step will be to create a searcher that will search the index:

```
IndexSearcher indexSearcher = new IndexSearcher(reader);
```

6. As your analyzer, create a standard analyzer:

```
Analyzer analyzer = new StandardAnalyzer();
```

7. Create a query parser by providing two arguments to the `QueryParser` constructor, the field where you will be searching and the analyzer you have created:

```
QueryParser queryParser = new QueryParser(FIELD_CONTENTS,
  analyzer);
```

8. In this recipe, you will be using a predefined search term. In this search, you are trying to find the documents that contain both `"over-full"` and `"persuasion"`:

```
String searchString = "over-full AND persuasion";
```

9. Using the search string, create a query:

```
Query query = queryParser.parse(searchString);
```

10. The searcher will be looking into the index to see whether it can find out the search term. You are also mentioning how many search results will be coming as a result, which in our case is 5:

```
TopDocs results = indexSearcher.search(query, 5);
```

11. Create an array to hold the `hits`:

```
ScoreDoc[] hits = results.scoreDocs;
```

12. Note that during indexing, we have used only one document, `shakespeare.txt`. So the length of this array, in our case, can be a maximum of 1.

13. You will also be interested in knowing the number of documents where the search was found as a hit:

```
int numTotalHits = results.totalHits;
System.out.println(numTotalHits + " total matching documents");
```

14. Finally, iterate through the hits. You get the document ID for which a hit was found. With the document ID, you will then create the document and print the path of the document and the score calculated by Lucene for a document for the search term you have used:

```
for(int i=0;i<hits.length;++i) {
  int docId = hits[i].doc;
  Document d = indexSearcher.doc(docId);
  System.out.println((i + 1) + ". " + d.get("path") + " score="
    + hits[i].score);
}
```

15. Close the method and the class:

```
}
}
```

16. If you run the code, you will see the following output:

```
[J] IndexFiles.java      [J] SearchFiles.java ⊠

28  import org.apache.lucene.queryparser.classic.QueryParser;
29  import org.apache.lucene.search.IndexSearcher;
30  import org.apache.lucene.search.Query;
31  import org.apache.lucene.search.ScoreDoc;
32  import org.apache.lucene.search.TopDocs;
33  import org.apache.lucene.store.FSDirectory;
34
35  public class SearchFiles {
36      public static final String INDEX_DIRECTORY = "index";
37      public static final String FIELD_CONTENTS = "contents";
38
39⊝     public static void main(String[] args) throws Exception {
40          IndexReader reader = DirectoryReader.open(FSDirectory.open(Path
41          IndexSearcher indexSearcher = new IndexSearcher(reader);
42
43          Analyzer analyzer = new StandardAnalyzer();
44          QueryParser queryParser = new QueryParser(FIELD_CONTENTS, analy
45          String searchString = "over-full AND persuasion";
46          Query query = queryParser.parse(searchString);
47
48          TopDocs results = indexSearcher.search(query, 5);
49          ScoreDoc[] hits = results.scoreDocs;
50
51          int numTotalHits = results.totalHits;
52          System.out.println(numTotalHits + " total matching documents");
53
54          for(int i=0;i<hits.length;++i) {
55              int docId = hits[i].doc;
```

```
📋 Problems  @ Javadoc  ⓖ Declaration  🖵 Console ⊠
<terminated> SearchFiler [Java Application] C:\Program Files\Java\jre1.8.0_111\bin\javaw.exe (Feb 16,
1 total matching documents
1. input\shakespeare.txt score=1.8491187
```

17. Open the `shakespeare.txt` file in the input folder of your project folder. Search manually, and you will find that both `"over-full"` and `"persuasion"` are present in the document.

18. Change the `searchString` in step 8, as follows:

```
String searchString = "shakespeare";
```

19. By keeping the rest of the codes as they are, whether you run the code, you will see the following output:

```
IndexFiles.java    SearchFiles.java ⊠

28  import org.apache.lucene.queryparser.classic.QueryParser;
29  import org.apache.lucene.search.IndexSearcher;
30  import org.apache.lucene.search.Query;
31  import org.apache.lucene.search.ScoreDoc;
32  import org.apache.lucene.search.TopDocs;
33  import org.apache.lucene.store.FSDirectory;
34
35  public class SearchFiles {
36      public static final String INDEX_DIRECTORY = "index";
37      public static final String FIELD_CONTENTS = "contents";
38
39      public static void main(String[] args) throws Exception {
40          IndexReader reader = DirectoryReader.open(FSDirectory.open(Paths
41          IndexSearcher indexSearcher = new IndexSearcher(reader);
42
43          Analyzer analyzer = new StandardAnalyzer();
44          QueryParser queryParser = new QueryParser(FIELD_CONTENTS, analyz
45          String searchString = "shakespeare";
46          Query query = queryParser.parse(searchString);
47
48          TopDocs results = indexSearcher.search(query, 5);
49          ScoreDoc[] hits = results.scoreDocs;
50
51          int numTotalHits = results.totalHits;
52          System.out.println(numTotalHits + " total matching documents");
53
54          for(int i=0;i<hits.length;++i) {
55              int docId = hits[i].doc;
```

```
Problems  @ Javadoc  Declaration  Console ⊠
<terminated> SearchFiles [Java Application] C:\Program Files\Java\jre1.8.0_111\bin\javaw.exe (Feb 16,
0 total matching documents
```

20. Open the `Shakespeare.txt` file again and double-check if the term Shakespeare appears in it. You will find none.

The complete code for this recipe is as follows:

```
package org.apache.lucene.demo;
import java.nio.file.Paths;
import org.apache.lucene.analysis.Analyzer;
import org.apache.lucene.analysis.standard.StandardAnalyzer;
```

```java
import org.apache.lucene.document.Document;
import org.apache.lucene.index.DirectoryReader;
import org.apache.lucene.index.IndexReader;
import org.apache.lucene.queryparser.classic.QueryParser;
import org.apache.lucene.search.IndexSearcher;
import org.apache.lucene.search.Query;
import org.apache.lucene.search.ScoreDoc;
import org.apache.lucene.search.TopDocs;
import org.apache.lucene.store.FSDirectory;

public class SearchFiles {
    public static final String INDEX_DIRECTORY = "index";
    public static final String FIELD_CONTENTS = "contents";

    public static void main(String[] args) throws Exception {
        IndexReader reader = DirectoryReader.open(FSDirectory.open
            (Paths.get(INDEX_DIRECTORY)));
        IndexSearcher indexSearcher = new IndexSearcher(reader);

        Analyzer analyzer = new StandardAnalyzer();
        QueryParser queryParser = new QueryParser(FIELD_CONTENTS,
            analyzer);
        String searchString = "shakespeare";
        Query query = queryParser.parse(searchString);

        TopDocs results = indexSearcher.search(query, 5);
        ScoreDoc[] hits = results.scoreDocs;

        int numTotalHits = results.totalHits;
        System.out.println(numTotalHits + " total matching documents");

        for(int i=0;i<hits.length;++i) {
            int docId = hits[i].doc;
            Document d = indexSearcher.doc(docId);
            System.out.println((i + 1) + ". " + d.get("path") + " score="
                + hits[i].score);
        }
    }
}
```

 You can visit
https://lucene.apache.org/core/2_9_4/queryparsersyntax.html for
the query syntaxes supported by Apache Lucene.

3
Analyzing Data Statistically

In this chapter, we will cover the following recipes:

- Generating descriptive statistics
- Generating summary statistics
- Generating summary statistics from multiple distributions
- Computing frequency distribution
- Counting word frequency in a string
- Counting word frequency in a string using Java 8
- Computing simple regression
- Computing ordinary least squares regression
- Computing generalized least squares regression
- Calculating covariance of two sets of data points
- Calculating Pearson's correlation of two sets of data points
- Conducting a paired t-test
- Conducting a Chi-square test
- Conducting one-way ANOVA test
- Conducting a Kolmogorov-Smirnov test

Introduction

Statistical analysis is one of the regular activities of a data scientist. Such analysis includes but is not limited to analysis of descriptive statistics, frequency distributions, simple and multiple regression, correlation and covariance, and statistical significance among data distributions. Luckily, Java has many libraries that are capable of strong statistical analysis of data with only a few lines of coding efforts. This chapter outlines how a data scientist can use Java to make this analysis with 15 recipes.

Note that the focus of this chapter is only on fundamental statistical analysis of data using Java although it is possible use linear algebra, numerical analysis, special functions, complex numbers, geometry, curve fitting, differential equations using the language.

In order to perform the recipes in this chapter, we would require the following:

1. Apache Commons Math 3.6.1. Therefore, you need to download the JAR file from `http://commons.apache.org/proper/commons-math/download_math.cgi`.

2. If you want to use older versions, the older versions are in the archive at `http://archive.apache.org/dist/commons/math/binaries/`, as shown in the following screenshot:

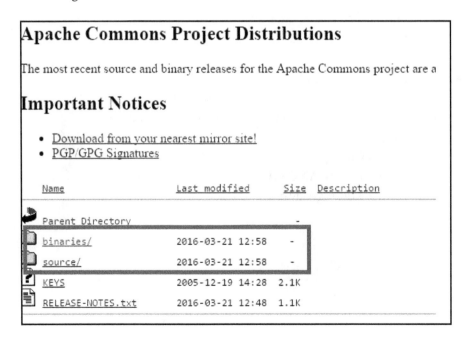

3. Include it as an external JAR file in your eclipse project:

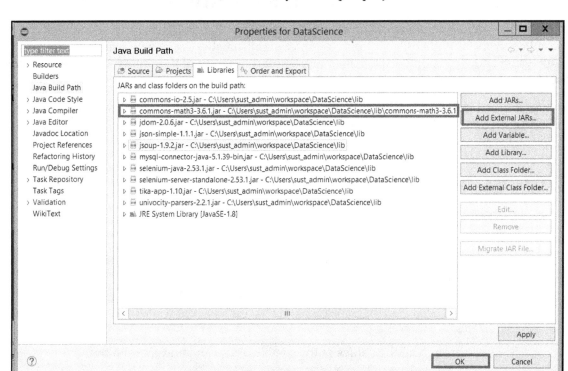

The `stat` package of Apache Commons Math 3.6.1 is very rich and well optimized. The package can generate the following descriptive statistics:

- Arithmetic and geometric means
- Variance and standard deviation
- Sum, product, log sum, sum of squared values
- Minimum, maximum, median, and percentiles
- Skewness and kurtosis
- First, second, third, and fourth moments

Furthermore, as per their website
`http://commons.apache.org/proper/commons-math/userguide/stat.html`, the methods are optimized and use as less memory as possible.

With the exception of percentiles and the median, all of these statistics can be computed without maintaining the full list of input data values in memory.

Generating descriptive statistics

Descriptive statistics are used to summarize a sample and are not generally developed based on probability theories. In contrast, inferential statistics are mostly used to draw a conclusion about the population from a representative *sample* of it. In this recipe, we will see how we can use Java to generate descriptive statistics from small samples.

Without broadening the scope of this recipe too much, we will be focusing only on a subset of descriptive statistics listed here.

How to do it...

1. Create a method that takes a `double` array as argument. The array will contain the values for which you are going to compute the descriptive statistics:

   ```
   public void getDescStats(double[] values){
   ```

2. Create an object of the `DescriptiveStatistics` type:

   ```
   DescriptiveStatistics stats = new DescriptiveStatistics();
   ```

3. Loop through all the values of the double array, and add them to the `DescriptiveStatistic` object:

   ```
   for( int i = 0; i < values.length; i++) {
       stats.addValue(values[i]);
   }
   ```

4. There are methods in the `DescriptiveStatistics` class of Apache Commons Math library to compute the mean, standard deviation, and median of a group of values. Call these methods to get the descriptive statistics of the values. Finally, close the method:

   ```
   double mean = stats.getMean();
   double std = stats.getStandardDeviation();
   double median = stats.getPercentile(50);
   System.out.println(mean + "\t" + std + "\t" + median);
   }
   ```

The complete piece of code including the driver method will look like this:

```java
import org.apache.commons.math3.stat.descriptive.DescriptiveStatistics;

public class DescriptiveStats {
    public static void main(String[] args){
        double[] values = {32, 39, 14, 98, 45, 44, 45, 34, 89, 67, 0,
            15, 0, 56, 88};
        DescriptiveStats descStatTest = new DescriptiveStats();
        descStatTest.getDescStats(values);
    }
    public void getDescStats(double[] values){
        DescriptiveStatistics stats = new DescriptiveStatistics();
        for( int i = 0; i < values.length; i++) {
                stats.addValue(values[i]);
        }
        double mean = stats.getMean();
        double std = stats.getStandardDeviation();
        double median = stats.getPercentile(50);
        System.out.println(mean + "\t" + std + "\t" + median);
    }
}
```

To compute statistics in a thread-safe way, you can create a `SynchronizedDescriptiveStatistics` instance as follows: `DescriptiveStatistics stats = new SynchronizedDescriptiveStatistics();`

Generating summary statistics

We can generate summary statistics for data by using the `SummaryStatistics` class. This is similar to the `DescriptiveStatistics` class used in the preceding recipe; the major difference is that unlike the `DescriptiveStatistics` class, the `SummaryStatistics` class does not store data in memory.

How to do it...

1. Like the preceding recipe, create a method that takes a `double` array as argument:

   ```
   public void getSummaryStats(double[] values){
   ```

2. Create an object of class `SummaryStatistics`:

   ```
   SummaryStatistics stats = new SummaryStatistics();
   ```

3. Add all the values to this object of the `SummaryStatistics` class:

   ```
   for( int i = 0; i < values.length; i++) {
       stats.addValue(values[i]);
   }
   ```

4. Finally, use methods in the `SummaryStatistics` class to generate the summary statistics for the values. Close the method when you are done using the statistics:

   ```
   double mean = stats.getMean();
   double std = stats.getStandardDeviation();
   System.out.println(mean + "\t" + std);
   }
   ```

The complete code with the driver method will look like the following:

```
import org.apache.commons.math3.stat.descriptive.SummaryStatistics;

public class SummaryStats {
    public static void main(String[] args){
        double[] values = {32, 39, 14, 98, 45, 44, 45, 34, 89, 67, 0, 15,
            0, 56, 88};
        SummaryStats summaryStatTest = new SummaryStats();
        summaryStatTest.getSummaryStats(values);
    }
    public void getSummaryStats(double[] values){
        SummaryStatistics stats = new SummaryStatistics();
        for( int i = 0; i < values.length; i++) {
                stats.addValue(values[i]);
        }
        double mean = stats.getMean();
        double std = stats.getStandardDeviation();
        System.out.println(mean + "\t" + std);
    }
}
```

Generating summary statistics from multiple distributions

In this recipe, we will be creating an AggregateSummaryStatistics instance to accumulate the overall statistics and SummaryStatistics for the sample data.

How to do it...

1. Create a method that takes two double array arguments. Each array will contain two different sets of data:

   ```
   public void getAggregateStats(double[] values1, double[]
       values2){
   ```

2. Create an object of class AggregateSummaryStatistics:

   ```
   AggregateSummaryStatistics aggregate = new
   AggregateSummaryStatistics();
   ```

3. To generate summary statistics from the two distributions, create two objects of the SummaryStatistics class:

   ```
   SummaryStatistics firstSet =
       aggregate.createContributingStatistics();
   SummaryStatistics secondSet =
       aggregate.createContributingStatistics();
   ```

4. Add the values of the two distributions in the two objects created in the preceding step:

   ```
   for(int i = 0; i < values1.length; i++) {
      firstSet.addValue(values1[i]);
   }
   for(int i = 0; i < values2.length; i++) {
      secondSet.addValue(values2[i]);
   }
   ```

5. Generate aggregated statistics from the two distributions using methods of the `AggregateSummaryStatistics` class. Finally, close the method after using the generated statistics:

```
double sampleSum = aggregate.getSum();
double sampleMean = aggregate.getMean();
double sampleStd= aggregate.getStandardDeviation();
System.out.println(sampleSum + "\t" + sampleMean + "\t" +
  sampleStd);
}
```

The complete codebase for the recipe is as follows:

```
import org.apache.commons.math3.stat.descriptive.
  AggregateSummaryStatistics;
import org.apache.commons.math3.stat.descriptive.SummaryStatistics;

public class AggregateStats {
   public static void main(String[] args){
      double[] values1 = {32, 39, 14, 98, 45, 44, 45};
      double[] values2 = {34, 89, 67, 0, 15, 0, 56, 88};
      AggregateStats aggStatTest = new AggregateStats();
      aggStatTest.getAggregateStats(values1, values2);
   }
   public void getAggregateStats(double[] values1, double[] values2){
      AggregateSummaryStatistics aggregate = new
      AggregateSummaryStatistics();
      SummaryStatistics firstSet =
        aggregate.createContributingStatistics();
      SummaryStatistics secondSet =
        aggregate.createContributingStatistics();
      for(int i = 0; i < values1.length; i++) {
         firstSet.addValue(values1[i]);
      }
      for(int i = 0; i < values2.length; i++) {
         secondSet.addValue(values2[i]);
      }
      double sampleSum = aggregate.getSum();
      double sampleMean = aggregate.getMean();
      double sampleStd= aggregate.getStandardDeviation();
      System.out.println(sampleSum + "\t" + sampleMean + "\t" +
        sampleStd);
   }
}
```

There's more...

The approach in this recipe has a few disadvantages, which are discussed here:

- Every time we call the addValue() method, the call must be synchronized on the SummaryStatistics instance maintained by the aggregate
- Every time we add a value, it updates the aggregate as well as the sample

To overcome these disadvantages, a static aggregate method is available in the class.

Computing frequency distribution

The Frequency class has methods to count the number of data instances in a bucket, to count unique number of data instances, and so on. The interface to Frequency is very simple, and in most cases, it requires very few lines of code to get the desired calculations done.

As value types, Strings, integers, longs, and chars are all supported.

 Natural ordering is the default ordering for cumulative frequencies, but this can be overridden by supplying a Comparator to the constructor.

How to do it...

1. Create a method that takes a double array as argument. We will be computing the frequency distributions of the values of this array:

   ```
   public void getFreqStats(double[] values){
   ```

2. Create an object of the Frequency class:

   ```
   Frequency freq = new Frequency();
   ```

3. Add the values of the double array to this object:

   ```
   for( int i = 0; i < values.length; i++) {
       freq.addValue(values[i]);
   }
   ```

4. Generate the frequency for each value in the array:

```
for( int i = 0; i < values.length; i++) {
   System.out.println(freq.getCount(values[i]));
}
```

5. Finally, close the method:

```
}
```

The complete codebase for the recipe is as follows:

```
import org.apache.commons.math3.stat.Frequency;

public class FrequencyStats {
   public static void main(String[] args){
      double[] values = {32, 39, 14, 98, 45, 44, 45, 34, 89, 67, 0, 15,
          0, 56, 88};
      FrequencyStats freqTest = new FrequencyStats();
      freqTest.getFreqStats(values);

   }
   public void getFreqStats(double[] values){
      Frequency freq = new Frequency();
      for( int i = 0; i < values.length; i++) {
         freq.addValue(values[i]);
      }

      for( int i = 0; i < values.length; i++) {
         System.out.println(freq.getCount(values[i]));
      }
   }
}
```

Counting word frequency in a string

This recipe is quite different than the other recipes in this chapter as it deals with strings and counting word frequencies in a string. We will use both Apache Commons Math and Java 8 for this task. This recipe will use the external library while the next recipe will achieve the same with Java 8.

How to do it...

1. Create a method that takes a `String` array. The array contains all the words in a string:

```
public void getFreqStats(String[] words){
```

2. Create a `Frequency` class object:

```
Frequency freq = new Frequency();
```

3. Add all the words to the `Frequency` object:

```
for( int i = 0; i < words.length; i++) {
  freq.addValue(words[i].trim());
}
```

4. For each word, count the frequency using the `Frequency` class's `getCount()` method. Finally, after processing the frequencies, close the method:

```
for( int i = 0; i < words.length; i++) {
    System.out.println(words[i] + "=" +
      freq.getCount(words[i]));
    }
}
```

The working code for the recipe is as follows:

```
import org.apache.commons.math3.stat.Frequency;

public class WordFrequencyStatsApache {
  public static void main(String[] args){
    String str = "Horatio says 'tis but our fantasy, "
          + "And will not let belief take hold of him "
          + "Touching this dreaded sight, twice seen of us. "
          + "Therefore I have entreated him along, 35"
          + "With us to watch the minutes of this night, "
          + "That, if again this apparition come, "
          + "He may approve our eyes and speak to it.";
    String[] words = str.toLowerCase().split("\\W+");
    WordFrequencyStatsApache freqTest = new
      WordFrequencyStatsApache();
    freqTest.getFreqStats(words);

  }
  public void getFreqStats(String[] words){
```

```
Frequency freq = new Frequency();
for( int i = 0; i < words.length; i++) {
    freq.addValue(words[i].trim());
}

for( int i = 0; i < words.length; i++) {
    System.out.println(words[i] + "=" + freq.getCount(words[i]));
}
    }
}
```

How it works...

This recipe prints each word and their frequency in the string so that the output experiences duplicate words and their frequencies. You need to have a programming mechanism to avoid duplicated output when you are processing the frequencies in the last `for` loop.

The next recipe, for instance, uses a `Map` data structure to avoid duplication of words. If the ordering of the words does not matter, you can use a `HashMap`, and if the ordering of the words is important, you need to use a `TreeMap` data structure.

Counting word frequency in a string using Java 8

This recipe does not use the Apache Commons Math library to count frequencies of words in a given string; rather it uses core libraries and mechanisms introduced in Java 8.

There are many ways to implement a working example that counts word frequencies, and therefore, the readers are encouraged to look at many implementations of this recipe in Java versions released earlier than 8.

How to do it...

1. Create a method that takes a string argument. We will be counting frequencies of the words in this string:

```
public void getFreqStats(String str){
```

2. Create a `Stream` from the given string. In our case, we will be converting the string to lower case and identify words based on a regular expression `\W+`. The process of converting a string into a stream will be done in parallel:

```
Stream<String> stream =
    Stream.of(str.toLowerCase().split("\\W+")).parallel();
```

3. We will be collecting the words and their frequencies using the `collect()` method of the `Stream` class. Note that the collection will be sent to a `Map` object with a `String` and `Long` in its generics; the string will contain the word and long will contain its frequency:

```
Map<String, Long> wordFreq =
    stream.collect(Collectors.groupingBy
        (String::toString,Collectors.counting()));
```

4. Finally, we will be using `forEach` to print the content of the map in one go and close the method:

```
wordFreq.forEach((k,v)->System.out.println(k + "=" + v));
}
```

The working example for this recipe is as follows:

```
import java.util.Map;
import java.util.stream.Collectors;
import java.util.stream.Stream;
public class WordFrequencyStatsJava {

    public static void main(String[] args){
        String str = "Horatio says 'tis but our fantasy, "
            + "And will not let belief take hold of him "
            + "Touching this dreaded sight, twice seen of us. "
            + "Therefore I have entreated him along, 35"
            + "With us to watch the minutes of this night, "
            + "That, if again this apparition come, "
            + "He may approve our eyes and speak to it.";
        WordFrequencyStatsJava freqTest = new WordFrequencyStatsJava();
```

```
        freqTest.getFreqStats(str);
    }
    public void getFreqStats(String str){
        Stream<String> stream =
Stream.of(str.toLowerCase().split("\\W+")).parallel();
        Map<String, Long> wordFreq = stream
.collect(Collectors.groupingBy(String::toString,Collectors.counting()));
        wordFreq.forEach((k,v)->System.out.println(k + "=" + v));
    }
}
```

Computing simple regression

The `SimpleRegression` class supports ordinary least squares regression with one independent variable: $y = intercept + slope * x$, where `intercept` is an optional parameter. The class is also capable of providing standard error for `intercept`. Observations (x,y) pairs can either be added to the model one at a time or they can be provided in a two-dimensional array. In this recipe, the data points are added one at a time.

 The observations are not stored in memory and therefore there is no limit on the number of observations that can be added to the model.

How to do it...

1. To compute simple regression, create a method that takes a two-dimensional `double` array. The array represents a series of (x,y) values:

   ```
   public void calculateRegression(double[][] data){
   ```

2. Create a `SimpleRegression` object, and add the data:

   ```
   SimpleRegression regression = new SimpleRegression();
   regression.addData(data);
   ```

    If you do not have interception or if you want to exclude it from the calculation, you need to use a different constructor to create the `SimpleRegression` object `SimpleRegression regression = new SimpleRegression(false);`.

3. Find out the interception, slope, and standard error for interception and slope. Finally, close the method:

```
System.out.println(regression.getIntercept());
System.out.println(regression.getSlope());
  System.out.println(regression.getSlopeStdErr());
}
```

The complete codebase for this recipe is as follows:

```
import org.apache.commons.math3.stat.regression.SimpleRegression;

public class RegressionTest {
    public static void main(String[] args){
        double[][] data = { { 1, 3 }, {2, 5 }, {3, 7 }, {4, 14 }, {5, 11 }};
        RegressionTest test = new RegressionTest();
        test.calculateRegression(data);
    }
    public void calculateRegression(double[][] data){
        SimpleRegression regression = new SimpleRegression();
        regression.addData(data);
        System.out.println(regression.getIntercept());
        System.out.println(regression.getSlope());
        System.out.println(regression.getSlopeStdErr());
    }
}
```

All statistics will return NaN if the number of observations are less than two in the model or when all x values are the same.
Using the getter methods, if you add more data after you get statistics, you will be able to get updated statistics without using a new instance.

Computing ordinary least squares regression

The OLSMultipleLinearRegression provides *Ordinary Least Squares Regression* to fit the linear model $Y=X^*b+u$. Here, Y is an n-vector regress, and X is a [n,k] matrix, where k columns are called regressors, b is k-vector of regression parameters, and u is an n-vector of error terms or residuals.

How to do it...

1. Create a method that takes a two-dimensional `double` array and a one-dimensional `double` array:

```
public void calculateOlsRegression(double[][] x, double[] y){
```

2. Create an OLS regression object and add the data points x and y:

```
OLSMultipleLinearRegression regression = new
  OLSMultipleLinearRegression();
regression.newSampleData(y, x);
```

3. Calculate various regression parameters and diagnostics using the following methods in the `OLSMultipleLinearRegression` class. The usage of these information depends on your task in hand. Finally, close the method:

```
double[] beta = regression.estimateRegressionParameters();
double[] residuals = regression.estimateResiduals();
double[][] parametersVariance =
  regression.estimateRegressionParametersVariance();
double regressandVariance =
  regression.estimateRegressandVariance();
double rSquared = regression.calculateRSquared();
double sigma = regression.estimateRegressionStandardError();
}
```

4. The x and y data points can be created as follows. For this example, we have used fixed data, and therefore, the initialization of the array indices are not made automatically. You need to create a looping system to create the x array:

```
double[] y = new double[]{11.0, 12.0, 13.0, 14.0, 15.0, 16.0};
double[][] x = new double[6][];
x[0] = new double[]{0, 0, 0, 0, 0};
x[1] = new double[]{2.0, 0, 0, 0, 0};
x[2] = new double[]{0, 3.0, 0, 0, 0};
x[3] = new double[]{0, 0, 4.0, 0, 0};
x[4] = new double[]{0, 0, 0, 5.0, 0};
x[5] = new double[]{0, 0, 0, 0, 6.0};
```

The working example for the recipe is as follows:

```
import org.apache.commons.math3.stat.regression.
  OLSMultipleLinearRegression;
public class OLSRegressionTest {
    public static void main(String[] args){
        double[] y = new double[]{11.0, 12.0, 13.0, 14.0, 15.0, 16.0};
        double[][] x = new double[6][];
        x[0] = new double[]{0, 0, 0, 0, 0};
        x[1] = new double[]{2.0, 0, 0, 0, 0};
        x[2] = new double[]{0, 3.0, 0, 0, 0};
        x[3] = new double[]{0, 0, 4.0, 0, 0};
        x[4] = new double[]{0, 0, 0, 5.0, 0};
        x[5] = new double[]{0, 0, 0, 0, 6.0};
        OLSRegressionTest test = new OLSRegressionTest();
        test.calculateOlsRegression(x, y);
    }
    public void calculateOlsRegression(double[][] x, double[] y){
        OLSMultipleLinearRegression regression = new
          OLSMultipleLinearRegression();
        regression.newSampleData(y, x);
        double[] beta = regression.estimateRegressionParameters();
        double[] residuals = regression.estimateResiduals();
        double[][] parametersVariance =
          regression.estimateRegressionParametersVariance();
        double regressandVariance =
          regression.estimateRegressandVariance();
        double rSquared = regression.calculateRSquared();
        double sigma = regression.estimateRegressionStandardError();
//print out the values here
    }
}
```

Two events can throw `IllegalArgumentException` when the dimensions of the input data arrays do not match and the data arrays do not contain sufficient data to estimate the model.

Computing generalized least squares regression

In this recipe, we will see another variant of least squares regression named generalized least squares regression. `GLSMultipleLinearRegression` implements *Generalized Least Squares* to fit the linear model *Y=X*b+u*.

How to do it...

1. Create a method that takes a two-dimensional double array, a one-dimensional double array, and a two-dimensional double array for the regression's omega parameter:

```
public void calculateGlsRegression(double[][] x, double[] y,
    double[][] omega){
```

2. Create a GLS regression object, the data points, and the omega parameter:

```
GLSMultipleLinearRegression regression = new
    GLSMultipleLinearRegression();
regression.newSampleData(y, x, omega);
```

3. Using the methods of the `GLSMultipleLinearRegression` class, compute various statistics of the regression and finally, close the method:

```
double[] beta = regression.estimateRegressionParameters();
double[] residuals = regression.estimateResiduals();
double[][] parametersVariance =
    regression.estimateRegressionParametersVariance();
double regressandVariance =
    regression.estimateRegressandVariance();
double sigma = regression.estimateRegressionStandardError();
}
```

4. To see how we can populate the two arrays x and y, refer to the preceding recipe. For this recipe, we also will need omega values besides x and y data points. The omega values can be inserted in a two-dimensional double array as follows:

```
double[][] omega = new double[6][];
omega[0] = new double[]{1.1, 0, 0, 0, 0, 0};
omega[1] = new double[]{0, 2.2, 0, 0, 0, 0};
omega[2] = new double[]{0, 0, 3.3, 0, 0, 0};
```

```
        omega[3] = new double[]{0, 0, 0, 4.4, 0, 0};
        omega[4] = new double[]{0, 0, 0, 0, 5.5, 0};
        omega[5] = new double[]{0, 0, 0, 0, 0, 6.6};
```

The complete class, the method, and the driver method for this recipe are as follows:

```
import org.apache.commons.math3.stat.regression.
    GLSMultipleLinearRegression;
public class GLSRegressionTest {
    public static void main(String[] args){
        double[] y = new double[]{11.0, 12.0, 13.0, 14.0, 15.0, 16.0};
        double[][] x = new double[6][];
        x[0] = new double[]{0, 0, 0, 0, 0};
        x[1] = new double[]{2.0, 0, 0, 0, 0};
        x[2] = new double[]{0, 3.0, 0, 0, 0};
        x[3] = new double[]{0, 0, 4.0, 0, 0};
        x[4] = new double[]{0, 0, 0, 5.0, 0};
        x[5] = new double[]{0, 0, 0, 0, 6.0};
        double[][] omega = new double[6][];
        omega[0] = new double[]{1.1, 0, 0, 0, 0, 0};
        omega[1] = new double[]{0, 2.2, 0, 0, 0, 0};
        omega[2] = new double[]{0, 0, 3.3, 0, 0, 0};
        omega[3] = new double[]{0, 0, 0, 4.4, 0, 0};
        omega[4] = new double[]{0, 0, 0, 0, 5.5, 0};
        omega[5] = new double[]{0, 0, 0, 0, 0, 6.6};
        GLSRegressionTest test = new GLSRegressionTest();
        test.calculateGlsRegression(x, y, omega);
    }
    public void calculateGlsRegression(double[][] x, double[] y,
      double[][] omega){
        GLSMultipleLinearRegression regression = new
          GLSMultipleLinearRegression();
        regression.newSampleData(y, x, omega);
        double[] beta = regression.estimateRegressionParameters();
        double[] residuals = regression.estimateResiduals();
        double[][] parametersVariance =
          regression.estimateRegressionParametersVariance();
        double regressandVariance =
          regression.estimateRegressandVariance();
        double sigma = regression.estimateRegressionStandardError();
//print out the values here
    }
}
```

Calculating covariance of two sets of data points

Unbiased covariances are given by the formula $cov(X, Y) = sum [(xi - E(X))(yi - E(Y))] / (n - 1)$, where $E(X)$ is the mean of X and $E(Y)$ is the mean of the Y values. Non-bias-corrected estimates use n in place of $n - 1$. To determine if the covariance is bias corrected or not, we need to set an additional, optional parameter called `biasCorrected` which is set to true by default.

How to do it...

1. Create a method that takes two one-dimensional double arrays. Each array represents a set of data points:

```
public void calculateCov(double[] x, double[] y){
```

2. Calculate the covariance of the two sets of data points as follows:

```
double covariance = new Covariance().covariance(x, y, false);
```

For this recipe, we have used non-bias-corrected covariance, and therefore, we have used three parameters in the `covariace()` method. To use unbiased covariance between two `double` arrays, remove the third parameter,
```
double covariance = new Covariance().covariance(x, y);:
```

3. Use the covariance as per your requirement and close the method:

```
System.out.println(covariance);
}
```

The working code for this recipe is as follows:

```
import org.apache.commons.math3.stat.correlation.Covariance;

public class CovarianceTest {
    public static void main(String[] args){
        double[] x = {43, 21, 25, 42, 57, 59};
        double[] y = {99, 65, 79, 75, 87, 81};
        CovarianceTest test = new CovarianceTest();
        test.calculateCov(x, y);
```

```
    }
    public void calculateCov(double[] x, double[] y){
        double covariance = new Covariance().covariance(x, y, false);//If
            false is removed, we get unbiased covariance
        System.out.println(covariance);
    }
}
```

Calculating Pearson's correlation of two sets of data points

PearsonsCorrelation computes correlations defined by the formula cor(X, Y) = sum[(xi - E(X))(yi - E(Y))] / [(n - 1)s(X)s(Y)], where E(X) and E(Y) are means of X and Y, and s(X) and s(Y) are their respective standard deviations.

How to do it...

1. Create a method that takes two double arrays that represent two sets of data points:

   ```
   public void calculatePearson(double[] x, double[] y){
   ```

2. Create a PearsonsCorrelation object:

   ```
   PearsonsCorrelation pCorrelation = new PearsonsCorrelation();
   ```

3. Compute correlation of the two sets of data points:

   ```
   double cor = pCorrelation.correlation(x, y);
   ```

4. Use the correlation as per your requirements, and close the method:

   ```
   System.out.println(cor);
   }
   ```

The complete code for the recipe is as follows:

```
import org.apache.commons.math3.stat.correlation.PearsonsCorrelation;

public class PearsonTest {
    public static void main(String[] args){
        double[] x = {43, 21, 25, 42, 57, 59};
        double[] y = {99, 65, 79, 75, 87, 81};
        PearsonTest test = new PearsonTest();
        test.calculatePearson(x, y);
    }
    public void calculatePearson(double[] x, double[] y){
        PearsonsCorrelation pCorrelation = new PearsonsCorrelation();
        double cor = pCorrelation.correlation(x, y);
        System.out.println(cor);
    }
}
```

Conducting a paired t-test

Among the number of standard statistical significance test libraries offered by Apache Commons Math, we will be using only a few to demonstrate paired the t-test, Chi-square test, one-way ANOVA test, and the Kolmogorov-Smirnov test. Readers can carry out other significance tests as the codes will use the static methods in the TestUtils class to execute tests.

Apache Commons Math has support for both one-sample and two-sample t-tests. Besides, two sample tests can be either paired or unpaired. The unpaired two-sample tests can be conducted with and without the assumption that the subpopulation variances are equal.

How to do it...

1. Create a method that takes two sets of double values as arguments. We will be conducting a paired t-test to find out any statistical significance between these two sets of values:

```
public void getTtest(double[] sample1, double[] sample2){
```

2. The t-statistic of the two distributions can be found using the `pairedT()` method:

```
System.out.println(TestUtils.pairedT(sample1, sample2));
```

3. The p-value of the paired t-test can be found using `pairedTTest()` method:

```
System.out.println(TestUtils.pairedTTest(sample1, sample2));
```

4. Finally, the significance in difference between two distributions for any given confidence interval or alpha value can be found as follows:

```
System.out.println(TestUtils.pairedTTest(sample1, sample2,
    0.05));
```

In this example, the third parameter is set to 0.05, which denotes that we want to know whether the difference is significant at alpha level set to 0.05 or at 95% confidence interval.

5. In the end, close the method:

```
}
```

The working example for the recipe is as follows:

```
import org.apache.commons.math3.stat.inference.TestUtils;
public class TTest {
    public static void main(String[] args){
        double[] sample1 = {43, 21, 25, 42, 57, 59};
        double[] sample2 = {99, 65, 79, 75, 87, 81};
        TTest test = new TTest();
        test.getTtest(sample1, sample2);
    }
    public void getTtest(double[] sample1, double[] sample2){
        System.out.println(TestUtils.pairedT(sample1, sample2));//t
            statistics
        System.out.println(TestUtils.pairedTTest(sample1, sample2));//p
            value
        System.out.println(TestUtils.pairedTTest(sample1, sample2,
            0.05));
    }
}
```

Conducting a Chi-square test

For conducting a Chi-square test on two sets of data distributions, one distribution will be called the observed distribution and the other distribution will be called the expected distribution.

How to do it...

1. Create a method that takes these two distributions as arguments. Note that the observed distribution is a `long` array, while the expected distribution is a `double` array:

   ```
   public void getChiSquare(long[] observed, double[] expected){
   ```

2. Get the t-statistic of the Chi-square test as follows:

   ```
   System.out.println(TestUtils.chiSquare(expected, observed));
   ```

3. The p-value of the test can found in a similar way but with a different method:

   ```
   System.out.println(TestUtils.chiSquareTest(expected,
       observed));
   ```

4. We can also observe whether the difference between the expected and observed data distributions is significant for a given confidence interval, as follows:

   ```
   System.out.println(TestUtils.chiSquareTest(expected, observed,
       0.05));
   ```

   In this example, our confidence interval is set to 95%, and therefore, the third parameter of the `chiSquareTest()` method is set to the alpha value to 0.05.

5. Finally, close the method:

   ```
   }
   ```

The complete code for this recipe is here:

```
import org.apache.commons.math3.stat.inference.TestUtils;
public class ChiSquareTest {
    public static void main(String[] args){
        long[] observed = {43, 21, 25, 42, 57, 59};
        double[] expected = {99, 65, 79, 75, 87, 81};
        ChiSquareTest test = new ChiSquareTest();
```

```
        test.getChiSquare(observed, expected);
    }
    public void getChiSquare(long[] observed, double[] expected){
        System.out.println(TestUtils.chiSquare(expected, observed));//t
          statistics
        System.out.println(TestUtils.chiSquareTest(expected,
          observed));//p value
        System.out.println(TestUtils.chiSquareTest(expected, observed,
          0.05));
    }
}
```

Conducting the one-way ANOVA test

ANOVA stands for Analysis of Variance. In this recipe, we will see how to use Java to do a one-way ANOVA test to determine whether the means of three or more independent and unrelated sets of data points are significantly different.

How to do it...

1. Create a method that takes various data distributions. In our example, we will be applying ANOVA on relations of calories, fats, carbohydrates, and control:

   ```
   public void calculateAnova(double[] calorie, double[] fat,
       double[] carb, double[] control){
   ```

2. Create an ArrayList. This ArrayList will contain all the data. The data distributions the method takes as arguments can be seen as classes. Therefore, in our example, we have named them classes:

   ```
   List<double[]> classes = new ArrayList<double[]>();
   ```

3. Sequentially, add the data from the four classes into ArrayList:

   ```
   classes.add(calorie);
   classes.add(fat);
   classes.add(carb);
   classes.add(control);
   ```

4. The F-value of the one-way ANOVA test can be found as follows:

```
System.out.println(TestUtils.oneWayAnovaFValue(classes));
```

5. The p-value of the one-way ANOVA test can be found using the following line:

```
System.out.println(TestUtils.oneWayAnovaPValue(classes));
```

6. Finally, to find out whether the differences of the data points in the given four classes are significant or not, use the following piece of code:

```
System.out.println(TestUtils.oneWayAnovaTest(classes, 0.05));
```

7. Use a parenthesis to close the method:

```
}
```

The complete code for the one-way ANOVA test recipe is as follows:

```
import java.util.ArrayList;
import java.util.List;
import org.apache.commons.math3.stat.inference.TestUtils;
public class AnovaTest {
    public static void main(String[] args){
        double[] calorie = {8, 9, 6, 7, 3};
        double[] fat = {2, 4, 3, 5, 1};
        double[] carb = {3, 5, 4, 2, 3};
        double[] control = {2, 2, -1, 0, 3};
        AnovaTest test = new AnovaTest();
        test.calculateAnova(calorie, fat, carb, control);
    }
    public void calculateAnova(double[] calorie, double[] fat,
        double[]
    carb, double[] control){
    List<double[]> classes = new ArrayList<double[]>();
    classes.add(calorie);
    classes.add(fat);
    classes.add(carb);
    classes.add(control);
    System.out.println(TestUtils.oneWayAnovaFValue(classes));
    System.out.println(TestUtils.oneWayAnovaPValue(classes));
    System.out.println(TestUtils.oneWayAnovaTest(classes, 0.05));
    }
}
```

The p-values returned by t-, chi-square, and ANOVA tests are exact, based on numerical approximations to the t-, chi-square, and F-distributions in the `distribution` package.

Conducting a Kolmogorov-Smirnov test

The Kolmogorov-Smirnov test (or simply KS test) is a test of equality for one-dimensional probability distributions that are continuous in nature. It is one of the popular methods to determine whether two sets of data points differ significantly.

How to do it...

1. Create a method that takes two different data distributions. We will see if the difference of the two data distributions is significant by using Kolmogorov-Smirnov test:

```
public void calculateKs(double[] x, double[] y){
```

2. One of the key statistics in the test is d-statistic. It is a double value that we will need in order to calculate the p-value of the test:

```
double d = TestUtils.kolmogorovSmirnovStatistic(x, y);
```

3. To evaluate the null hypothesis that the values are drawn from a unit normal distribution, use the following code:

```
System.out.println(TestUtils.kolmogorovSmirnovTest(x, y,
    false));
```

4. Finally, the p-value of the significance test can be found in the following way:

```
System.out.println(TestUtils.exactP(d, x.length, y.length,
    false));
```

The complete code for the recipe is as follows:

```java
import org.apache.commons.math3.stat.inference.TestUtils;

public class KSTest {
    public static void main(String[] args){
        double[] x = {43, 21, 25, 42, 57, 59};
        double[] y = {99, 65, 79, 75, 87, 81};
        KSTest test = new KSTest();
        test.calculateKs(x, y);
    }
    public void calculateKs(double[] x, double[] y){
        double d = TestUtils.kolmogorovSmirnovStatistic(x, y);
        System.out.println(TestUtils.kolmogorovSmirnovTest(x, y, false));
        System.out.println(TestUtils.exactP(d, x.length, y.length,
            false));
    }
}
```

That is the end of the recipes in this chapter. There are so many different statistical analyses possible to do with the Apache Commons Math Library. For more use of the library, please refer to the Javadoc of the version used in this chapter that can be found at
http://commons.apache.org/proper/commons-math/javadocs/api-3.6.1/index.html.

4
Learning from Data - Part 1

In this chapter, we will cover the following recipes:

- Creating and saving an Attribute-Relation File Format file
- Cross-validating a machine-learning model
- Classifying unseen test data
- Classifying unseen test data with a filtered classifier
- Generating linear regression models
- Generating logistic regression models
- Clustering data using the KMeans algorithm
- Clustering data from classes
- Learning association rules from data
- Selecting features/attributes using the low-level method, the filtering method, and the meta-classifier method

Introduction

In this chapter and the following, chapter we will cover recipes that use machine-learning techniques to learn patterns from data. These patterns are the center of attention for at least three key machine-learning tasks: classification, regression, and clustering. Classification is the task of predicting a value from a nominal class. In contrast to classification, regression models attempt to predict a value from a numeric class. Finally, clustering is the technique of grouping of data points based on their proximity.

There are many Java-based tools, workbenches, libraries, and APIs that can be used for research and development in the areas of machine learning mentioned earlier. One of the most popular tools is **Waikato Environment of Knowledge Analysis** (**Weka**), which is a free software licensed under the GNU General Public License. It is written in Java and has a very good collection of data preparation and filtering options, classical machine learning algorithms with customizable parameter settings, and powerful data visualization options. Moreover, it has a very handy **Graphical User Interface** (**GUI**) for non-Java users besides its easy-to-use Java libraries.

Our focus, in this chapter, will be on demonstrating how to do regular data science activities such as dataset preparation for a tool, model generation for different types of machine-learning tasks, and model performance evaluation using Weka.

 Note that the codes in the recipes of this chapter will not implement any exception handling, and therefore, the catch blocks are intentionally left blank. The exception handling totally depends on the user and his/her needs.

Creating and saving an Attribute-Relation File Format (ARFF) file

Weka's native file format is called **Attribute-Relation File Format** (**ARFF**). There are two logical parts of an ARFF file. The first part is called *header*, and the second part is called *data*. The *header* part has three physical sections that must be present in an ARFF file–the name of the relation, the attributes or features, and their data types and ranges. The *data* part has one physical section that must also be present to generate a machine-learning model. The *header* part of an ARFF file looks like the following:

```
% 1. Title: Iris Plants Database
  %
% 2. Sources:
  %      (a) Creator: R.A. Fisher
  %      (b) Donor: Michael Marshall (MARSHALL%PLU@io.arc.nasa.gov)
  %      (c) Date: July, 1988
  %
@RELATION iris

@ATTRIBUTE sepallength      NUMERIC
@ATTRIBUTE sepalwidth       NUMERIC
@ATTRIBUTE petallength      NUMERIC
@ATTRIBUTE petalwidth       NUMERIC
@ATTRIBUTE class   {Iris-setosa,Iris-versicolor,Iris-virginica}
```

Here, the lines that start with the % symbol indicate a comment. The name of the relation is indicated by the @RELATION keyword. The next few lines starting with the @ATTRIBUTE keyword denotes the features or attributes. In the example, the name of the relation is iris ,and the dataset has five attributes–the first four attributes are of *numeric* type, and the last attribute is the *class* of a data point, which is a *nominal* attribute with three class values.

The *data* section of an ARFF file looks like this:

```
@DATA
5.1,3.5,1.4,0.2,Iris-setosa
4.9,3.0,1.4,0.2,Iris-setosa
4.7,3.2,1.3,0.2,Iris-setosa
4.6,3.1,1.5,0.2,Iris-setosa
5.0,3.6,1.4,0.2,Iris-setosa
5.4,3.9,1.7,0.4,Iris-setosa
4.6,3.4,1.4,0.3,Iris-setosa
```

The example shows that the data section starts with a keyword @DATA and then contains comma-separated values of the attributes. The order of the comma-separated values should be in line with the order of attributes in the *attribute* section.

The @RELATION, @ATTRIBUTE, and @DATA declarations are case insensitive.

To understand more about the ARFF file format, the types of attributes supported in Weka and sparse ARFF files, please refer to http://www.cs.waikato.ac.nz/ml/weka/arff.html.

In order to perform the recipes in this chapter, we will require the following:

To develop our codes, we will be using Eclipse IDE, and to successfully execute all codes in this chapter, we will be adding the Weka JAR file into a project. To do so, follow these steps:

1. To download Weka, go to
   http://www.cs.waikato.ac.nz/ml/weka/downloading.html and you will find download options for Windows, Mac, and other operating systems such as Linux. Read through the options carefully and download the appropriate version.

At the time of writing of this book, 3.9.0 was the latest version for the developers, and as the author already had version 1.8 JVM installed in his 64-bit Windows machine, he has chosen to download a self-extracting executable for 64-bit Windows without a Java VM as shown in the following screenshot:

- **Developer version**

    This is the trunk of Weka and continues from the stable-3-8 code line. It receives both bug fixes and new features.

    - **Windows x86**

        Click **here** to download a self-extracting executable that includes Java VM 1.8 (weka-3-9-0jre.exe; 100.7 MB)

        Click **here** to download a self-extracting executable without the Java VM (weka-3-9-0.exe; 50.1 MB)

        These executables will install Weka in your Program Menu. Download the second version if you already have Java 1.7 (or later) on your system.

    - **Windows x64**

        Click **here** to download a self-extracting executable that includes 64 bit Java VM 1.8 (weka-3-9-0jre-x64.exe; 105.4 MB)

        Click **here** to download a self-extracting executable without the Java VM (weka-3-9-0-x64.exe; 50.1 MB)

        These executables will install Weka in your Program Menu. Download the second version if you already have Java 1.7 (or later) on your system.

    - **Mac OS X**

        Click **here** to download a disk image for OS X that contains a Mac application including Oracle's Java 1.8 JVM (weka-3-9-0-oracle-jvm.dmg; 125.7 MB)

    - **Other platforms (Linux, etc.)**

        Click **here** to download a zip archive containing Weka (weka-3-9-0.zip; 50.4 MB)

2. After the download is complete, double-click on the executable file and follow the on screen instructions. You need to install the *full* version of Weka.

3. Once the installation is done, do not run the software. Instead, go to the directory where you have installed it and find the Java Archive File for Weka (`weka.jar`). Add this file to your Eclipse project as external library:

changelogs	10/27/2016 7:14 PM	File folder		
data	10/27/2016 7:14 PM	File folder		
doc	10/27/2016 7:14 PM	File folder		
COPYING	4/14/2016 3:04 AM	File	35 KB	
documentation	4/14/2016 3:04 AM	CSS File	1 KB	
documentation	4/14/2016 3:04 AM	Chrome HTML Do...	2 KB	
README	4/14/2016 3:04 AM	File	16 KB	
remoteExperimentServer	4/14/2016 3:04 AM	Executable Jar File	42 KB	
RunWeka	4/14/2016 3:04 AM	Windows Batch File	1 KB	
RunWeka.class	4/14/2016 3:04 AM	CLASS File	5 KB	
RunWeka	4/14/2016 3:04 AM	Configuration sett...	3 KB	
uninstall	10/27/2016 7:14 PM	Application	56 KB	
Weka 3.9 (with console)	10/27/2016 7:14 PM	Shortcut	2 KB	
Weka 3.9	10/27/2016 7:14 PM	Shortcut	2 KB	
weka	4/14/2016 3:04 AM	GIF image	30 KB	
weka	4/14/2016 3:04 AM	ICO File	351 KB	
weka	4/14/2016 3:04 AM	Executable Jar File	10,740 KB	
wekaexamples	4/14/2016 3:04 AM	WinRAR ZIP archive	14,245 KB	
WekaManual	4/14/2016 3:04 AM	Adobe Acrobat D...	6,467 KB	
weka-src	4/14/2016 3:04 AM	Executable Jar File	10,514 KB	

If you need to download older versions of Weka for some reason, all of them can be found at `https://sourceforge.net/projects/weka/files/`. Please note that there is a possibility that many of the methods from old versions are deprecated and therefore not supported any more.

How to do it...

1. We will be keeping all our codes in a `main()` method instead of creating a method. Therefore, create a class and a `main` method:

    ```
    public class WekaArffTest {
        public static void main(String[] args) throws Exception {
    ```

    Note that the `main` method will contain codes related to Weka's libraries and therefore throws exception

2. Create two ArrayLists. The first `ArrayList` will contain the attributes, and the second `ArrayList` will contain the class values. Therefore, the generic of the first `ArrayList` will be of type Attribute (which is, in fact, a Weka class to model attributes), while the generic of the second `ArrayList` can be string to denote the class labels:

    ```
    ArrayList<Attribute>     attributes;
    ArrayList<String>        classVals;
    ```

3. Next, create an Instances object. This object will be modelling the instances in the @DATA section of an ARFF file; each line in the @DATA section is an instance:

    ```
    Instances        data;
    ```

4. Create a double array. The array will be containing the values of the attributes:

    ```
    double[]         values;
    ```

5. Now is the time to set up the attributes. We will be creating the @ATTRIBUTE section of our ARFF file. First, instantiate the attributes:

    ```
    attributes = new ArrayList<Attribute>();
    ```

6. Next, we will be creating a numeric attribute named age and will add it to our attributes `ArrayList`:

    ```
    attributes.add(new Attribute("age"));
    ```

7. We will now be creating a string attribute named name and will add it to our attributes `ArrayList`. Before that, however, we will be creating an empty `ArrayList` of type String and assigning NULL to it. This empty `ArrayList` will be used in the constructor of the `Attribute` class to indicate that name is a string type attribute and not nominal, like a class attribute:

```
ArrayList<String> empty = null;
attributes.add(new Attribute("name", empty));
```

8. Weka supports date type attributes as well. Next we will be creating a dob attribute to denote date of birth:

```
attributes.add(new Attribute("dob", "yyyy-MM-dd"));
```

9. We will then be instantiating the class value `ArrayList` and will create five class values–class1, class2, class3, class4, and class5:

```
classVals = new ArrayList<String>();
for (int i = 0; i < 5; i++){
   classVals.add("class" + (i + 1));
}
```

10. With these class values, we will next create an attribute and add it to our attributes `ArrayList`:

```
Attribute classVal = new Attribute("class", classVals);
attributes.add(classVal);
```

11. With this line of code, we have completed creating our @ATTRIBUTE section of the ARFF file. Next, we will be populating the @DATA section.

12. First, we will be creating an Instances object with a name MyRelation (which is the parameter in the @RELATION section of our ARFF file), and all the attributes:

```
data = new Instances("MyRelation", attributes, 0);
```

13. We will be using the double array that we created earlier to generate four values for our four attributes; we will be assigning age, name, date of birth, and a class value (randomly chosen it has no significance in this example):

```
values = new double[data.numAttributes()];
values[0] = 35;
values[1] = data.attribute(1).addStringValue("John Doe");
values[2] = data.attribute(2).parseDate("1981-01-20");
values[3] = classVals.indexOf("class3");
```

14. Then, we add these values to our data section:

```
data.add(new DenseInstance(1.0, values));
```

15. In a similar way, we will be creating a second instance for our data section as follows:

```
values = new double[data.numAttributes()];
values[0] = 30;
values[1] = data.attribute(1).addStringValue("Harry Potter");
values[2] = data.attribute(2).parseDate("1986-07-05");
values[3] = classVals.indexOf("class1");
data.add(new DenseInstance(1.0, values));
```

16. If we want to save the ARFF file somewhere, add the following segment of code:

```
BufferedWriter writer = new BufferedWriter(new
  FileWriter("c:/training.arff"));
writer.write(data.toString());
writer.close();
```

17. The entire content of the ARFF file that we just created can be displayed on console output as well:

```
System.out.println(data);
```

18. At this point, close the method and the class:

```
    }
  }
```

The complete code for the recipe is as follows:

```java
import java.io.BufferedWriter;
import java.io.FileWriter;
import java.util.ArrayList;

import weka.core.Attribute;
import weka.core.DenseInstance;
import weka.core.Instances;

public class WekaArffTest {
    public static void main(String[] args) throws Exception {
        ArrayList<Attribute>      attributes;
        ArrayList<String>      classVals;
        Instances         data;
        double[]          values;

        // Set up attributes
        attributes = new ArrayList<Attribute>();
        // Numeric attribute
        attributes.add(new Attribute("age"));
        // String attribute
        ArrayList<String> empty = null;
        attributes.add(new Attribute("name", empty));
        // Date attribute
        attributes.add(new Attribute("dob", "yyyy-MM-dd"));
        classVals = new ArrayList<String>();
        for (int i = 0; i < 5; i++){
           classVals.add("class" + (i + 1));
        }
        Attribute classVal = new Attribute("class", classVals);
        attributes.add(classVal);

        // Create Instances object
        data = new Instances("MyRelation", attributes, 0);

        // Data fill up
        // First instance
        values = new double[data.numAttributes()];
        values[0] = 35;
        values[1] = data.attribute(1).addStringValue("John Doe");
        values[2] = data.attribute(2).parseDate("1981-01-20");
        values[3] = classVals.indexOf("class3");

        // add
        data.add(new DenseInstance(1.0, values));

        // Second instance
```

```
        values = new double[data.numAttributes()];
        values[0] = 30;
        values[1] = data.attribute(1).addStringValue("Harry Potter");
        values[2] = data.attribute(2).parseDate("1986-07-05");
        values[3] = classVals.indexOf("class1");

        // add
        data.add(new DenseInstance(1.0, values));

        //writing arff file to disk
        BufferedWriter writer = new BufferedWriter(new
          FileWriter("c:/training.arff"));
        writer.write(data.toString());
        writer.close();
        // Output data
        System.out.println(data);
    }
}
```

The output of the code is as follows:

```
@relation MyRelation

@attribute age numeric
@attribute name string
@attribute dob date yyyy-MM-dd
@attribute class {class1,class2,class3,class4,class5}

@data
35,'John Doe',1981-01-20,class3
30,'Harry Potter',1986-07-05,class1
```

Cross-validating a machine learning model

In this recipe, we will be creating four methods that will be doing four different things–one method will load an ARFF file (assuming that the ARFF file is already created and saved somewhere); the second method will read the data in the ARFF file and generate a machine-learning model (we have arbitrarily chosen Naive Bayes model); the third method will be saving the model by using serialization, and the last method will be evaluating the model on the ARFF file using a 10-fold cross-validation.

How to do it...

1. Create two instance variables. The first will contain all the instances of the iris dataset. The iris ARFF dataset can be found in the data folder of your installed Weka directory. The second variable will be a `NaiveBayes` classifier:

```
Instances iris = null;
NaiveBayes nb;
```

2. Our first method will be loading the iris ARFF file using the `DataSource` class, reading the content with the `getDataSet()` method of the class, and setting the position of the class attribute. If you open the `iris.arff` dataset using a notepad, you will see that the class attribute is the last attribute, which is a convention, not a mandatory rule. Therefore, `iris.setClassIndex(iris.numAttributes() - 1);` has been used to assign the last attribute as class attribute. For any classification task in Weka, this is very important:

```
public void loadArff(String arffInput){
  DataSource source = null;
  try {
    source = new DataSource(arffInput);
    iris = source.getDataSet();
    if (iris.classIndex() == -1)
    iris.setClassIndex(iris.numAttributes() - 1);
  } catch (Exception e1) {
  }
}
```

3. Our next method will be generating a `NaiveBayes` classifier using the `buildClassifier(dataset)` method of the `NaiveBayes` class, based on the iris dataset:

```
public void generateModel(){
  nb = new NaiveBayes();
  try {
    nb.buildClassifier(iris);
  } catch (Exception e) {
  }
}
```

4. Weka has a facility to save any model that is generated using Weka. These saved models can be later used to classify unseen, unlabeled test data. We need to use Weka's `SerializationHelper` class, which has a particular method named write that takes the path to save the uses model and the model as its parameter:

```
public void saveModel(String modelPath){
    try {
        weka.core.SerializationHelper.write(modelPath, nb);
    } catch (Exception e) {
    }
}
```

5. Our final method for this recipe will be cross-validating the model for its performance evaluation using the iris dataset. For this purpose, we will be using a 10-fold cross-validation. This popular technique of model performance evaluation is very useful if we have only a small amount of data. However, it has some limitation, too. The discussion of this method's pros and cons is beyond the scope of this cookbook. Interested readers may refer to `https://en.wikipedia.org/wiki/Cross-validation_(statistics)` for more details:

```
public void crossValidate(){
    Evaluation eval = null;
    try {
        eval = new Evaluation(iris);
        eval.crossValidateModel(nb, iris, 10, new Random(1));
        System.out.println(eval.toSummaryString());
    } catch (Exception e1) {
    }
}
```

The line `eval.crossValidateModel(nb, iris, 10, new Random(1));` uses the model and the dataset as its first two parameters. The third parameter denotes that this is a 10-fold cross-validation. The last parameter is to introduce randomization into the process, which is very important since, in most cases, the data instances in our datasets are not randomized.

The complete executable code for this recipe is as follows:

```
import java.util.Random;

import weka.classifiers.Evaluation;
import weka.classifiers.bayes.NaiveBayes;
import weka.core.Instances;
import weka.core.converters.ConverterUtils.DataSource;

public class WekaCVTest {
    Instances iris = null;
    NaiveBayes nb;

    public void loadArff(String arffInput){
        DataSource source = null;
        try {
            source = new DataSource(arffInput);
            iris = source.getDataSet();
            if (iris.classIndex() == -1)
                iris.setClassIndex(iris.numAttributes() - 1);
        } catch (Exception e1) {
        }
    }

    public void generateModel(){
        nb = new NaiveBayes();
        try {
            nb.buildClassifier(iris);
        } catch (Exception e) {

        }
    }

    public void saveModel(String modelPath){
        try {
            weka.core.SerializationHelper.write(modelPath, nb);
        } catch (Exception e) {
        }
    }

    public void crossValidate(){
        Evaluation eval = null;
        try {
            eval = new Evaluation(iris);
            eval.crossValidateModel(nb, iris, 10, new Random(1));
            System.out.println(eval.toSummaryString());
        } catch (Exception e1) {
        }
```

```
    }
    public static void main(String[] args){
        WekaCVTest test = new WekaCVTest();
        test.loadArff("C:/Program Files/Weka-3-6/data/iris.arff");
        test.generateModel();
        test.saveModel("c:/nb.model");
        test.crossValidate();
    }
}
```

The output of the code is as follows:

```
Correctly Classified Instances          144               96      %
Incorrectly Classified Instances          6                4      %
Kappa statistic                          0.94
Mean absolute error                      0.0342
Root mean squared error                  0.155
Relative absolute error                  7.6997 %
Root relative squared error             32.8794 %
Total Number of Instances              150
```

In this recipe, we saved a machine-learning model. If you need to load a model, you need to know what type of learning algorithm (for example, Naive Bayes in this recipe) was used to generate the model so that you can load the model to the appropriate learning-algorithm object. The loading of a model can be done using the following method:

```
public void loadModel(String modelPath){
try {
nb = (NaiveBayes)
weka.core.SerializationHelper.read(modelPath);
} catch (Exception e) {
}
}
```

Classifying unseen test data

The classic supervised machine-learning classification task is to train a classifier on labeled training instances and to apply the classifier on unseen test instances. The key thing to remember here is that the number of attributes in the training set, their types, their names, and their range of values (if they are regular nominal attributes or nominal class attributes) in the training dataset must be exactly the same as those in the test dataset.

Getting ready

It is possible to have a key difference between a training dataset and a testing dataset in Weka. The @DATA section of an ARFF file in the testing section can look similar to the @DATA section of an ARFF file. It can have attribute values and class labels as follows:

```
@DATA
    5.1,3.5,1.4,0.2,Iris-setosa
    4.9,3.0,1.4,0.2,Iris-setosa
    4.7,3.2,1.3,0.2,Iris-setosa
```

When a classifier is applied on such labeled test data, the classifier ignores the class labels when predicting the class of an instance. Also note that if your test data are labeled, you can compare your classifier's predicted labels with the actual labels. This gives you an opportunity to generate evaluation metrics of your classifier. However, the most common case will be that your test data will not have any class information and, based on its learning from training data, a classifier will be predicting and assigning a class label. The @DATA section of such a test dataset will look like the following, where the class labels are unknown and represented with a question mark (?):

```
@DATA
    5.1,3.5,1.4,0.2,?
    4.9,3.0,1.4,0.2,?
    4.7,3.2,1.3,0.2,?
```

Weka's *Data* directory does not contain any such test file. So, you can create your own test file that is similar to the iris.arff file. Copy the following contents, put them in a text file by opening notepad, and save the file as iris-test.arff file in your file system (say, in C:/ drive):

```
@RELATION iris-test

@ATTRIBUTE sepallength   REAL
@ATTRIBUTE sepalwidth    REAL
@ATTRIBUTE petallength   REAL
@ATTRIBUTE petalwidth    REAL
@ATTRIBUTE class    {Iris-setosa,Iris-versicolor,Iris-virginica}
@DATA
3.1,1.2,1.2,0.5,?
2.3,2.3,2.3,0.3,?
4.2,4.4,2.1,0.2,?
3.1,2.5,1.0,0.2,?
2.8,1.6,2.0,0.2,?
3.0,2.6,3.3,0.3,?
4.5,2.0,3.4,0.1,?
```

```
5.3,2.0,3.1,0.2,?
3.2,1.3,2.1,0.3,?
2.1,6.4,1.2,0.1,?
```

How to do it...

1. We will have the following instance variables:

   ```
   NaiveBayes nb;
   Instances train, test, labeled;
   ```

   To make this recipe a bit challenging as well as a good learning experience for us, we will load a previously built and saved model and assign the model to our `NaiveBayes` classifier. This classifier will be applied on unlabeled testing instances. The testing instances will be copied to the classifier as labeled instances. Without altering the testing instances, the class labels predicted by the classifier will be assigned as class labels to respective labeled instances.

2. First, we will be creating a method to load a prebuilt and saved model. We, in fact, can load the classifier we built and saved in the preceding recipe named *Cross-validating a machine learning model*:

   ```
   public void loadModel(String modelPath){
     try {
       nb = (NaiveBayes)
         weka.core.SerializationHelper.read(modelPath);
     } catch (Exception e) {
     }
   }
   ```

3. Then, we need to read the training and test datasets. As a training dataset, we will be using the `iris.arff` file in the *Data* directory of the installed files of Weka in our file system. As test file, we will be using the `iris-test.arff` file we created earlier in this recipe:

   ```
   public void loadDatasets(String training, String testing){
   ```

4. To read the training dataset, we have used Weka's DataSource class. The key advantage in using this class is that it can deal with all file types supported by Weka. However, Weka users can use Java's `BufferedReader` class also to read the contents of a dataset. In this recipe, just to introduce a new way to read datasets, we will be using the `BufferedReader` class instead of the `DataSource` class.

We will be treating the ARFF file as a regular file and using a `BufferedReader` reader to point the training dataset. The reader will then be used to create training instances using the constructor of the Instances class of Weka. Finally, we will set the last attribute as the class attribute for the dataset:

```
BufferedReader reader = null;
  try {
    reader = new BufferedReader(new FileReader(training));
    train = new Instances (reader);
    train.setClassIndex(train.numAttributes() -1);
  } catch (IOException e) {

}
```

5. In a similar way, we will be reading the test dataset:

```
try {
    reader = new BufferedReader(new FileReader(testing));
    test = new Instances (reader);
    test.setClassIndex(train.numAttributes() -1);
  } catch (IOException e) {
  }
```

Note that you do not need to create a new `BufferedReader` object.

6. Finally, close the open `BufferedReader` object and end the method:

```
try {
    reader.close();
  } catch (IOException e) {
  }
}
```

7. Our next method will be creating a `NaiveBayes` classifier from the training data and applying the classifier on unseen, unlabeled instances of our test dataset. The method will also display the probability of the class value predicted by the `NaiveBayes` classifier:

```
public void classify(){
    try {
        nb.buildClassifier(train);
    } catch (Exception e) {
    }
}
```

8. We will be creating labeled instances, which are the copies of testing instances. The labels predicted by the classifier we generated in the preceding step will be assigned to these instances, leaving the testing instances unaltered:

```
labeled = new Instances(test);
```

9. Now, for each instance of our test dataset, we will be creating a class label, which is a double variable. Then, Naive Bayes will apply its `classifyInstance()` method that takes an instance as the parameter. The class label will be assigned to the class label variable and the value of this variable, will be assigned as the class label of this particular instance in the labeled instances. In other words, the ? value of the test instance in the labeled instances will be replaced by the value predicted by Naive Bayes:

```
for (int i = 0; i < test.numInstances(); i++) {
    double clsLabel;
    try {
        clsLabel = nb.classifyInstance(test.instance(i));
        labeled.instance(i).setClassValue(clsLabel);
        double[] predictionOutput =
            nb.distributionForInstance(test.instance(i));
        double predictionProbability = predictionOutput[1];
        System.out.println(predictionProbability);
    } catch (Exception e) {
    }
}
```

10. Finally, we will be writing the labeled test dataset (that is, `labeled`) in the file system:

```
public void writeArff(String outArff){
    BufferedWriter writer;
    try {
```

```
        writer = new BufferedWriter(new FileWriter(outArff));
        writer.write(labeled.toString());
        writer.close();
    } catch (IOException e) {
    }
}
```

The complete executable code for this recipe is as follows:

```java
import java.io.BufferedReader;
import java.io.BufferedWriter;
import java.io.FileReader;
import java.io.FileWriter;
import java.io.IOException;

import weka.classifiers.bayes.NaiveBayes;
import weka.core.Instances;

public class WekaTrainTest {
    NaiveBayes nb;
    Instances train, test, labeled;
    public void loadModel(String modelPath){
        try {
            nb = (NaiveBayes)
               weka.core.SerializationHelper.read(modelPath);
        } catch (Exception e) {
        }
    }
    public void loadDatasets(String training, String testing){
        BufferedReader reader = null;
        try {
            reader = new BufferedReader(new FileReader(training));
            train = new Instances (reader);
            train.setClassIndex(train.numAttributes() -1);
        } catch (IOException e) {
        }


        try {
            reader = new BufferedReader(new FileReader(testing));
            test = new Instances (reader);
            test.setClassIndex(train.numAttributes() -1);
        } catch (IOException e) {
        }

        try {
            reader.close();
```

```
        } catch (IOException e) {
        }
    }

    public void classify(){
        try {
            nb.buildClassifier(train);
        } catch (Exception e) {
        }

        labeled = new Instances(test);

        for (int i = 0; i < test.numInstances(); i++) {
            double clsLabel;
            try {
                clsLabel = nb.classifyInstance(test.instance(i));
                labeled.instance(i).setClassValue(clsLabel);
                double[] predictionOutput =
                    nb.distributionForInstance(test.instance(i));
                double predictionProbability = predictionOutput[1];
                System.out.println(predictionProbability);
            } catch (Exception e) {
            }
        }
    }

    public void writeArff(String outArff){
        BufferedWriter writer;
        try {
            writer = new BufferedWriter(new FileWriter(outArff));
            writer.write(labeled.toString());
            writer.close();
        } catch (IOException e) {
        }
    }
    public static void main(String[] args) throws Exception{
        WekaTrainTest test = new WekaTrainTest();
        test.loadModel("path to your Naive Bayes Model");
        test.loadDatasets("path to iris.arff dataset", "path to iris-
            test.arff dataset");
        test.classify();
        test.writeArff("path to your output ARFF file");
    }
}
```

On the console, you will see the probability values predicted by our model:

```
5.032582653870928E-13
2.1050052853672135E-4
5.177104804026096E-16
1.2459904922893976E-16
3.1771015903129274E-10
0.9999993509430146
0.999999944638627
0.9999999844862647
3.449759371835354E-8
4.0178483420981394E-77
```

If you open the ARFF file that is generated by the code with the class values of the previously unknown instances, you should see contents as follows:

```
@relation iris-test

@attribute sepallength numeric
@attribute sepalwidth numeric
@attribute petallength numeric
@attribute petalwidth numeric
@attribute class {Iris-setosa,Iris-versicolor,Iris-virginica}

@data
3.1,1.2,1.2,0.5,Iris-setosa
2.3,2.3,2.3,0.3,Iris-setosa
4.2,4.4,2.1,0.2,Iris-setosa
3.1,2.5,1,0.2,Iris-setosa
2.8,1.6,2,0.2,Iris-setosa
3,2.6,3.3,0.3,Iris-versicolor
4.5,2,3.4,0.1,Iris-versicolor
5.3,2,3.1,0.2,Iris-versicolor
3.2,1.3,2.1,0.3,Iris-setosa
2.1,6.4,1.2,0.1,Iris-setosa
```

Classifying unseen test data with a filtered classifier

Many times, you will need to use a filter before you develop a classifier. The filter can be used for removing, transforming, discretizing, and adding attributes, removing misclassified instances, randomizing or normalizing instances, and so on. The usual way to do that is to use Weka's Filter class and then perform a series of filtering with the class methods. Besides, Weka has a class named `FilteredClassifier`, which is a *class for running an arbitrary classifier on data that has been passed through an arbitrary filter*.

In this recipe, we will see how we can use a filter and a classifier at the same time to classify unseen test examples.

How to do it...

1. This time, we will be using a Random Forest classifier. As our dataset, we will be using `weather.nominal.arff` that can be found in the `Data` directory of the installed Weka folder in your file system.

   The following two will be our instance variables:

   ```
   Instances weather = null;
   RandomForest rf;
   ```

2. Next in our code, we will have a method to load a dataset. We will be sending the directory path for the `weather.nominal.arff` file to this method from our driver method. Using the `DataSource` class of Weka, we will be reading the data of the `weather.nominal.arff` file and setting the last attribute of the dataset as the class attribute:

   ```
   public void loadArff(String arffInput){
     DataSource source = null;
     try {
       source = new DataSource(arffInput);
       weather = source.getDataSet();
       weather.setClassIndex(iris.numAttributes() - 1);
     } catch (Exception e1) {
     }
   }
   ```

3. Next, we will be creating the method that is central to this recipe:

```
public void buildFilteredClassifier(){
```

4. To create this method we will first be creating a Random Forest classifier:

```
rf = new RandomForest();
```

5. We will be creating a filter that removes a specific attribute from the `weather.nominal.arff` file. To do so, we will be using Weka's Remove class. The following code will create a filter that will be used to remove the first attribute of our dataset:

```
Remove rm = new Remove();
rm.setAttributeIndices("1");
```

6. With our next lines of code, create a `FilteredClassifier`, add the filter that we created in the previous step, and add the `RandomForest` classifier:

```
FilteredClassifier fc = new FilteredClassifier();
fc.setFilter(rm);
fc.setClassifier(rf);
```

7. Using the Filtered classifier, we can build a Random Forest classifier from the nominal weather dataset. Then, for each instance of the nominal weather dataset, the classifier will be predicting the class values. In the try block, we will be printing the actual and predicted values for the instance:

```
try{
  fc.buildClassifier(weather);
  for (int i = 0; i < iris.numInstances(); i++){
      double pred = fc.classifyInstance(weather.instance(i));
      System.out.print("given value: " +
          weather.classAttribute().value((int)
          weather.instance(i).classValue()));
      System.out.println("---predicted value: " +
      weather.classAttribute().value((int) pred));
  }
} catch (Exception e) {
  }
}
```

The complete code for the recipe is as follows:

```
import weka.classifiers.meta.FilteredClassifier;
import weka.classifiers.trees.RandomForest;
import weka.core.Instances;
import weka.core.converters.ConverterUtils.DataSource;
import weka.filters.unsupervised.attribute.Remove;


public class WekaFilteredClassifierTest {
   Instances weather = null;
   RandomForest rf;

   public void loadArff(String arffInput){
      DataSource source = null;
      try {
         source = new DataSource(arffInput);
         weather = source.getDataSet();
         weather.setClassIndex(weather.numAttributes() - 1);
      } catch (Exception e1) {
      }
   }

   public void buildFilteredClassifier(){
      rf = new RandomForest();
      Remove rm = new Remove();
      rm.setAttributeIndices("1");
      FilteredClassifier fc = new FilteredClassifier();
      fc.setFilter(rm);
      fc.setClassifier(rf);
      try{
         fc.buildClassifier(weather);
         for (int i = 0; i < weather.numInstances(); i++){
            double pred = fc.classifyInstance(weather.instance(i));
            System.out.print("given value: " +
              weather.classAttribute().value((int)
                weather.instance(i).classValue()));
            System.out.println("---predicted value: " +
              weather.classAttribute().value((int) pred));
         }
      } catch (Exception e) {
      }
   }
   public static void main(String[] args){
      WekaFilteredClassifierTest test = new
        WekaFilteredClassifierTest();
      test.loadArff("C:/Program Files/Weka-3-
        6/data/weather.nominal.arff");
```

```
        test.buildFilteredClassifier();
    }
}
```

The output of the code will be as follows:

```
given value: no---predicted value: yes
given value: no---predicted value: no
given value: yes---predicted value: yes
given value: yes---predicted value: yes
given value: yes---predicted value: yes
given value: no---predicted value: yes
given value: yes---predicted value: yes
given value: no---predicted value: yes
given value: yes---predicted value: yes
given value: yes---predicted value: yes
given value: yes---predicted value: yes
given value: yes---predicted value: yes
given value: yes---predicted value: yes
given value: no---predicted value: yes
```

Generating linear regression models

Most of the linear regression modelling follows a general pattern–there will be many independent variables that will collectively produce a result, which is a dependent variable. For instance, we can generate a regression model to predict the price of a house based on different attributes/features of a house (mostly numeric, real values) such as its size in square feet, number of bedrooms, number of washrooms, importance of its location, and so on.

In this recipe, we will use Weka's linear regression classifier to generate a regression model.

How to do it...

1. In this recipe, the linear regression model we will be creating is based on the `cpu.arff` dataset, which can be found in the `data` directory of the Weka installation directory.

Our code will have two instance variables: the first variable will contain the data instances of the `cpu.arff` file, and the second variable will be our linear regression classifier:

```
Instances cpu = null;
LinearRegression lReg ;
```

2. Next, we will be creating a method to load the ARFF file and will assign the last attribute of the ARFF file as its class attribute:

```
public void loadArff(String arffInput){
  DataSource source = null;
  try {
    source = new DataSource(arffInput);
    cpu = source.getDataSet();
    cpu.setClassIndex(cpu.numAttributes() - 1);
  } catch (Exception e1) {
  }
}
```

3. We will be creating a method to build the linear regression model. To do so, we simply need to call the `buildClassifier()` method of our linear regression variable. The model can directly be sent as a parameter to `System.out.println()`:

```
public void buildRegression(){
  lReg = new LinearRegression();
  try {
    lReg.buildClassifier(cpu);
  } catch (Exception e) {
  }
  System.out.println(lReg);
}
```

The complete code for the recipe is as follows:

```
import weka.classifiers.functions.LinearRegression;
import weka.core.Instances;
import weka.core.converters.ConverterUtils.DataSource;

public class WekaLinearRegressionTest {
    Instances cpu = null;
    LinearRegression lReg ;

    public void loadArff(String arffInput){
        DataSource source = null;
        try {
```

```
        source = new DataSource(arffInput);
        cpu = source.getDataSet();
        cpu.setClassIndex(cpu.numAttributes() - 1);
    } catch (Exception e1) {

    }
}

public void buildRegression(){
    lReg = new LinearRegression();
    try {
        lReg.buildClassifier(cpu);
    } catch (Exception e) {

    }
    System.out.println(lReg);
}

public static void main(String[] args) throws Exception{
    WekaLinearRegressionTest test = new WekaLinearRegressionTest();
    test.loadArff("path to the cpu.arff file");
    test.buildRegression();
}
}
```

The output of the code is as follows:

```
Linear Regression Model

class =

        0.0491 * MYCT +
        0.0152 * MMIN +
        0.0056 * MMAX +
        0.6298 * CACH +
        1.4599 * CHMAX +
     -56.075
```

Generating logistic regression models

Weka has a class named Logistic, which can be used for building and using a multinomial logistic regression model with a ridge estimator. Although the original logistic regression does not deal with instance weights, the algorithm in Weka has been modified to handle the instance weights.

In this recipe, we will use Weka to generate a logistic regression model on the iris dataset.

How to do it...

1. We will be generating a logistic regression model from the `iris` dataset, which can be found in the `data` directory in the installed folder of Weka.

   Our code will have two instance variables: one will be containing the data instances of the iris dataset, and the other will be the logistic regression classifier:

   ```
   Instances iris = null;
   Logistic logReg ;
   ```

2. We will be using a method to load and read the dataset, as well as to assign its class attribute (the last attribute of the `iris.arff` file):

   ```
   public void loadArff(String arffInput){
     DataSource source = null;
     try {
       source = new DataSource(arffInput);
       iris = source.getDataSet();
       iris.setClassIndex(iris.numAttributes() - 1);
     } catch (Exception e1) {
     }
   }
   ```

3. Next, we will be creating the most important method of our recipe that builds a logistic regression classifier from the `iris` dataset:

   ```
   public void buildRegression(){
     logReg = new Logistic();
     try {
       logReg.buildClassifier(iris);
     } catch (Exception e) {
     }
     System.out.println(logReg);
   }
   ```

The complete executable code for the recipe is as follows:

```
import weka.classifiers.functions.Logistic;
import weka.core.Instances;
import weka.core.converters.ConverterUtils.DataSource;

public class WekaLogisticRegressionTest {
    Instances iris = null;
    Logistic logReg ;
```

```
public void loadArff(String arffInput){
    DataSource source = null;
    try {
        source = new DataSource(arffInput);
        iris = source.getDataSet();
        iris.setClassIndex(iris.numAttributes() - 1);
    } catch (Exception e1) {
    }
}

public void buildRegression(){
    logReg = new Logistic();

    try {
        logReg.buildClassifier(iris);
    } catch (Exception e) {
    }
    System.out.println(logReg);
}

public static void main(String[] args) throws Exception{
    WekaLogisticRegressionTest test = new
        WekaLogisticRegressionTest();
    test.loadArff("path to the iris.arff file ");
    test.buildRegression();
}
}
```

The output of the code is as follows:

```
Logistic Regression with ridge parameter of 1.0E-8
Coefficients...
                        Class
Variable        Iris-setosa    Iris-versicolor
=================================================
sepallength         21.8065             2.4652
sepalwidth           4.5648             6.6809
petallength        -26.3083            -9.4293
petalwidth         -43.887            -18.2859
Intercept            8.1743            42.637


Odds Ratios...
                        Class
Variable        Iris-setosa    Iris-versicolor
=================================================
sepallength  2954196659.8892            11.7653
sepalwidth           96.0426           797.0304
```

petallength	0	0.0001
petalwidth	0	0

The interpretation of the results from the recipe is beyond the scope of this book. Interested readers are encouraged to see a Stack Overflow discussion, which can be found here: http://stackoverflow.com/questions/19136213/how-to-interpret-weka-logistic-regression-output

Clustering data points using the KMeans algorithm

In this recipe, we will be using the KMeans algorithm to cluster or group data points of a dataset together.

How to do it...

1. We will be using the cpu dataset to cluster its data points based on a simple KMeans algorithm. The cpu dataset can be found in the data directory of the installed folder in the Weka directory.

   We will be having two instance variables as in the previous recipes. The first variable will be containing the data points of the cpu dataset, and the second variable will be our Simple KMeans clusterer:

   ```
   Instances cpu = null;
   SimpleKMeans kmeans;
   ```

2. Then, we will be creating a method to load the cpu dataset, and to read its contents. Please note that as clustering is an unsupervised method, we do not need to specify the class attribute of our dataset:

   ```
   public void loadArff(String arffInput){
     DataSource source = null;
     try {
       source = new DataSource(arffInput);
       cpu = source.getDataSet();
     } catch (Exception e1) {
     }
   }
   ```

3. Next, we will be creating our method to develop the clusterer:

```
public void clusterData(){
```

4. We instantiate the cluster and set the value of seed to 10. The seed will be used to generate a random number, and it takes an integer value:

```
kmeans = new SimpleKMeans();
kmeans.setSeed(10);
```

5. Then, we tell the clusterer to preserve the order of the data instances as it is. If you feel that you will not maintain the order of the instances in the dataset, you can set the parameter of the setPreserveInstancesOrder() method to false. We also set the number of clusters to 10. And finally, we build the clusters from the cpu dataset:

```
try {
    kmeans.setPreserveInstancesOrder(true);
    kmeans.setNumClusters(10);
    kmeans.buildClusterer(cpu);
```

6. Next, we get each instance and cluster number assigned to them by the simple KMeans algorithm, using a for loop:

```
int[] assignments = kmeans.getAssignments();
    int i = 0;
    for(int clusterNum : assignments) {
        System.out.printf("Instance %d -> Cluster %d\n", i,
            clusterNum);
        i++;
    }
} catch (Exception e1) {
}
```

The complete code for the recipe is as follows:

```
import weka.clusterers.SimpleKMeans;
import weka.core.Instances;
import weka.core.converters.ConverterUtils.DataSource;

public class WekaClusterTest {
    Instances cpu = null;
    SimpleKMeans kmeans;

    public void loadArff(String arffInput){
        DataSource source = null;
        try {
```

```
            source = new DataSource(arffInput);
            cpu = source.getDataSet();
        } catch (Exception e1) {
        }
    }

    public void clusterData(){
        kmeans = new SimpleKMeans();
        kmeans.setSeed(10);
        try {
            kmeans.setPreserveInstancesOrder(true);
            kmeans.setNumClusters(10);
            kmeans.buildClusterer(cpu);
            int[] assignments = kmeans.getAssignments();
            int i = 0;
            for(int clusterNum : assignments) {
                System.out.printf("Instance %d -> Cluster %d\n", i,
                    clusterNum);
                i++;
            }
        } catch (Exception e1) {
        }
    }

    public static void main(String[] args) throws Exception{
        WekaClusterTest test = new WekaClusterTest();
        test.loadArff("path to cpu.arff file");
        test.clusterData();
    }
}
```

The `cpu.arff` file has 209 data instances. The output for the first 10 will be as follows:

```
Instance 0 -> Cluster 7
Instance 1 -> Cluster 5
Instance 2 -> Cluster 5
Instance 3 -> Cluster 5
Instance 4 -> Cluster 1
Instance 5 -> Cluster 5
Instance 6 -> Cluster 5
Instance 7 -> Cluster 5
Instance 8 -> Cluster 4
Instance 9 -> Cluster 4
```

Clustering data from classes

If you have a dataset with classes, which is an unusual case for unsupervised learning, Weka has a method called clustering from classes. In this method, Weka first ignores the class attribute and generates the clustering. Then during the test phase, it assigns classes to the clusters based on the majority value of the class attribute within each cluster. We will cover this method in this recipe.

How to do it...

1. In this recipe, we will use a dataset with class values for instances. We will use a `weather.nominal.arff` file, which can be found in the *data* directory of the installed Weka directory.

   In our code, we will have two instance variables. The first variable will contain the instances of our dataset and the second variable will contain an Expectation-Minimization clusterer:

   ```
   Instances weather = null;
   EM clusterer;
   ```

2. Next, we will be loading our dataset, reading it, and setting the last index as its class index:

   ```
   public void loadArff(String arffInput){
     DataSource source = null;
     try {
       source = new DataSource(arffInput);
       weather = source.getDataSet();
       weather.setClassIndex(weather.numAttributes() - 1);
     } catch (Exception e1) {
     }
   }
   ```

3. Then, we will create our key method in this recipe that will generate clusters from classes:

   ```
   public void generateClassToCluster(){
   ```

4. To do this we will first create a remove filter. This filter will be used to remove the class attribute from the dataset as Weka ignores this attribute during clustering:

```
Remove filter = new Remove();
filter.setAttributeIndices("" + (weather.classIndex() + 1));
```

5. Then, we will apply the filter to our dataset:

```
try {
    filter.setInputFormat(weather);
```

6. We will get the dataset without the class variable and can create an Expectation-Maximization clusterer from the data:

```
Instances dataClusterer = Filter.useFilter(weather, filter);
clusterer = new EM();
clusterer.buildClusterer(dataClusterer);
```

7. We will then evaluate the cluster by using the classes of our original dataset:

```
ClusterEvaluation eval = new ClusterEvaluation();
eval.setClusterer(clusterer);
eval.evaluateClusterer(weather);
```

8. Finally, we will print the clustering results on the console:

```
System.out.println(eval.clusterResultsToString());
    } catch (Exception e) {
  }
}
```

The complete code for the recipe is as follows:

```
import weka.clusterers.ClusterEvaluation;
import weka.clusterers.EM;
import weka.core.Instances;
import weka.core.converters.ConverterUtils.DataSource;
import weka.filters.Filter;
import weka.filters.unsupervised.attribute.Remove;

public class WekaClassesToClusterTest {
    Instances weather = null;
    EM clusterer;

    public void loadArff(String arffInput){
        DataSource source = null;
```

```
    try {
        source = new DataSource(arffInput);
        weather = source.getDataSet();
        weather.setClassIndex(weather.numAttributes() - 1);
    } catch (Exception e1) {

    }
}

public void generateClassToCluster(){
    Remove filter = new Remove();
    filter.setAttributeIndices("" + (weather.classIndex() + 1));
    try {
        filter.setInputFormat(weather);
        Instances dataClusterer = Filter.useFilter(weather, filter);
        clusterer = new EM();
        clusterer.buildClusterer(dataClusterer);
        ClusterEvaluation eval = new ClusterEvaluation();
        eval.setClusterer(clusterer);
        eval.evaluateClusterer(weather);

        System.out.println(eval.clusterResultsToString());
    } catch (Exception e) {

    }
}
public static void main(String[] args){
    WekaClassesToClusterTest test = new WekaClassesToClusterTest();
    test.loadArff("path to weather.nominal.arff file");
    test.generateClassToCluster();
}
}
```

Learning association rules from data

Association rule learning is a machine-learning technique to discover associations and rules between various features or variables in a dataset. A similar technique in statistics is known as correlation, which is covered in Chapter 3, *Analyzing Data Statistically*, but association rule learning is more useful in decision making. For instance, by analyzing big supermarket data, a machine-learning learner can discover that if a person buys onions, tomatoes, chicken patty, and mayonnaise, she will most likely buy buns (to make burgers).

In this recipe, we will see how we can use Weka to learn association rules from datasets.

Getting ready

We will be using the supermarket dataset that can be found in the data directory of our installed Weka directory. The total number of instances in the dataset is 4,627 instances with 217 binary attributes each. The attributes have a value of true or missing. There is a nominal class attribute called total that has the value low if the transaction was less than $100, or high if the transaction was greater than $100.

How to do it...

1. Declare two instance variables to contain the data of the supermarket dataset and to denote Apriori learner:

   ```
   Instances superMarket = null;
   Apriori apriori;
   ```

2. Create a method to load the dataset, and to read it. For this recipe, you do not need to set the class attribute of the dataset:

   ```
   public void loadArff(String arffInput){
     DataSource source = null;
     try {
       source = new DataSource(arffInput);
       superMarket = source.getDataSet();
     } catch (Exception e1) {
     }
   }
   ```

3. Create a method to instantiate the Apriori learner. The method then builds associations from the given dataset. Finally, display the learner on the console:

   ```
   public void generateRule(){
     apriori = new Apriori();
     try {
       apriori.buildAssociations(superMarket);
       System.out.println(apriori);
     } catch (Exception e) {
     }
   }
   ```

The default number of rules produced by an Apriori learner is set to 10. If you need more rules to be produced, you can enter the following line of code before you build the associations, where n is an integer denoting the number of rules `learn-apriori.setNumRules(n);`

The complete code for the recipe is as follows:

```
import weka.associations.Apriori;
import weka.core.Instances;
import weka.core.converters.ConverterUtils.DataSource;

public class WekaAssociationRuleTest {
    Instances superMarket = null;
    Apriori apriori;
    public void loadArff(String arffInput){
        DataSource source = null;
        try {
            source = new DataSource(arffInput);
            superMarket = source.getDataSet();
        } catch (Exception e1) {
        }
    }
    public void generateRule(){
        apriori = new Apriori();
        try {
            apriori.buildAssociations(superMarket);
            System.out.println(apriori);
        } catch (Exception e) {
        }
    }
    public static void main(String args[]){
        WekaAssociationRuleTest test = new WekaAssociationRuleTest();
        test.loadArff("path to supermarket.arff file");
        test.generateRule();
    }
}
```

The rules found by the Apriori learner will be as follows:

```
 1. biscuits=t frozen foods=t fruit=t total=high 788 ==> bread and cake=t
723    <conf:(0.92)> lift:(1.27) lev:(0.03) [155] conv:(3.35)
 2. baking needs=t biscuits=t fruit=t total=high 760 ==> bread and cake=t
696    <conf:(0.92)> lift:(1.27) lev:(0.03) [149] conv:(3.28)
 3. baking needs=t frozen foods=t fruit=t total=high 770 ==> bread and
cake=t 705    <conf:(0.92)> lift:(1.27) lev:(0.03) [150] conv:(3.27)
 4. biscuits=t fruit=t vegetables=t total=high 815 ==> bread and cake=t 746
<conf:(0.92)> lift:(1.27) lev:(0.03) [159] conv:(3.26)
 5. party snack foods=t fruit=t total=high 854 ==> bread and cake=t 779
<conf:(0.91)> lift:(1.27) lev:(0.04) [164] conv:(3.15)
 6. biscuits=t frozen foods=t vegetables=t total=high 797 ==> bread and
cake=t 725    <conf:(0.91)> lift:(1.26) lev:(0.03) [151] conv:(3.06)
 7. baking needs=t biscuits=t vegetables=t total=high 772 ==> bread and
cake=t 701    <conf:(0.91)> lift:(1.26) lev:(0.03) [145] conv:(3.01)
 8. biscuits=t fruit=t total=high 954 ==> bread and cake=t 866
<conf:(0.91)> lift:(1.26) lev:(0.04) [179] conv:(3)
 9. frozen foods=t fruit=t vegetables=t total=high 834 ==> bread and cake=t
757    <conf:(0.91)> lift:(1.26) lev:(0.03) [156] conv:(3)
10. frozen foods=t fruit=t total=high 969 ==> bread and cake=t 877
<conf:(0.91)> lift:(1.26) lev:(0.04) [179] conv:(2.92)
```

Selecting features/attributes using the low-level method, the filtering method, and the meta-classifier method

Feature selection is an important machine-learning process that identifies the most important attributes in a dataset from a set of attributes, so that if a classifier is generated based on the selected attributes, the classifier produces better results than the one with all the attributes.

In Weka, there are three ways of selecting attributes. This recipe will use all of the three ways of attribute selection techniques available in Weka: the low-level attribute selection method, attribute selection using a filter, and attribute selection using a meta-classifier.

Getting ready

The recipe will select important attributes of the `iris` dataset that can be found in the `data` directory of Weka's installed directory.

To perform attribute selection, two elements are required: a search method and an evaluation method. In our recipe, we will use Best First Search as our search method and a subset evaluation method named Correlation-based Feature Subset Selection.

How to do it...

1. Declare an instance variable to hold the data from the iris dataset. Declare another variable for a `NaiveBayes` classifier:

   ```
   Instances iris = null;
   NaiveBayes nb;
   ```

2. Create a method to load our dataset. The method will also read the data instances and set the last attribute of the dataset as the class attribute:

   ```
   public void loadArff(String arffInput){
     DataSource source = null;
     try {
       source = new DataSource(arffInput);
       iris = source.getDataSet();
       iris.setClassIndex(iris.numAttributes() - 1);
     } catch (Exception e1) {
     }
   }
   ```

3. We will start simple–we will create a method that uses Weka's low-level attribute selection method:

   ```
   public void selectFeatures(){
   ```

4. Create an `AttributeSelection` object:

   ```
   AttributeSelection attSelection = new AttributeSelection();
   ```

5. Next, create objects for the search and evaluator, and set the evaluator and the search object for the attribute `selection` object:

```
CfsSubsetEval eval = new CfsSubsetEval();
BestFirst search = new BestFirst();
attSelection.setEvaluator(eval);
attSelection.setSearch(search);
```

6. Then, use the attribute selection object to select attributes from the iris dataset using the search and evaluator. We will get the index of the attributes that are selected by this technique and will display the selected attribute numbers (the attribute numbers start from 0):

```
try {
    attSelection.SelectAttributes(iris);
    int[] attIndex = attSelection.selectedAttributes();
    System.out.println(Utils.arrayToString(attIndex));
} catch (Exception e) {
}
}
```

The output of this method will be as follows:

```
2, 3, 4
```

The output means that the attribute selection technique selects attribute numbers 2, 3, and 4 from all the attributes of the iris dataset.

7. Now, we will create a method that implements the second technique of selecting attributes based on filters:

```
public void selectFeaturesWithFilter(){
```

8. Create an attribute selection filter. Note that the package for this filter is not the one we used in the first method of this recipe:

```
weka.filters.supervised.attribute.AttributeSelection filter =
    new weka.filters.supervised.attribute.AttributeSelection();
```

9. Next, create objects for the search and evaluator, and set the evaluator and the search object for the filter:

```
CfsSubsetEval eval = new CfsSubsetEval();
BestFirst search = new BestFirst();
filter.setEvaluator(eval);
filter.setSearch(search);
```

10. Then, apply the filter to the iris dataset, and retrieve new data using the `useFilter()` of the Filter class, which takes the dataset and filter as its two arguments. This is something different than what we saw in the previous method. This is very useful if we want to create a new ARFF file by selecting the attributes selected by the filtering technique on the fly:

```
try {
    filter.setInputFormat(iris);
    Instances newData = Filter.useFilter(iris, filter);
    System.out.println(newData);
} catch (Exception e) {

}
}
```

From the output on the console, we can see that the attribute section of the ARFF file data now has the following entries:

```
@attribute petallength numeric
@attribute petalwidth numeric
@attribute class {Iris-setosa,Iris-versicolor,Iris-virginica}
```

This means that the two attributes listed along with the class attributes were selected by the attribute selection method we just used.

11. Finally, we will create a method that selects attributes before handing over the dataset to a classifier (in our case, it is a `NaiveBayes` classifier):

```
public void selectFeaturesWithClassifiers(){
```

12. Create a meta-classifier that reduces the dimensionality of data (that is, selects attributes) before passing them to a `NaiveBayes` classifier:

```
AttributeSelectedClassifier classifier = new
    AttributeSelectedClassifier();
```

13. Create an evaluator, a search object, and a `NaiveBayes` classifier:

```
CfsSubsetEval eval = new CfsSubsetEval();
BestFirst search = new BestFirst();
nb = new NaiveBayes();
```

14. Set the evaluator, the search object, and the `NaiveBayes` classifier to the meta-classifier:

```
classifier.setClassifier(nb);
classifier.setEvaluator(eval);
classifier.setSearch(search);
```

15. Now, we will be evaluating the performance of the `NaiveBayes` classifier with the attributes selected by the meta-classifier technique. Note that the attributes selected by the meta-classifier are like a *black box* in this example. For the evaluation, a 10-fold cross-validation has been used:

```
Evaluation evaluation;
try {
    evaluation = new Evaluation(iris);
    evaluation.crossValidateModel(classifier, iris, 10, new
      Random(1));
    System.out.println(evaluation.toSummaryString());
} catch (Exception e) {
}
}
```

The complete code for the recipe is as follows:

```
import java.util.Random;
import weka.attributeSelection.AttributeSelection;
import weka.attributeSelection.BestFirst;
import weka.attributeSelection.CfsSubsetEval;
import weka.classifiers.Evaluation;
import weka.classifiers.bayes.NaiveBayes;
import weka.classifiers.meta.AttributeSelectedClassifier;
import weka.core.Instances;
import weka.core.Utils;
import weka.core.converters.ConverterUtils.DataSource;
import weka.filters.Filter;

public class WekaFeatureSelectionTest {
    Instances iris = null;
    NaiveBayes nb;
    public void loadArff(String arffInput){
        DataSource source = null;
```

```
      try {
         source = new DataSource(arffInput);
         iris = source.getDataSet();
         iris.setClassIndex(iris.numAttributes() - 1);
      } catch (Exception e1) {
      }
   }

   public void selectFeatures(){
      AttributeSelection attSelection = new AttributeSelection();
      CfsSubsetEval eval = new CfsSubsetEval();
      BestFirst search = new BestFirst();
      attSelection.setEvaluator(eval);
      attSelection.setSearch(search);
      try {
         attSelection.SelectAttributes(iris);
         int[] attIndex = attSelection.selectedAttributes();
         System.out.println(Utils.arrayToString(attIndex));
      } catch (Exception e) {
      }
   }

   public void selectFeaturesWithFilter(){
      weka.filters.supervised.attribute.AttributeSelection filter = new
       weka.filters.supervised.attribute.AttributeSelection();
      CfsSubsetEval eval = new CfsSubsetEval();
      BestFirst search = new BestFirst();
      filter.setEvaluator(eval);
      filter.setSearch(search);
      try {
         filter.setInputFormat(iris);
         Instances newData = Filter.useFilter(iris, filter);
         System.out.println(newData);
      } catch (Exception e) {
      }
   }
   public void selectFeaturesWithClassifiers(){
      AttributeSelectedClassifier classifier = new
        AttributeSelectedClassifier();
      CfsSubsetEval eval = new CfsSubsetEval();
      BestFirst search = new BestFirst();
      nb = new NaiveBayes();
      classifier.setClassifier(nb);
      classifier.setEvaluator(eval);
      classifier.setSearch(search);
      Evaluation evaluation;
      try {
         evaluation = new Evaluation(iris);
```

```
            evaluation.crossValidateModel(classifier, iris, 10, new
                Random(1));
            System.out.println(evaluation.toSummaryString());
        } catch (Exception e) {
        }
    }
    public static void main(String[] args){
        WekaFeatureSelectionTest test = new WekaFeatureSelectionTest();
        test.loadArff("C:/Program Files/Weka-3-6/data/iris.arff");
        test.selectFeatures();
        test.selectFeaturesWithFilter();
        test.selectFeaturesWithClassifiers();
    }
}
```

The output of this method will be as follows:

```
Correctly Classified Instances        144             96      %
Incorrectly Classified Instances        6              4      %
Kappa statistic                       0.94
Mean absolute error                   0.0286
Root mean squared error               0.1386
Relative absolute error               6.4429 %
Root relative squared error          29.4066 %
Total Number of Instances             150
```

 The following channel has tutorials on doing many different machine-learning tasks using Weka, including its API and GUI: https://www.yout ube.com/c/rushdishams.

5
Learning from Data - Part 2

In this chapter, we will cover the following recipes:

- Applying machine learning on data using Java Machine Learning library
- Dataset import and export
- Clustering and evaluation
- Classification
- Cross-validation and held-out testing
- Feature scoring
- Feature selection
- Classifying data points using the Stanford Classifier
- Classifying data points using Massive Online Analysis

Introduction

In Chapter 4, *Learn from Data – Part 1*, we used the Weka machine learning workbench for different recipes for classification, clustering, association rule mining, feature selection, and so on. We also mentioned in that chapter that Weka is not the only tool that is written in Java to learn patterns from data. There are other tools that can perform similar tasks. Examples of such tools include but are not limited to **Java Machine Learning (Java-ML)** library, **Massive Online Analysis (MOA)**, and Stanford machine learning libraries.

In this chapter, we will be focusing on bits and pieces of these other tools to conduct machine learning analysis on data.

Applying machine learning on data using Java Machine Learning (Java-ML) library

Java Machine Learning (**Java-ML**) library is a collection of standard machine learning algorithms. Unlike Weka, the library does not have any GUI because it is primarily aimed at software developers. A particularly advantageous feature of Java-ML is that it has a common interface for each type of algorithm, and therefore, implementation of the algorithms is fairly easy and straightforward. The support for the library is another key feature of it since the source codes are well documented and hence extendable, and there are plenty of code samples and tutorials for all sorts of machine learning tasks that can be accomplished using the library. The website `http://java-ml.sourceforge.net/` has all the details regarding the library.

In this recipe, we will use this library to do the following tasks:

- Dataset import and export
- Clustering and evaluation
- Classification
- Cross-validation and held-out testing
- Feature scoring
- Feature selection

Getting ready

In order to perform this recipe, we will require the following:

1. In this recipe, we will be using the **0.1.7** version of the library. Download this version from `https://sourceforge.net/projects/java-ml/files/java-ml/`:

2. The file you downloaded is a compressed zip file. Extract the files to a directory. The directory structure looks like the following:

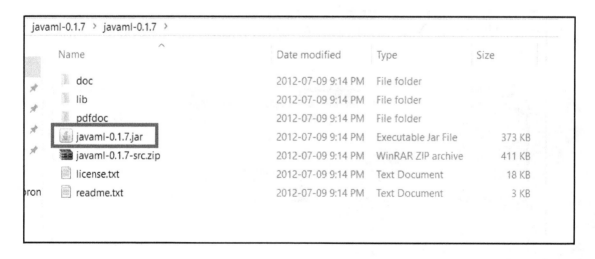

We will need the `javaml-0.1.7.jar` file to be included as an external JAR file in the Eclipse project that we will be using to implement the recipe.

3. The directory also has a folder named `lib`. By opening the lib folder, we will see that it contains several other JAR files:

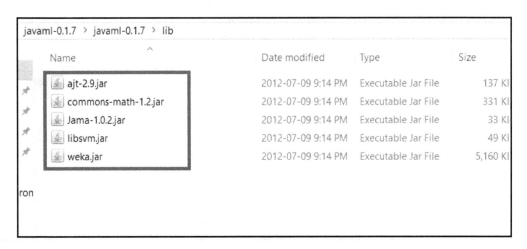

These JAR files are Java-ML's dependencies and, therefore, must also be included in the project as an external JAR file:

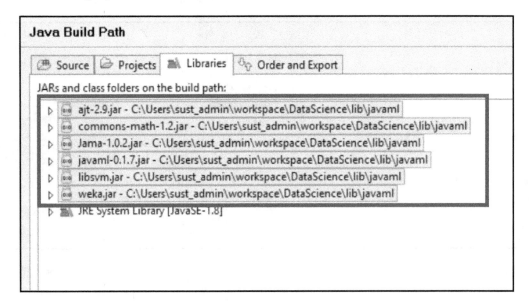

4. In our recipe, we will also be using a sample Iris dataset that is compatible with Java-ML's native file format. Iris and other data files, however, do not come with the library's distribution; they need to be downloaded from a different repository. To download the datasets, go to `http://java-l.sourceforge.net/content/databases`. Java-ML has two types of datasets: 111 small UCI datasets and 7 large UCI datasets. For your practice, it is highly recommended to download both types of datasets. For the recipe, click 111 small UCI datasets and you will be prompted for its download:

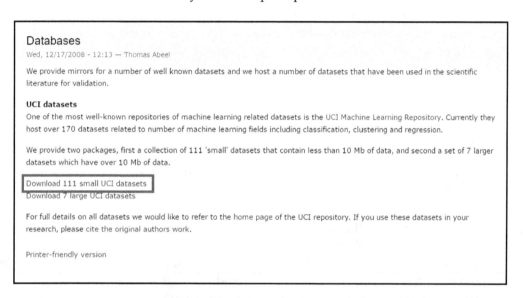

5. Once the download finishes, extract the folders. You will see that there are 111 folders in the distribution, each representing a dataset. Find the iris dataset folder and open it. You will see that there are two data files and one name file. In our recipe, we will be using the `iris.data` file. The path to this file needs to be noted as we will be using the path in our recipe:

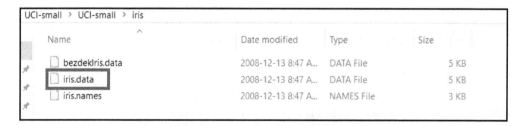

If you use any of the UCI datasets, you need to acknowledge and provide reference to the original work accordingly. Details can be found at `http ://archive.ics.uci.edu/ml/citation_policy.html`.

How to do it...

1. Create a class named `JavaMachineLearning`. We will be using a main method to implement all of the machine learning tasks. The method will be throwing an `IOException`:

```
public class JavaMachineLearning {
    public static void main(String[] args) throws IOException{
```

2. First, we will be reading the iris dataset using Java-ML's `FileHandler` class's `loadDataset()` method:

```
Dataset data = FileHandler.loadDataset(new File("path to your
iris.data"), 4, ",");
```

The parameters for the method is the path to the `dataset`, the position of class attribute, and the delimiter that separates the values. The `dataset` can be read with any standard text editor. The starting index of the attributes is 0 and the iris `dataset` has the class attribute as its fifth attribute. Therefore, the second parameter is set to 4. Also, the data values are separated by comma, in our case. So, the third parameter is set to comma. The content of the file is taken to a `Dataset` object.

3. Print the `dataset` content by simply passing the object to the `System.out.println()` method:

```
System.out.println(data);
```

4. The partial output of the code will be as follows:

```
[{[5.1, 3.5, 1.4, 0.2];Iris-setosa}, {[4.9, 3.0, 1.4,
  0.2];Iris-setosa}, {[4.7, 3.2, 1.3, 0.2];Iris-setosa}, {[4.6,
    3.1, 1.5, 0.2];Iris-setosa}, {[5.0, 3.6, 1.4, 0.2];Iris-
      setosa}, {[5.4, 3.9, 1.7, 0.4];Iris-setosa}, {[4.6, 3.4,
        1.4, 0.3];Iris-setosa}, {[5.0, 3.4, 1.5, 0.2];Iris-
          setosa}, {[4.4, 2.9, 1.4, 0.2];Iris-setosa}, ...]
```

5. If at any point, you need to export your `dataset` from the .data format to a .txt format, Java-ML has a very simple way to accomplish it using its `exportDataset()` method of the `FileHandler` class. The method takes the data and the output file as its parameter. The following line of code creates a text file in the `C:/` drive with the contents of the iris `dataset`:

```
FileHandler.exportDataset(data, new File("c:/javaml-
    output.txt"));
```

Partial output of the text file produced by the preceding code is as follows:

```
Iris-setosa 5.1    3.5    1.4    0.2
Iris-setosa 4.9    3.0    1.4    0.2
Iris-setosa 4.7    3.2    1.3    0.2
Iris-setosa 4.6    3.1    1.5    0.2
. . . . . . . . . . . . . . . . . . . . . . . . . . . . . . .
```

There are two key things to notice for the data file generated by Java-ML. First, the class value is the first attribute, and second, the values are no more comma-separated as they were in the .data file; rather, they are separated by tabs.

6. To read a data file created by the preceding step, we can use the `loadDataset()` method again. But this time the values of the parameter will be different:

```
data = FileHandler.loadDataset(new File("c:/javaml-
    output.txt"), 0,"\t");
```

7. If we print the data:

```
System.out.println(data);
```

Then it will be the same output as we saw in step 3:

```
[{[5.1, 3.5, 1.4, 0.2];Iris-setosa}, {[4.9, 3.0, 1.4,
    0.2];Iris-setosa}, {[4.7, 3.2, 1.3, 0.2];Iris-setosa}, {[4.6,
        3.1, 1.5, 0.2];Iris-setosa}, {[5.0, 3.6, 1.4, 0.2];Iris-
            setosa}, {[5.4, 3.9, 1.7, 0.4];Iris-setosa}, {[4.6, 3.4,
                1.4, 0.3];Iris-setosa}, {[5.0, 3.4, 1.5, 0.2];Iris-
                    setosa}, {[4.4, 2.9, 1.4, 0.2];Iris-setosa}, ...]
```

8. Java-ML provides very easy interface to apply clustering, display the clusters, and evaluate the clustering. We will be using the KMeans clustering in our recipe. Create a KMeans clusterer:

```
Clusterer km = new KMeans();
```

9. Provide your data to the clusterer using the cluster() method. The resultant will be multiple clusters of data points (or multiple datasets). Put the results into an array of Dataset:

```
Dataset[] clusters = km.cluster(data);
```

10. If you want to see the data points in each cluster, use a for loop to iterate over the array of datasets:

```
for(Dataset cluster:clusters){
    System.out.println("Cluster: " + cluster);
}
```

Partial output for the code in this step would be as follows:

```
Cluster: [{[6.3, 3.3, 6.0, 2.5];Iris-virginica}, {[7.1, 3.0,
    5.9, 2.1];Iris-virginica}, ...]
Cluster: [{[5.5, 2.3, 4.0, 1.3];Iris-versicolor}, {[5.7, 2.8,
    4.5, 1.3];Iris-versicolor}, ...]
Cluster: [{[5.1, 3.5, 1.4, 0.2];Iris-setosa}, {[4.9, 3.0, 1.4,
    0.2];Iris-setosa}, ...]
Cluster: [{[7.0, 3.2, 4.7, 1.4];Iris-versicolor}, {[6.4, 3.2,
    4.5, 1.5];Iris-versicolor}, ...]
```

From the output, we can see that the KMeans algorithm created four clusters from the iris dataset.

11. Sum of squared errors is one of the measures to evaluate the performance of a clusterer. We will be using the ClusterEvaluation class to measure the error of clustering:

```
ClusterEvaluation sse = new SumOfSquaredErrors();
```

12. Next, we simply send the clusters to the score method of the object to get the sum of squared errors of clustering:

```
double score = sse.score(clusters);
```

13. Print the error score:

```
System.out.println(score);
```

The following will be displayed in the output:

114.9465465309897

This is the sum of squared error of KMeans clustering for the iris dataset.

14. Classification in Java-ML is also very easy and requires only a few lines of codes. The following code creates a **K-nearest neighbour (KNN)** classifier. The classifier will predict the label of unseen data points based on the majority voting from the five nearest neighbors. The `buildClassifier()` method is used to train a classifier that takes the dataset (in our case, it is iris) as argument:

```
Classifier knn = new KNearestNeighbors(5);
knn.buildClassifier(data);
```

15. After a model is built, the recipe will then continue to evaluate the model. We will see two evaluation methods that can be accomplished using Java-ML:
    - K-fold cross validation and
    - Held-out testing

16. For k-fold cross-validation of the KNN classifier, we will use the classifier to create a `CrossValidation` instance. The `CrossValidation` class has a method named `crossValidation()` that takes the dataset as parameter. The method returns a map that has object as its first parameter and the evaluation metric as its second parameter:

```
CrossValidation cv = new CrossValidation(knn);
Map<Object, PerformanceMeasure> cvEvaluation =
    cv.crossValidation(data);
```

17. Now that we have the cross-validation results, we can simply print them by using the following:

```
System.out.println(cvEvaluation);
```

This will display the true positives, false positives, true negatives, and false negatives for each class:

```
{Iris-versicolor=[TP=47.0, FP=1.0, TN=99.0, FN=3.0], Iris-
    virginica=[TP=49.0, FP=3.0, TN=97.0, FN=1.0], Iris-setosa=
    [TP=50.0, FP=0.0, TN=100.0, FN=0.0]}
```

18. In order to do a held-out testing, we need to have a test dataset. Unfortunately, we do not have any test dataset for iris. Therefore, we will be using the same iris.data file (that was used to train our KNN classifier) as our test dataset. But note that in real life, you will have a test dataset with the exact number of attributes as in your training dataset, while the labels of the data points will be unknown.

First, we load the test dataset:

```
Dataset testData = FileHandler.loadDataset(new File("path to
    your iris.data "), 4, ",");
```

Then we get the performance of the classifier on the test data using the following code:

```
Map<Object, PerformanceMeasure> testEvaluation =
    EvaluateDataset.testDataset(knn, testData);
```

19. Then, we can simply print the results for each class by iterating over the map object:

```
for(Object classVariable:testEvaluation.keySet()){
    System.out.println(classVariable + " class has " +
        testEvaluation.get(classVariable).getAccuracy());
}
```

The preceding code will be printing the accuracy of the KNN classifier for each class:

```
Iris-versicolor class has 0.9666666666666667
Iris-virginica class has 0.9666666666666667
Iris-setosa class has 1.0
```

20. Feature scoring is a key aspect of machine learning to reduce dimensionality. In Java-ML, we will be implementing the following method that generates a score for a given attribute:

```
public double score(int attIndex);
```

First, create a feature scoring algorithm instance. In our recipe, we will be using Gain Ratio algorithm:

```
GainRatio gainRatio = new GainRatio();
```

21. Next, apply the algorithm to the data:

```
gainRatio.build(data);
```

22. Finally, print the scores of each feature using a for loop and by iterating through sending the attribute index to the `score()` method, one by one:

```
for (int i = 0; i < gainRatio.noAttributes(); i++){
  System.out.println(gainRatio.score(i));
}
```

The scores of the features of the iris dataset will be as follows:

```
0.2560110727706682
0.1497001925156687
0.508659832906763
0.4861382158327255
```

23. We can also rank features based on some feature-ranking algorithms. To do this, we will be implementing the `rank()` method of Java-ML that works in a similar way like the `score()` method–both take the index of an attribute:

```
public int rank(int attIndex);
```

Create a feature ranking algorithm instance. In our example, we will be depending on SVM's ranking of features based on recursive elimination method of features. The parameter of the constructor denotes the percentage of the worst ranked features that are going to be eliminated:

```
RecursiveFeatureEliminationSVM featureRank = new
  RecursiveFeatureEliminationSVM(0.2);
```

- Next, apply the algorithm on the dataset:

```
featureRank.build(data);
```

- Finally, print the ranking of each feature using a for loop and by iterating through sending the attribute index to the `rank()` method sequentially:

```
for (int i = 0; i < featureRank.noAttributes(); i++){
    System.out.println(featureRank.rank(i));
}
```

- The ranking of the features of the iris dataset will be as follows:

```
3
2
0
1
```

24. While for the scoring and ranking of the features we get information for individual features, we only get the subset of features selected from a dataset when we apply feature subset selection of Java-ML.

    First, create a feature selection algorithm. In our recipe, we will be using a forward selection method using the `greedy` method. In the process of selecting features, we need a distance measure, which in our case is Pearson's correlation measure. The first parameter of the constructor stands for number of attributes to select in the subset:

```
GreedyForwardSelection featureSelection = new
GreedyForwardSelection(5, new PearsonCorrelationCoefficient());
```

- Then, apply the algorithm to the dataset:

```
featureSelection.build(data);
```

- Finally, you can easily print the features selected by the algorithm:

```
System.out.println(featureSelection.selectedAttributes());
```

The output subset of features will be as follows:

```
[0]
```

The complete code for the recipe is as follows:

```java
import java.io.File;
import java.io.IOException;
import java.util.Map;
import net.sf.javaml.classification.Classifier;
import net.sf.javaml.classification.KNearestNeighbors;
import net.sf.javaml.classification.evaluation.CrossValidation;
import net.sf.javaml.classification.evaluation.EvaluateDataset;
import net.sf.javaml.classification.evaluation.PerformanceMeasure;
import net.sf.javaml.clustering.Clusterer;
import net.sf.javaml.clustering.KMeans;
import net.sf.javaml.clustering.evaluation.ClusterEvaluation;
import net.sf.javaml.clustering.evaluation.SumOfSquaredErrors;
import net.sf.javaml.core.Dataset;
import net.sf.javaml.distance.PearsonCorrelationCoefficient;
import net.sf.javaml.featureselection.ranking.
    RecursiveFeatureEliminationSVM;
import net.sf.javaml.featureselection.scoring.GainRatio;
import net.sf.javaml.featureselection.subset.GreedyForwardSelection;
import net.sf.javaml.tools.data.FileHandler;

public class JavaMachineLearning {
    public static void main(String[] args) throws IOException{
        Dataset data = FileHandler.loadDataset(new File("path to
            iris.data"), 4, ",");
        System.out.println(data);
        FileHandler.exportDataset(data, new File("c:/javaml-
            output.txt"));
        data = FileHandler.loadDataset(new File("c:/javaml-output.txt"),
            0,"\t");
        System.out.println(data);
        //Clustering
        Clusterer km = new KMeans();
        Dataset[] clusters = km.cluster(data);
        for(Dataset cluster:clusters){
            System.out.println("Cluster: " + cluster);
        }
        ClusterEvaluation sse= new SumOfSquaredErrors();
        double score = sse.score(clusters);
        System.out.println(score);
        //Classification
        Classifier knn = new KNearestNeighbors(5);
```

```
knn.buildClassifier(data);
//Cross validation
CrossValidation cv = new CrossValidation(knn);
Map<Object, PerformanceMeasure> cvEvaluation =
  cv.crossValidation(data);
System.out.println(cvEvaluation);
//Held-out testing
Dataset testData = FileHandler.loadDataset(new File("path to
  iris.data"), 4, ",");
Map<Object, PerformanceMeasure> testEvaluation =
      EvaluateDataset.testDataset(knn, testData);
for(Object classVariable:testEvaluation.keySet()){
   System.out.println(classVariable + " class has
     "+testEvaluation.get(classVariable).getAccuracy());
}
//Feature scoring
GainRatio gainRatio = new GainRatio();
gainRatio.build(data);
for (int i = 0; i < gainRatio.noAttributes(); i++){
   System.out.println(gainRatio.score(i));
}
//Feature ranking
RecursiveFeatureEliminationSVM featureRank = new
  RecursiveFeatureEliminationSVM(0.2);
featureRank.build(data);
for (int i = 0; i < featureRank.noAttributes(); i++){
   System.out.println(featureRank.rank(i));
}
//Feature subset selection
GreedyForwardSelection featureSelection = new
  GreedyForwardSelection(5, new
      PearsonCorrelationCoefficient());
featureSelection.build(data);
System.out.println(featureSelection.selectedAttributes());
}
}
```

Classifying data points using the Stanford classifier

The Stanford classifier is a machine learning classifier developed in the University of Stanford by the Stanford Natural Language Processing group. The software is implemented in Java, and as its classifier, the software uses Maximum Entropy. Maximum Entropy is equivalent to multiclass logistic regression models with some slight differences in parameter settings. The advantage of using the Stanford classifier is that the technology used in the software is the same basic technology that is used by Google or Amazon.

Getting ready

In this recipe, we will be using the Stanford classifier to classify data points based on its learning using Maximum Entropy. We will be using the 3.6.0 version of the software. For details, please refer to http://nlp.stanford.edu/software/classifier.html. To run the code of this recipe, you will need Java 8. In order to perform this recipe, we would require to do the following:

1. Go to http://nlp.stanford.edu/software/classifier.html, and download version 3.6.0. This is the latest version at the time of writing of this book. The software distribution is a compressed zip file:

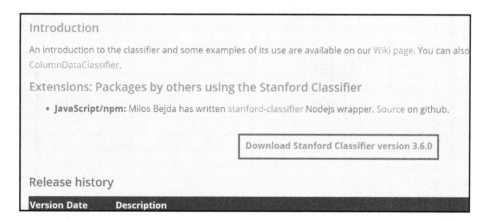

Introduction

An introduction to the classifier and some examples of its use are available on our Wiki page. You can also ColumnDataClassifier.

Extensions: Packages by others using the Stanford Classifier

- **JavaScript/npm:** Milos Bejda has written stanford-classifier Nodejs wrapper. Source on github.

Download Stanford Classifier version 3.6.0

Release history

| Version Date | Description |

2. Once downloaded, decompress the files. You will see a list of files and folders as follows:

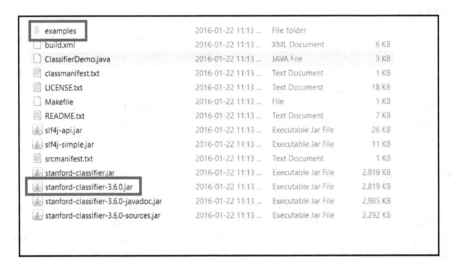

The `stanford-classifier-3.6.0.jar` file needs to be included in your Eclipse project:

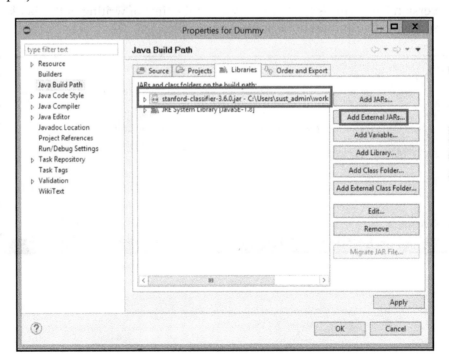

The distribution also has a folder named examples. We will be using the contents of this file in our recipe. The examples folder contains two datasets: the cheese-disease dataset and the Iris dataset. Each dataset contains three associated files: a training file (with .train extension), a testing file (with .test extension), and a properties (with `.prop` extension). In our recipe, we will be using the cheese-disease dataset:

Name	Date modified	Type	Size
cheese2007.prop	2016-01-22 11:13 ...	PROP File	1 KB
cheeseDisease.test	2016-01-22 11:13 ...	TEST File	4 KB
cheeseDisease.train	2016-01-22 11:13 ...	TRAIN File	33 KB
iris.test	2016-01-22 11:13 ...	TEST File	1 KB
iris.train	2016-01-22 11:13 ...	TRAIN File	4 KB
iris2007.prop	2016-01-22 11:13 ...	PROP File	1 KB

If you open the cheeseDisease.train file, the contents will be something as follows:

```
2 Back Pain
2 Dissociative Disorders
2 Lipoma
1 Blue Rathgore
2 Gallstones
1 Chevrotin des Aravis
2 Pulmonary Embolism
2 Gastroenteritis
2 Ornithine Carbamoyltransferase Deficiency Disease ...........
```

The first column, which is denoting either 1 or 2, is the class of a data instance, while the second column, which is a string value, is a name. The class 1 denotes that the name followed by it is a name of cheese, and the class 2 denotes that the name followed by it is a name of a disease. The goal of applying supervised classification on the dataset is to build a classifier that can separate cheese names from disease names.

 The columns in the dataset are separated by a tab character. Here, there is just one class column and one predictive column. This is the minimum for training a classifier. However, you can have any number of predictive columns and specify their roles.

3. The `Cheese2007.prop` file is the property file of the dataset. You need to understand the contents of the file since this file will be contacted by the code in our recipe to get necessary information about class features, types of features to be used by the classifier, display format on the console, parameters of the classifier, and so on. Therefore, we will be examining the contents of this file now.

The first few lines of the property file list the feature options. The lines with # denote comments. The lines tell the classifier to use the class feature (which is column 1 in the training file) during its learning. It also provides information, such as the classifier will be using N-gram feature where the minimum length of N-gram being 1 and maximum being 4. The classifier will also use prefixes and suffixes during its calculation of N-gram and binned lengths of 10, 20, and 30:

```
# # Features
# useClassFeature=true
1.useNGrams=true
1.usePrefixSuffixNGrams=true
1.maxNGramLeng=4
1.minNGramLeng=1
1.binnedLengths=10,20,30
```

The next important block of lines is the mapping where the property file communicates to the classifier that the ground truth for evaluation will be column 0 and predictions need to be made for column 1:

```
# # Mapping
# goldAnswerColumn=0
displayedColumn=1
```

Next, the property file saves the optimization parameter for the Maximum Entropy classifier:

```
#
# Optimization
# intern=true
  sigma=3
  useQN=true
  QNsize=15
  tolerance=1e-4
```

Finally, the property file has entries for the path of training and testing files:

```
#   Training input
# trainFile=./examples/cheeseDisease.train
testFile=./examples/cheeseDisease.test
```

How to do it...

1. For the recipe, we will be creating a class in our project. We will only use a `main()` method to demonstrate the classification. The method will be throwing an exception:

    ```
    public class StanfordClassifier { public static void
        main(String[] args) throws Exception {
    ```

2. The Stanford classifier is implemented in the `ColumnDataClassifier` class. Create a classifier by providing the path of the property file for the cheese-disease dataset:

    ```
    ColumnDataClassifier columnDataClassifier = new
        ColumnDataClassifier("examples/cheese2007.prop");
    ```

3. Next, using the training data, build a classifier. The generics for the `Classifier` class is `<String, String>` since the first column is the class and the second column is the name of cheese/disease. Note that even though the class column has 1 and 2 as its nominal values, they are treated as strings:

    ```
    Classifier<String,String> classifier =
        columnDataClassifier.makeClassifier
            (columnDataClassifier.readTrainingExamples
                ("examples/cheeseDisease.train"));
    ```

4. Finally, iterate through each line of the test dataset. The test dataset is similar to the training dataset: the first column is the actual class and the second column is the name. A first few lines of the test dataset are as follows:

> 2 Psittacosis
>
> 2 Cushing Syndrome
>
> 2 Esotropia
>
> 2 Jaundice, Neonatal
>
> 2 Thymoma...............

How it works...

The column data classifier is applied to each line of the test set, and the result is sent to a `Datum` object. The classifier predicts the class of the `Datum` object and it prints the prediction on console:

```
for (String line :
ObjectBank.getLineIterator("examples/cheeseDisease.test", "utf-8")) {
Datum<String,String> d = columnDataClassifier.makeDatumFromLine(line);
System.out.println(line + " ==> " + classifier.classOf(d)); }
```

The output on the console will be as follows (outputs are chopped):

```
2 Psittacosis ==> 2 2 Cushing Syndrome ==> 2 2 Esotropia ==> 2 2 Jaundice,
Neonatal ==> 2 2 Thymoma ==> 2 1 Caerphilly ==> 1 2 Teratoma ==> 2 2
Phantom Limb ==> 1 2 Iron Overload ==> 1 ..............
```

The first column is the actual class, the second column is the name, and the value on the right hand side of ==> symbol is the class of the predicted by the classifier.

The complete code for the recipe is as follows:

```
import edu.stanford.nlp.classify.Classifier;
import edu.stanford.nlp.classify.ColumnDataClassifier;
import edu.stanford.nlp.ling.Datum;
import edu.stanford.nlp.objectbank.ObjectBank;
public class StanfordClassifier {
public static void main(String[] args) throws Exception {
ColumnDataClassifier columnDataClassifier = new
ColumnDataClassifier("examples/cheese2007.prop"); Classifier<String,String>
classifier =
columnDataClassifier.makeClassifier(columnDataClassifier.readTrainingExampl
es("examples/cheeseDisease.train"));
  for (String line :
ObjectBank.getLineIterator("examples/cheeseDisease.test", "utf-8")) {
Datum<String,String> d = columnDataClassifier.makeDatumFromLine(line);
System.out.println(line + " ==> " + classifier.classOf(d));
}
}
}
```

This recipe does not demonstrate the loading and saving of the Stanford classifier model. If you are interested, take a look at the `ClassifierDemo.java` file in the distribution.

Classifying data points using Massive Online Analysis (MOA)

Massive Online Analysis or MOA is related to Weka, but it comes with more scalability. It is a notable Java workbench for data stream mining. With a strong community in place, MOA has implementations of classification, clustering, regression, concept drift identification, and recommender systems. Among other key advantages of MOA are its capability of being extended by the developers and its capacity of having bi-directional interactions with Weka.

Getting ready

In order to perform this recipe, we would require the following:

1. MOA can be downloaded from `https://sourceforge.net/projects/moa-data stream/`, which eventually is accessible from the MOA *getting started* webpage at `http://moa.cms.waikato.ac.nz/getting-started/`:

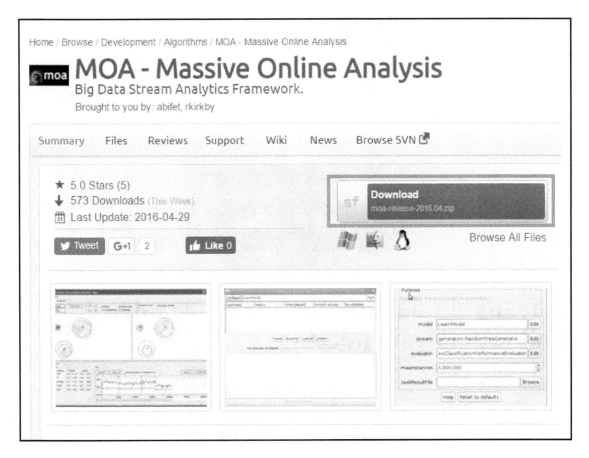

This will download a zip file named `moa-release-2016.04.zip` to your system. Save it anywhere you like.

2. Once downloaded, extract the files. You will see files and folders as follows:

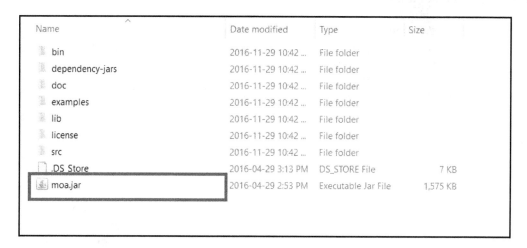

3. You will need to put the `moa.jar` file as an external library to your project:

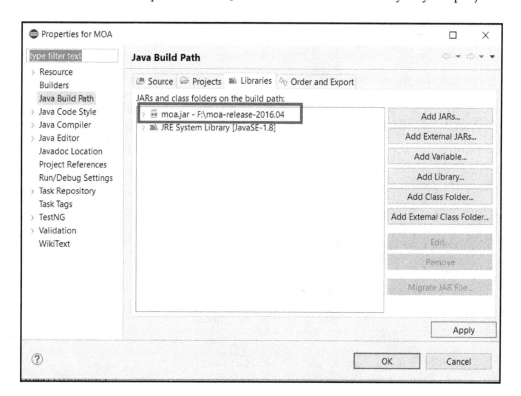

How to do it...

1. First, create the class and a method that takes two arguments: the first argument denotes number of instances that we are going to handle, and the second denotes whether we will be testing the classifier or not:

```
public class MOA { public void run(int numInstances, boolean
    isTesting){
```

2. Create a HoeffdingTree classifier:

```
Classifier learner = new HoeffdingTree();
```

 MOA has implementations of the following classifiers: Naive Bayes, Hoeffding Tree, Hoeffding Option Tree, Hoeffding Adaptive Tree, Bagging, Boosting, Bagging using ADWIN, Leveraging Bagging, SGD, Perceptron, SPegasos.

3. Next, create a random radial basis function stream.

4. Prepare the stream to be used:

```
stream.prepareForUse();
```

5. Set the reference to the header of the data stream. The header of the data stream can be found using the getHeader() method:

```
learner.setModelContext(stream.getHeader());
```

6. Then, prepare the classifier to be used:

```
learner.prepareForUse();
```

7. Declare two variables for tracking the number of samples and the number of samples correctly classified:

```
int numberSamplesCorrect = 0; int numberSamples = 0;
```

8. Declare another variable to track the time taken for the classification:

```
long evaluateStartTime =
    TimingUtils.getNanoCPUTimeOfCurrentThread();
```

9. Next, loop through until the stream has more instances and the number of samples being classified does not reach the total number of instances. In the loop, get the data of the stream's each instance. Then, check whether the classifier correctly classified the instance. If it did, increase the `numberSamplesCorrect` variable by 1. Check this only if testing is turned on (through the second parameter of this method).

10. Then, go to the next sample by increasing the sample number and training your learner with the next train instance:

```
while (stream.hasMoreInstances() && numberSamples < numInstances)
  {
  Instance trainInst = stream.nextInstance().getData();
  if (isTesting)
    {
    if (learner.correctlyClassifies(trainInst)){
      numberSamplesCorrect++;
      }
    }
  numberSamples++; learner.trainOnInstance(trainInst);
  }
```

10. Calculate the accuracy:

```
double accuracy = 100.0 * (double) numberSamplesCorrect/
  (double) numberSamples;
```

11. Also, compute the time taken for the classification:

```
double time = TimingUtils.nanoTimeToSeconds(TimingUtils.
  getNanoCPUTimeOfCurrentThread()- evaluateStartTime);
```

12. Finally, display these evaluation metrics and close the method:

```
System.out.println(numberSamples + " instances processed with "
  + accuracy + "% accuracy in "+time+" seconds."); }
```

13. To execute the method, you can have a `main()` method as follows. Close your class:

```
public static void main(String[] args) throws IOException { MOA
  exp = new MOA(); exp.run(1000000, true); } }
```

The entire code for the recipe is as follows:

```java
import moa.classifiers.trees.HoeffdingTree;
import moa.classifiers.Classifier;
import moa.core.TimingUtils;
import moa.streams.generators.RandomRBFGenerator;
import com.yahoo.labs.samoa.instances.Instance;
import java.io.IOException;


public class MOA {
        public void run(int numInstances, boolean isTesting){
                Classifier learner = new HoeffdingTree();
                RandomRBFGenerator stream = new RandomRBFGenerator();
                stream.prepareForUse();

                learner.setModelContext(stream.getHeader());
                learner.prepareForUse();

                int numberSamplesCorrect = 0;
                int numberSamples = 0;
                long evaluateStartTime = Tim-
                   ingUtils.getNanoCPUTimeOfCurrentThread();
                while (stream.hasMoreInstances() && numberSamples <
                   numIn-stances) {
                        Instance trainInst =
                            stream.nextInstance().getData();
                        if (isTesting) {
                                if
                        (learner.correctlyClassifies(trainInst)){
                                numberSamplesCorrect++;
                                }
                        }
                        numberSamples++;
                        learner.trainOnInstance(trainInst);
                }
                double accuracy = 100.0 * (double)
                   numberSamplesCorrect/ (double) numberSamples;
                double time = Tim-in-
                   gUtils.nanoTimeToSeconds(TimingUtils.
                    getNanoCPUTimeOfCurrentThread()- evaluateStartTime);
                System.out.println(numberSamples + " instances
                 processed with " + accuracy + "% accuracy in "+time+"
                    seconds.");
        }

        public static void main(String[] args) throws IOException {
                MOA exp = new MOA();
```

```
        exp.run(1000000, true);
    }
}
```

The output of the code in the recipe will be something as follows (the output might vary from machine to machine):

```
1000000 instances processed with 91.0458% accuracy in 6.769871032 seconds.
```

Classifying multilabeled data points using Mulan

So far, we have seen multiclass classification that aims to classify a data instance into one of several classes. Multilabeled data instances are data instances that can have multiple classes or labels. The machine learning tools that we have used so far are not capable of handling data points that have this characteristic of having multiple target classes.

For classifying multilabeled data points, we will be using an open source Java library named Mulan. Mulan has implementations of various classification, ranking, feature selection, and evaluation of models. As Mulan does not have GUI, the only way to use it is either by command line or using its API. In this recipe, we will limit our focus on classification and evaluation of classification of a multilabeled dataset using two different classifiers.

Getting ready

In order to perform this recipe, we will require the following:

1. First, download Mulan. In our recipe, we will be using its version 1.5. The compressed files for the library can be found at
   `https://sourceforge.net/projects/mulan/files/mulan-1-5/mulan-1.5.0.zip/download`, which is accessible through
   `http://mulan.sourceforge.net/download.html`.

2. Unzip the compressed files. You will see a data folder as follows. Take a look inside the `dist` folder:

Name	Date modified	Type	Size
.settings	2016-11-29 11:17 ...	File folder	
apidoc	2016-11-29 11:17 ...	File folder	
data	2016-11-29 11:17 ...	File folder	
dist	2016-11-29 11:17 ...	File folder	
lib	2016-11-29 11:17 ...	File folder	
nbproject	2016-11-29 11:17 ...	File folder	
src	2016-11-29 11:17 ...	File folder	
target	2016-11-29 11:17 ...	File folder	
test	2016-11-29 11:17 ...	File folder	
.classpath	2015-02-22 7:05 PM	CLASSPATH File	1 KB
.project	2015-02-22 5:44 PM	PROJECT File	1 KB
build.xml	2015-02-22 5:44 PM	XML Document	9 KB
changelog.txt	2015-02-22 5:44 PM	Text Document	5 KB
license.txt	2015-02-22 5:44 PM	Text Document	35 KB
readme.txt	2015-02-22 5:44 PM	Text Document	1 KB

3. You will see three files there. Among the three files, there is another compressed file named `Mulan-1.5.0.zip`. Unzip the files:

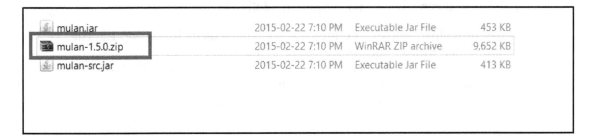

mulan.jar	2015-02-22 7:10 PM	Executable Jar File	453 KB
mulan-1.5.0.zip	2015-02-22 7:10 PM	WinRAR ZIP archive	9,652 KB
mulan-src.jar	2015-02-22 7:10 PM	Executable Jar File	413 KB

4. This time, you will see three or four JAR files. From the four JAR files, we will be using the JAR files highlighted in the following image:

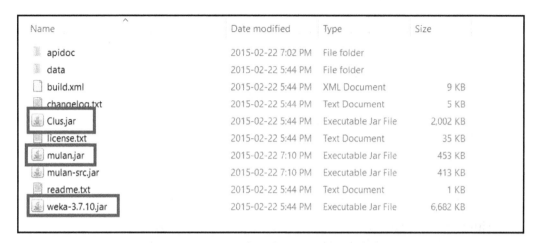

5. Add these three JAR files into your project as external libraries:

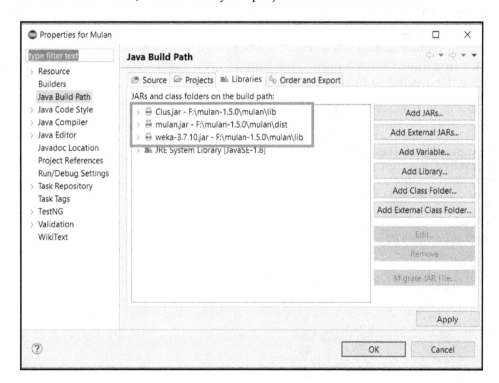

6. The data folder of the Mulan distribution contains an example multi labeled dataset. In our recipe, we will be using the `emotions.arff` file and the `emotions.xml` file:

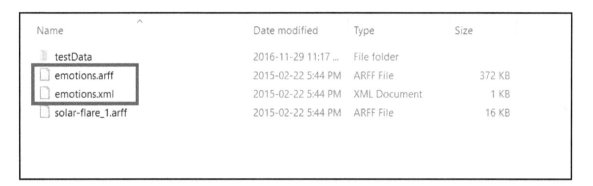

Before we jump into our recipe, let's take a look at the dataset format for Mulan. Mulan requires two files to specify a multi-labeled dataset. The first one is an ARFF file (take a look at `Chapter 4`, *Learn from Data – part 1*. The labels should be specified as nominal attributes with two values "0" and "1", where the prior denotes the absence of the label and latter denotes the presence of the label. The following example demonstrates that the dataset has three numeric features, and each instance can have five classes or labels. In the `@data` section, the first three values represent the actual feature values and then we have five 0s or 1s denoting the absence or presence of the classes:

```
@relation MultiLabelExample

@attribute feature1 numeric
@attribute feature2 numeric
@attribute feature3 numeric
@attribute label1 {0, 1}
@attribute label2 {0, 1}
@attribute label3 {0, 1}
@attribute label4 {0, 1}
@attribute label5 {0, 1}

@data
2.3,5.6,1.4,0,1,1,0,0
```

The XML file, on the other hand, specifies the labels and any hierarchical relationship among them. The following example is an XML file corresponding to the preceding example:

```
<labels xmlns="http://mulan.sourceforge.net/labels">
<label name="label1"></label>
  <label name="label2"></label>
  <label name="label3"></label>
  <label name="label4"></label>
  <label name="label5"></label>
</labels>
```

For more details, please refer to `http://mulan.sourceforge.net/format.html`.

How to do it...

1. Create a class and a `main()` method. We will be writing all of our codes inside the `main()` method:

   ```
   public class Mulan { public static void main(String[] args){
   ```

2. Create a dataset and read the `emotions.arff` and `emotions.xml` file to the dataset:

   ```
   MultiLabelInstances dataset = null;
     try {
       dataset = new  MultiLabelInstances("path to
         emotions.arff",
         "path to emotions.xml");
     } catch (InvalidDataFormatException e) {
     }
   ```

3. Next, we will be creating a RAkEL classifier and a MLkNN classifier. Note that RAkEL is a meta-classifier, which means it can have a multilabel learner and it is typically used with `LabelPowerset` algorithm. `LabelPowerset` is a transform-based algorithm and can take a single-label classifier (in our case, J48) as parameter. MLkNN is an adaptation classifier and based on k-nearest neighbour:

   ```
   RAkEL learner1 = new RAkEL(new LabelPowerset(new J48()));
     MLkNN
     learner2 = new MLkNN();
   ```

4. Create an evaluator to evaluate the classification performances:

```
Evaluator eval = new Evaluator();
```

5. As we will be having evaluations for two classifiers, we need to declare a variable that can have multiple evaluation results:

```
MultipleEvaluation results;
```

6. We will be having a 10-fold cross validation evaluation. Therefore, declare a variable with number of folds you are going to create:

```
int numFolds = 10;
```

7. Next, evaluate your first learner and display the results:

```
results = eval.crossValidate(learner1, dataset, numFolds);
System.out.println(results);
```

8. Finally, evaluate your second learner and display the results:

```
results = eval.crossValidate(learner2, dataset, numFolds);
System.out.println(results);
```

9. Close the method and class:

```
} }
```

The complete code for the recipe is as follows:

```
import mulan.classifier.lazy.MLkNN;
import mulan.classifier.meta.RAkEL;
import mulan.classifier.transformation.LabelPowerset;
import mulan.data.InvalidDataFormatException;
import mulan.data.MultiLabelInstances;
import mulan.evaluation.Evaluator;
import mulan.evaluation.MultipleEvaluation;
import weka.classifiers.trees.J48;

public class Mulan {
        public static void main(String[] args){
                MultiLabelInstances dataset = null;
                try {
                    dataset = new MultiLabelInstances("path to emo-
                        tions.arff", "path to emotions.xml");
                } catch (InvalidDataFormatException e) {
                }
```

```
RAkEL learner1 = new RAkEL(new LabelPowerset(new
    J48()));
MLkNN learner2 = new MLkNN();
Evaluator eval = new Evaluator();
MultipleEvaluation results;
int numFolds = 10;
results = eval.crossValidate(learner1, dataset, num-
    Folds);
System.out.println(results);
results = eval.crossValidate(learner2, dataset, num-
    Folds);
System.out.println(results);
    }
  }
```

The output of the code will be the performance of the two learners of your choice:

```
Fold 1/10
Fold 2/10
Fold 3/10
Fold 4/10
Fold 5/10
Fold 6/10
Fold 7/10
Fold 8/10
Fold 9/10
Fold 10/10
Hamming Loss: 0.2153±0.0251
Subset Accuracy: 0.2562±0.0481
Example-Based Precision: 0.6325±0.0547
Example-Based Recall: 0.6307±0.0560
Example-Based F Measure: 0.5990±0.0510
Example-Based Accuracy: 0.5153±0.0484
Example-Based Specificity: 0.8607±0.0213

. . . . . . . . . . . . . . . . . . . . . . . . . . . . . . . . . . . . . .
Fold 1/10
Fold 2/10
Fold 3/10
Fold 4/10
Fold 5/10
Fold 6/10
Fold 7/10
Fold 8/10
Fold 9/10
Fold 10/10
Hamming Loss: 0.1951±0.0243
Subset Accuracy: 0.2831±0.0538
Example-Based Precision: 0.6883±0.0655
```

```
Example-Based Recall: 0.6050±0.0578
Example-Based F Measure: 0.6138±0.0527
Example-Based Accuracy: 0.5326±0.0515
Example-Based Specificity: 0.8994±0.0271

. . . . . . . . . . . . . . . . . . . . . . . . . . . . . . . . . . .
```

6
Retrieving Information from Text Data

In this chapter, we will cover the following recipes:

- Detecting tokens (words) using Java
- Detecting sentences using Java
- Detecting tokens (words) and sentences using OpenNLP
- Retrieving lemma and part-of-speech and recognizing named entities from tokens using Stanford CoreNLP
- Measuring text similarity with Cosine Similarity measure using Java 8
- Extracting topics from text documents using Mallet
- Classifying text documents using Mallet
- Classifying text documents using Weka

Introduction

Due to the availability of web data, as most of them are in text format, the type of data that a data scientist handles nowadays the most is text. There are many dimensions of text data that can be retrieved from documents, articles, blog posts, social media updates, newswires, and you name it.

Many Java-based tools are available for data scientists to retrieve information from text data. Also, there are tools that achieve a variety of data science tasks. In this chapter, we have limited our scope to a few data science tasks like trivial text feature extractions like sentences and words, document classification using machine learning, topic extraction and modelling, keyword extraction from documents, and named entity recognition.

Detecting tokens (words) using Java

One of the most common tasks that a data scientist needs to do using text data is to detect tokens from it. This task is called *tokenization*. Although "token" can mean a word, symbol, phrase or any other meaningful text unit, in this chapter, we will consider words as tokens since a word is a reasonable text unit to deal with. However, the notion of word tokens varies from person to person; some need words only, some prefer symbols to be omitted during detection, while some want to keep punctuation in the words for getting more context. Based on the variety of needs, in this recipe, we will be using three different techniques that, when applied to the same string, yield three different results. The techniques will involve string tokenization, break iterator, and regular expressions. It is you who needs to decide which technique to use.

Remember that we have selectively chosen only three methods though there are many other options out there; they are for you to explore.

Getting ready

1. Go to `https://docs.oracle.com/javase/7/docs/api/java/util/regex/Patte rn.html` and go through the documentation on the regular expression patterns supported by the `Pattern` class.
2. Go to `https://docs.oracle.com/javase/7/docs/api/java/text/BreakIterat or.html` and see the examples. This will give you an idea on the usage of a break iterator.

How to do it...

1. First, we will create a method that uses Java's `StringTokenzier` class to detect tokens. This method will take the input sentence and tokenize the sentence using this class. Finally, the method will print the tokens:

   ```
   public void useTokenizer(String input){
   ```

2. Call the `StringTokenizer` constructor by sending the input sentence as parameter:

   ```
   StringTokenizer tokenizer = new StringTokenizer(input);
   ```

3. Create a string object to hold the tokens:

```
String word ="";
```

4. Iterate through the tokenizer to get each word and print them on the console:

```
while(tokenizer.hasMoreTokens()){
    word = tokenizer.nextToken();
    System.out.println(word);
}
```

5. Close the method:

```
}
```

The output of this method for a sentence like *Let's get this vis-a-vis, he said, "these boys' marks are really that well?"* will be as follows:

```
"Let's
get
this
vis-a-vis",
he
said,
"these
boys'
marks
are
really
that
well?"
```

6. Second, we will create a method that will use Java's `BreakIterator` class to iterate through each word in a text. You will see that the code is slightly more complex than the first method we have created in this recipe.

   The method will get the input sentence as its argument:

   ```
   public void useBreakIterator(String input){
   ```

7. Then, use the `BreakIterator` class to create a `tokenizer`:

   ```
   BreakIterator tokenizer = BreakIterator.getWordInstance();
   ```

8. Apply the `tokenizer` on the input sentence:

```
tokenizer.setText(input);
```

9. Get the starting index of the `tokenizer`:

```
int start = tokenizer.first();
```

10. Get each token using a for loop as a string and print them on console as follows:

```
for (int end = tokenizer.next();
    end != BreakIterator.DONE;
    start = end, end = tokenizer.next()) {
    System.out.println(input.substring(start,end));
}
```

11. Close the method:

```
}
```

The output of this method for a sentence like *"Let's get this vis-a-vis", he said, "these boys' marks are really that well?"* will be as follows:

```
"
Let's
get
this
vis-a-vis
"

'
he
said

'
"

these
boys
'

marks
are
really
that
well
?
"
```

12. Finally, we will create a method that tokenizes an input text using regular expression:

```
public void useRegEx(String input){
```

13. Use a pattern using a regular expression that can capture punctuations, single or multiple hyphenated words, quotation marks, apostrophes in the end, and so on. If you need some specific patterns, just use your own regular expression in the following line:

```
Pattern pattern = Pattern.compile("\\w[\\w-]+('\\w*)?");
```

14. Apply a `matcher` on the `pattern`:

```
Matcher matcher = pattern.matcher(input);
```

15. Use the `matcher` to retrieve all the words from the input text:

```
while ( matcher.find() ) {
  System.out.println(input.substring(matcher.start(),
    matcher.end()));
}
```

16. Close the method:

```
}
```

The output of this method for a sentence like *Let's get this vis-a-vis,he said, these boys' marks are really that well?* will be as follows:

```
Let's
get
this
vis-a-vis
he
said
these
boys'
marks
are
really
that
well
```

The full code for this recipe will be as follows:

```java
import java.text.BreakIterator;
import java.util.StringTokenizer;
import java.util.regex.Matcher;
import java.util.regex.Pattern;

public class WordDetection {
    public static void main(String[] args){
        String input = ""Let's get this vis-a-vis", he said, "these boys'
          marks are really that well?"";
        WordDetection wordDetection = new WordDetection();
        wordDetection.useTokenizer(input);
        wordDetection.useBreakIterator(input);
        wordDetection.useRegEx(input);
    }
    public void useTokenizer(String input){
        System.out.println("Tokenizer");
        StringTokenizer tokenizer = new StringTokenizer(input);
        String word ="";
        while(tokenizer.hasMoreTokens()){
            word = tokenizer.nextToken();
            System.out.println(word);
        }
    }
    public void useBreakIterator(String input){
        System.out.println("Break Iterator");
        BreakIterator tokenizer = BreakIterator.getWordInstance();
         tokenizer.setText(input);
         int start = tokenizer.first();
         for (int end = tokenizer.next();
              end != BreakIterator.DONE;
              start = end, end = tokenizer.next()) {
              System.out.println(input.substring(start,end));
         }
    }
    public void useRegEx(String input){
        System.out.println("Regular Expression");
        Pattern pattern = Pattern.compile("\\w[\\w-]+('\\w*)?");
        Matcher matcher = pattern.matcher(input);

        while ( matcher.find() ) {
            System.out.println(input.substring(matcher.start(),
              matcher.end()));
        }
    }
}
```

Detecting sentences using Java

In this recipe, we will see how we can detect sentences so that we can use them for further analysis. Sentences are a very important text unit for data scientists to experiment different routing exercises, such as classification. To detect sentences from texts, we will be using Java's `BreakIterator` class.

Getting ready

Go to `https://docs.oracle.com/javase/7/docs/api/java/text/BreakIterator.html` and see the examples. This will give you an idea on the usage of a break iterator.

How to do it...

As a test for this recipe's code, we will use two sentences that can create confusion to many regular-expression-based solutions. The two sentences for test are: *My name is Rushdi Shams. You can use Dr. before my name as I have a PhD. but I am a bit shy to use it.* Interestingly, we will see that Java's `BreakIterator` class handles them with great efficiency.

Create a method that takes the test string as argument.

```
public void useSentenceIterator(String source){
```

1. Create a `sentenceiterator` object of the `BreakIterator` class:

```
BreakIterator iterator =
    BreakIterator.getSentenceInstance(Locale.US);
```

2. Apply the `iterator` on the test string:

```
iterator.setText(source);
```

3. Get the `start` index of the test string to an integer variable:

```
int start = iterator.first();
```

4. Finally, iterate through all the sentences in the iterator and print them. To loop through the sentences in the iterator, you will need another variable named `end` to point to the end index of a sentence:

```
for (int end = iterator.next(); end != BreakIterator.DONE;
    start = end, end = iterator.next()) {
    System.out.println(source.substring(start,end));
}
```

The output of the code will be as follows:

```
My name is Rushdi Shams.
You can use Dr. before my name as I have a Ph.D. but I am a bit shy to use
it.
```

The complete code for the recipe is as follows:

```
import java.text.BreakIterator;
import java.util.Locale;
public class SentenceDetection {
    public void useSentenceIterator(String source){
        BreakIterator iterator =
          BreakIterator.getSentenceInstance(Locale.US);
        iterator.setText(source);
        int start = iterator.first();
        for (int end = iterator.next();
            end != BreakIterator.DONE;
            start = end, end = iterator.next()) {
          System.out.println(source.substring(start,end));
        }
    }
    public static void main(String[] args){
        SentenceDetection detection = new SentenceDetection();
        String test = "My name is Rushdi Shams. You can use Dr. before my
          name as I have a Ph.D. but I am a bit shy to use it.";
        detection.useSentenceIterator(test);
    }
}
```

Detecting tokens (words) and sentences using OpenNLP

The previous two recipes in this chapter detected tokens (words) and sentences using legacy Java classes and methods in them. In this recipe, we will combine the two tasks of detecting tokens and sentences with an open-source library of Apache named OpenNLP. The reason for introducing OpenNLP with these two tasks that can be accomplished well with the legacy methods is to introduce data scientists to a tool that is really handy and has very high accuracy in several information retrieval tasks on standard and classic corpora. The homepage for OpenNLP can be found at https://opennlp.apache.org/. One strong argument of using this library for tokenization, sentence segmentation, part-of-speech tagging, named entity recognition, chunking, parsing, and co-reference resolution is that you can have your own classifier trained on your corpora of articles or documents.

Getting ready

1. At the time of writing this book, the 1.6.0 version was the latest for OpenNLP and therefore you are encouraged to use this version. Download the 1.6.0 version of the library from https://opennlp.apache.org/download.html. Go to this webpage and download the binary zip files:

> ### Download
>
> ### Last Offical Release
>
> Apache OpenNLP 1.6.0 is now available for download.
>
> | File | Signatures |
> |------|-----------|
> | apache-opennlp-1.6.0-bin.tar.gz | md5 sha1 asc |
> | apache-opennlp-1.6.0-bin.zip | md5 sha1 asc |
> | apache-opennlp-1.6.0-src.tar.gz | md5 sha1 asc |
> | apache-opennlp-1.6.0-src.zip | md5 sha1 asc |

2. After downloading the files, unzip them. In the distribution, you will find a directory named `lib`.

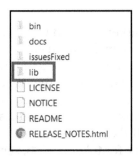

3. In the `lib` directory, you will find the following two Jar files:

From that directory, add the `opennlp-tools-1.6.0.jar` file as an external library to your Eclipse project that you need to create for this recipe:

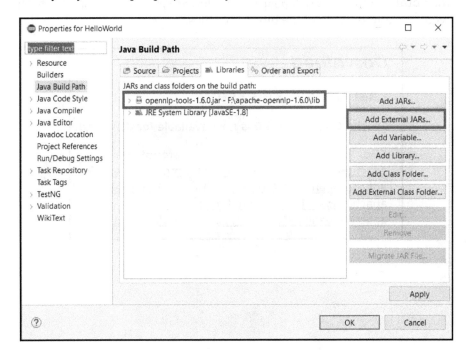

For this recipe, you will be using the pre-built models for token and sentence detection provided by OpenNLP. Therefore, you need to download and save the models in your hard drive. Remember the location of these models so that you can include the models in your code.

Go to `http://opennlp.sourceforge.net/models-1.5/` and download the English tokenizer and sentence detector models. Save them in your `C:/` drive. Now, you are ready to write some code:

de	POS Tagger	Perceptron model trained on tiger corpus.	de-pos-perceptron.bin
en	Tokenizer	Trained on opennlp training data.	en-token.bin
en	Sentence Detector	Trained on opennlp training data.	en-sent.bin
en	POS Tagger	Maxent model with tag dictionary.	en-pos-maxent.bin

How to do it...

1. In this recipe, you will create a method that uses the `tokenizer` and sentence detector models of OpenNLP to tokenize and fragment a source text into sentences. As parameters, you will send the following:
   - A string that will contain the source text.
   - The path of the model(s).
   - A string denoting whether you want to tokenize the source text or to fragment it into sentence units. For the former, the choice you will be sending is *word*, and for the latter, the choice will be *sentence*.

```
public void useOpenNlp(String sourceText, String modelPath,
    String choice) throws IOException{
```

2. First, read the models treating them as input streams:

```
InputStream modelIn = null;
modelIn = new FileInputStream(modelPath);
```

3. Then, create an if block for the choice *sentence* that will contain codes to detect sentence fragments of the source text:

```
if(choice.equalsIgnoreCase("sentence")){
```

4. Create a sentence model from the pre-built model and then close the variable that was used to hold the pre-built model:

```
SentenceModel model = new SentenceModel(modelIn);
modelIn.close();
```

5. Using the model, create a sentence detector:

```
SentenceDetectorME sentenceDetector = new
    SentenceDetectorME(model);
```

6. Detect the sentences of the source text using the sentence detector. The resultant sentences will be taken to be an array of string:

```
String sentences[] = sentenceDetector.sentDetect(sourceText);
```

7. Now, print the sentences on the console and close the if block:

```
System.out.println("Sentences: ");
  for(String sentence:sentences){
      System.out.println(sentence);
  }
}
```

8. Next, create an else if block that will hold your code for tokenization of the source text:

```
else if(choice.equalsIgnoreCase("word")){
```

9. Create a `tokenizer` model from the pre-built model and close the pre-built model:

```
TokenizerModel model = new TokenizerModel(modelIn);
modelIn.close();
```

10. Using the model, create a `tokenizer`:

```
Tokenizer tokenizer = new TokenizerME(model);
```

11. Extract tokens (words) from the source text using the `tokenizer`. The extracted tokens will be taken to an array of string:

```
String tokens[] = tokenizer.tokenize(sourceText);
```

12. Finally, print the tokens on console and close the else if block:

```
System.out.println("Words: ");
  for(String token:tokens){
      System.out.println(token);
  }
}
```

13. You will need an else block just in case an invalid choice comes from the user:

```
else{
  System.out.println("Error in choice");
  modelIn.close();
  return;
}
```

14. Close the method:

```
}
```

The complete source code for the recipe is as follows:

```
import java.io.FileInputStream;
import java.io.IOException;
import java.io.InputStream;

import opennlp.tools.sentdetect.SentenceDetectorME;
import opennlp.tools.sentdetect.SentenceModel;
import opennlp.tools.tokenize.Tokenizer;
import opennlp.tools.tokenize.TokenizerME;
import opennlp.tools.tokenize.TokenizerModel;

public class OpenNlpSenToken {
    public static void main(String[] args){
        OpenNlpSenToken openNlp = new OpenNlpSenToken();
        try {
            openNlp.useOpenNlp("My name is Rushdi Shams. "
                    + "You can use Dr. before my name as I have a Ph.D. "
                    + "but I am a bit shy to use it.", "C:/en-sent.bin",
                        "sentence");
            openNlp.useOpenNlp(""Let's get this vis-a-vis", he said,
                "these boys' marks are really that well?"", "C:/en-
                    token.bin", "word");
        } catch (IOException e) {
        }
    }
}
```

```java
public void useOpenNlp(String sourceText, String modelPath, String
    choice) throws IOException{
  InputStream modelIn = null;
  modelIn = new FileInputStream(modelPath);

  if(choice.equalsIgnoreCase("sentence")){
     SentenceModel model = new SentenceModel(modelIn);
     modelIn.close();
     SentenceDetectorME sentenceDetector = new
        SentenceDetectorME(model);
     String sentences[] = sentenceDetector.sentDetect(sourceText);
     System.out.println("Sentences: ");
     for(String sentence:sentences){
        System.out.println(sentence);
     }
  }
  else if(choice.equalsIgnoreCase("word")){
     TokenizerModel model = new TokenizerModel(modelIn);
     modelIn.close();
     Tokenizer tokenizer = new TokenizerME(model);
     String tokens[] = tokenizer.tokenize(sourceText);
     System.out.println("Words: ");
     for(String token:tokens){
        System.out.println(token);
     }
  }
  else{
     System.out.println("Error in choice");
     modelIn.close();
     return;
  }
}
```

You can now compare the output of this source code with the previous two recipes since the same source text was used for those two recipes.

 For other uses of the OpenNLP library, the readers of this book are highly encouraged to look at `https://opennlp.apache.org/documentation/1.6.0/manual/opennlp.html`.

Retrieving lemma, part-of-speech, and recognizing named entities from tokens using Stanford CoreNLP

Now that we know how to extract tokens or words from a given text, we will see how we can get different types of information from the tokens such as their lemmas, part-of-speech, and whether the token is a named entity.

The process of lemmatization group inflected forms of a word together so that they can be analyzed as a single text unit. This is similar to the process of stemming with a big difference that stemming does not consider context during its grouping. Therefore, lemmatization is particularly more useful for text data analysis than stemming but requires more computation power.

Part-of-speech tags of the tokens in an article or document are widely used as features for many machine-learning models that can be useful for data scientists.

Named entities, on the other hand, are very important for news article data analysis and have very high impact on researches related to business corporations.

In this recipe, we will be retrieving this information from text using Stanford CoreNLP 3.7.0, which was the latest version at the time the chapter was written.

Getting ready

1. Go to `http://stanfordnlp.github.io/CoreNLP/download.html` and download Stanford CoreNLP 3.7.0.

2. The files that you have downloaded in step 1 are compressed. If you decompress them, you will find a directory structure as follows:

patterns	12/12/2016 10:29 ...	File folder	
sutime	12/12/2016 10:31 ...	File folder	
tokensregex	12/12/2016 10:31 ...	File folder	
StanfordDependenciesManual	12/12/2016 10:29 ...	Adobe Acrobat D...	196 KB
ejml-0.23	12/12/2016 10:29 ...	Executable Jar File	207 KB
javax.json	12/12/2016 10:29 ...	Executable Jar File	84 KB
javax.json-api-1.0-sources	12/12/2016 10:29 ...	Executable Jar File	54 KB
joda-time	12/12/2016 10:29 ...	Executable Jar File	615 KB
joda-time-2.9-sources	12/12/2016 10:29 ...	Executable Jar File	757 KB
jollyday	12/12/2016 10:29 ...	Executable Jar File	209 KB
jollyday-0.4.9-sources	12/12/2016 10:29 ...	Executable Jar File	193 KB
protobuf	12/12/2016 10:29 ...	Executable Jar File	581 KB
slf4j-api	12/12/2016 10:29 ...	Executable Jar File	26 KB
slf4j-simple	12/12/2016 10:29 ...	Executable Jar File	11 KB
stanford-corenlp-3.7.0	12/12/2016 10:29 ...	Executable Jar File	7,644 KB
stanford-corenlp-3.7.0-javadoc	12/12/2016 10:31 ...	Executable Jar File	9,480 KB
stanford-corenlp-3.7.0-models	12/12/2016 10:30 ...	Executable Jar File	353,647 KB
stanford-corenlp-3.7.0-sources	12/12/2016 10:29 ...	Executable Jar File	5,099 KB
xom	12/12/2016 10:29 ...	Executable Jar File	306 KB
xom-1.2.10-src	12/12/2016 10:29 ...	Executable Jar File	657 KB
LIBRARY-LICENSES	12/12/2016 10:29 ...	File	2 KB
Makefile	12/12/2016 10:29 ...	File	1 KB
SemgrexDemo.java	12/12/2016 10:30 ...	JAVA File	3 KB
ShiftReduceDemo.java	12/12/2016 10:30 ...	JAVA File	2 KB
StanfordCoreNlpDemo.java	12/12/2016 10:30 ...	JAVA File	6 KB

3. Include all the jar files as indicated in the exhibit into your existing project as external Jar files and you will be ready to write some code:

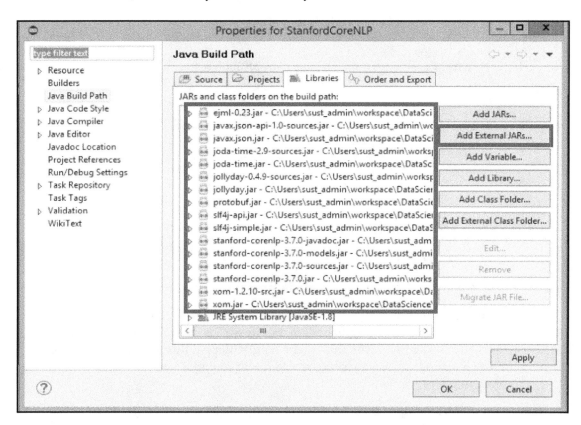

How to do it...

1. Create a class and a `main()` method where you will be keeping all of your codes for this recipe:

```
public class Lemmatizer {
  public static void main(String[] args){
```

2. Next, create a Stanford CoreNLP pipeline. Through this pipeline, you will be providing many property value to the CoreNLP engine:

```
StanfordCoreNLP pipeline;
```

3. Create a `Properties` object and add a few properties to it. In our case, we will be tokenizing with part-of-speech tagging and lemmatization:

```
Properties props = new Properties();
props.put("annotators", "tokenize, ssplit, pos, lemma, ner");
```

4. Next, with these properties, create a CoreNLP object:

```
pipeline = new StanfordCoreNLP(props, false);
```

5. Create a string for which you need to generate lemmas:

```
String text = "Hamlet's mother, Queen Gertrude, says this
    famous line while watching The Mousetrap. "
        + "Gertrude is talking about the queen in the play. "
        + "She feels that the play-queen seems insincere because
            she repeats so dramatically that she'll never remarry
            due to her undying love of her husband.";
```

6. Next, create an `Annotation` with the given text:

```
Annotation document = pipeline.process(text);
```

7. Finally, for each token, get the original token and get the lemma of the token. You do not need to get the original token, but to see the difference between the word form and the lemma form, this can be handy. Repeat this for all the sentences using the `Annotation` variable named document that you have created in the previous step:

```
for(CoreMap sentence: document.get(SentencesAnnotation.class))
{
    for(CoreLabel token: sentence.get(TokensAnnotation.class))
    {
        String word = token.get(TextAnnotation.class);
        String lemma = token.get(LemmaAnnotation.class);
        String pos = token.get(PartOfSpeechAnnotation.class);
        String ne = token.get(NamedEntityTagAnnotation.class);
        System.out.println(word + "-->" + lemma + "-->" + pos
        + "-->" + ne);
    }
}
```

8. Close the method and the class:

```
    }
}
```

Partial output of the code will be as follows:

```
. . .
Queen-->Queen-->NNP-->PERSON
Gertrude-->Gertrude-->NNP-->PERSON
,-->,-->,-->O
says-->say-->VBZ-->O
this-->this-->DT-->O
famous-->famous-->JJ-->O
line-->line-->NN-->O
while-->while-->IN-->O
watching-->watch-->VBG-->O
The-->the-->DT-->O
Mousetrap-->mousetrap-->NN-->O
.-->.-->.-->O
Gertrude-->Gertrude-->NNP-->PERSON
is-->be-->VBZ-->O
talking-->talk-->VBG-->O
. . .
```

The complete code for this recipe is as follows:

```
import edu.stanford.nlp.ling.CoreAnnotations.LemmaAnnotation;
import edu.stanford.nlp.ling.CoreAnnotations.NamedEntityTagAnnotation;
import edu.stanford.nlp.ling.CoreAnnotations.PartOfSpeechAnnotation;
import edu.stanford.nlp.ling.CoreAnnotations.SentencesAnnotation;
import edu.stanford.nlp.ling.CoreAnnotations.TextAnnotation;
import edu.stanford.nlp.ling.CoreAnnotations.TokensAnnotation;
import edu.stanford.nlp.ling.CoreLabel;
import edu.stanford.nlp.pipeline.Annotation;
import edu.stanford.nlp.pipeline.StanfordCoreNLP;
import edu.stanford.nlp.util.CoreMap;
import java.util.Properties;

public class Lemmatizer {
    public static void main(String[] args){
      StanfordCoreNLP pipeline;
        Properties props = new Properties();
        props.put("annotators", "tokenize, ssplit, pos, lemma, ner");
        pipeline = new StanfordCoreNLP(props, false);
        String text = "Hamlet's mother, Queen Gertrude, says this
          famous line while watching The Mousetrap. "
            + "Gertrude is talking about the queen in the play. "
```

```
            + "She feels that the play-queen seems insincere because
              she repeats so dramatically that she'll never remarry
                due to her undying love of her husband.";
    Annotation document = pipeline.process(text);

    for(CoreMap sentence: document.get(SentencesAnnotation.class))
      {
        for(CoreLabel token: sentence.get(TokensAnnotation.class))
          {
            String word = token.get(TextAnnotation.class);
            String lemma = token.get(LemmaAnnotation.class);
            String pos = token.get(PartOfSpeechAnnotation.class);
            String ne = token.get(NamedEntityTagAnnotation.class);
            System.out.println(word + "-->" + lemma + "-->" + pos
            + "-->" + ne);
          }
      }
  }
}
```

Measuring text similarity with Cosine Similarity measure using Java 8

Data scientists often measure the distance or similarity between two data points–sometimes for classification or clustering, sometimes for detecting outliers, and for many other cases. When they deal with texts as data points, the traditional distance or similarity measurements cannot be used. There are many standard and classic as well as emerging and novel similarity measures available for comparing two or more text data points. In this recipe, we will be using a measurement named Cosine Similarity to compute distance between two sentences. Cosine Similarity is considered to be a *de facto* standard in the information retrieval community and therefore widely used. In this recipe, we will use this measurement to find the similarity between two sentences in string format.

Getting ready

Although the readers can get a comprehensive outlook of the measurement from https://en.wikipedia.org/wiki/Cosine_similarity, let us see the algorithm for using the formula for two sentences:

1. First, extract the words from the two strings.

2. For each word in the respective strings, calculate their frequency. Frequency here denotes number of times the words are present in each sentence. Let A be the vector of the words and their frequencies from first string and B be the vector of words and their frequencies from second string.

3. Find out unique words in each string by removing duplicates.

4. Find out a list of words that are in intersection of the two strings.

5. The numerator of the Cosine Similarity formula will be the dot product of the vectors A and B.

6. The denominator of the formula will be the arithmetic product of the magnitudes of the vectors A and B.

Note that the Cosine Similarity score of two sentences will be between −1 meaning exactly opposite and 1 meaning exactly the same, while a 0 score indicates decorrelation.

How to do it...

1. Create a method that takes two string arguments. These are the strings for which you will be `calculateCosine` similarity:

```
public double calculateCosine(String s1, String s2){
```

2. Use the power of regular expressions and Java 8's parallelization facility to tokenize the given strings. This gives you two streams of words in the two strings:

```
Stream<String> stream1 =
  Stream.of(s1.toLowerCase().split("\\W+")).parallel();
Stream<String> stream2 =
  Stream.of(s2.toLowerCase().split("\\W+")).parallel();
```

For tokenization, you can use any method in the first recipe of this chapter, but the method shown in this step is also handy, short, and leverages the power of both Regular Expressions and Java 8.

3. Get the frequency of each word in each string. Again, you will be using Java 8 to achieve this. The resultant will be two maps:

```
Map<String, Long> wordFreq1 = stream1
  .collect(Collectors.groupingBy
  (String::toString,Collectors.counting()));
Map<String, Long> wordFreq2 = stream2
  .collect(Collectors.groupingBy
  (String::toString,Collectors.counting()));
```

4. From the list of words in each sentence, only keep the unique ones by removing the duplicates. To do that, you will be creating two sets with the maps you have created in the previous step:

```
Set<String> wordSet1 = wordFreq1.keySet();
Set<String> wordSet2 = wordFreq2.keySet();
```

5. As you will be calculating dot product of the two maps in step 3 to use in the numerator of the Cosine similarity measure, you need to create a list of words common to both strings:

```
Set<String> intersection = new HashSet<String>(wordSet1);
intersection.retainAll(wordSet2);
```

6. Next, calculate the numerator of the formula, which is the dot product of the two maps:

```
double numerator = 0;
  for (String common: intersection){
  numerator += wordFreq1.get(common) * wordFreq2.get(common);
}
```

7. From this point on, you will be preparing to compute the denominator of the formula, which is the arithmetic product of the magnitudes of the two maps.

First, create the variables to hold the values of the magnitude of your vectors (which is in the map data structure):

```
double param1 = 0, param2 = 0;
```

8. Now, compute the magnitude of your first vector:

```
for(String w1: wordSet1){
   param1 += Math.pow(wordFreq1.get(w1), 2);
}
param1 = Math.sqrt(param1);
```

9. Next, compute the magnitude of your second vector:

```
for(String w2: wordSet2){
   param2 += Math.pow(wordFreq2.get(w2), 2);
}
param2 = Math.sqrt(param2);
```

10. Now that you have all the parameters for your `denominator`, multiply the magnitudes to get it:

```
double denominator = param1 * param2;
```

11. Finally, put the numerator and denominator in place to compute the Cosine Similarity of the two strings. Return the score to the caller. Close the method:

```
double cosineSimilarity = numerator/denominator;
return cosineSimilarity;
}
```

12. The complete code for this recipe is given here:

```
import java.util.HashSet;
import java.util.Map;
import java.util.Set;
import java.util.stream.Collectors;
import java.util.stream.Stream;

public class CosineSimilarity {
   public double calculateCosine(String s1, String s2){
      //tokenization in parallel with Java 8
      Stream<String> stream1 =
        Stream.of(s1.toLowerCase().split("\\W+")).parallel();
      Stream<String> stream2 =
        Stream.of(s2.toLowerCase().split("\\W+")).parallel();
      //word frequency maps for two strings
      Map<String, Long> wordFreq1 = stream1
         .collect(Collectors.groupingBy
           (String::toString,Collectors.counting()));
      Map<String, Long> wordFreq2 = stream2
         .collect(Collectors.groupingBy
```

```
            (String::toString,Collectors.counting()));
      //unique words for each string
      Set<String> wordSet1 = wordFreq1.keySet();
      Set<String> wordSet2 = wordFreq2.keySet();
      //common words of two strings
      Set<String> intersection = new HashSet<String>(wordSet1);
      intersection.retainAll(wordSet2);
      //numerator of cosine formula. s1.s2
      double numerator = 0;
      for (String common: intersection){
          numerator += wordFreq1.get(common) * wordFreq2.get(common);
      }
      //denominator of cosine formula has two parameters
      double param1 = 0, param2 = 0;
      //sqrt (sum of squared of s1 word frequencies)
      for(String w1: wordSet1){
          param1 += Math.pow(wordFreq1.get(w1), 2);
      }
      param1 = Math.sqrt(param1);
      //sqrt (sum of squared of s2 word frequencies)
      for(String w2: wordSet2){
          param2 += Math.pow(wordFreq2.get(w2), 2);
      }
      param2 = Math.sqrt(param2);
      //denominator of cosine formula. sqrt(sum(s1^2)) X
        sqrt(sum(s2^2))
      double denominator = param1 * param2;
      //cosine measure
      double cosineSimilarity = numerator/denominator;
      return cosineSimilarity;
   }//end method to calculate cosine similarity of two strings
   public static void main(String[] args){
      CosineSimilarity cos = new CosineSimilarity();
      System.out.println(cos.calculateCosine("To be, or not to be: that
        is the question.", "Frailty, thy name is woman!"));
      System.out.println(cos.calculateCosine("The lady doth protest too
        much, methinks.", "Frailty, thy name is woman!"));
   }
}
```

If you run the code, you will find the following output:

```
0.11952286093343936
0.0
```

The output means that the cosine similarity between the sentences *To be, or not to be: that is the question.* and *Frailty, thy name is woman!* is about 0.11; and between*The lady doth protest too much, methinks.* and *Frailty, thy name is woman!* it is 0.0.

> In this recipe, you have not removed stop words from the strings. To get a bias-free outcome, it is better to remove stop words from the two text units.

Extracting topics from text documents using Mallet

With an ever-increasing amount of documents in text format nowadays, an important task for any data scientist is to get an overview of a large number of articles with abstracts, summaries, or a list of abstract topics, not because this saves time to read through the articles but to do clustering, classification, semantic relatedness measurement, sentiment analysis, and so on.

In machine learning and natural language processing domain, topic modelling refers to retrieving abstract topics or keywords from text articles using statistical models. In this recipe, we will be using a sophisticated Java-based machine learning and natural language processing library named Mallet, which is an acronym for Machine Learning for Language Toolkit (see http://mallet.cs.umass.edu/). Mallet is widely used in the academia as well as in the industry for the following:

- document classification,
- clustering,
- topic modelling, and
- information extraction.

However, the scope of this book is limited to topic modelling and document classification. In this recipe, we will cover how to extract topics using Mallet while the next recipe will focus on classification of text documents using Mallet with supervised machine learning.

Note that you will use only command prompt to use the tool and you will not be involved in coding for this recipe and next. This is because Mallet is easier to use with command prompts. Interested readers who want to use the Java API are encouraged to read Mallet's resourceful API documentation at `http://mallet.cs.umass.edu/api/`.

Getting ready

1. First, you will be installing Mallet. We will be providing installation instructions only for Windows operating systems in this recipe. Go to `http://mallet.cs.umass.edu/download.php` and download Mallet. At the time of writing this book, version 2.0.8 was the latest version and therefore you are encouraged to download it (preferably the zip file):

Current release: The following packaged release of MALLET 2.0 is available:

mallet-2.0.8.tar.gz mallet-2.0.8.zip

Windows installation: After unzipping MALLET, set the environment variable %MALLET_HOME% to point to the MALLET directory. In all command line examples, substitute bin\mallet for bin/mallet.

Development release: To download the most current version of MALLET 2.0, use our public GitHub repository:

git clone https://github.com/mimno/Mallet.git

2. Unzip Mallet into your `C:/` directory. Your `C:/` drive will have a directory named `C:\mallet-2.0.8RC2` or similar:

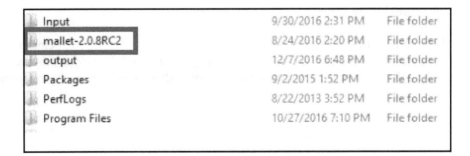

Input	9/30/2016 2:31 PM	File folder	
mallet-2.0.8RC2	8/24/2016 2:20 PM	File folder	
output	12/7/2016 6:48 PM	File folder	
Packages	9/2/2015 1:52 PM	File folder	
PerfLogs	8/22/2013 3:52 PM	File folder	
Program Files	10/27/2016 7:10 PM	File folder	

3. Inside the directory, the files and folders will look something as the following screenshot shows. The actual runnable file is in the bin folder and there are some sample datasets in the sample-data folder:

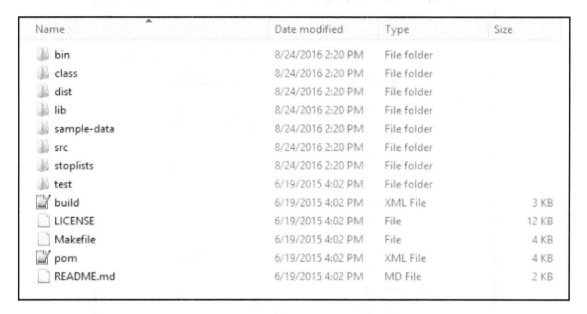

4. Go to `Control Panel\System and Security\System` in your Windows PC. Click on **Advanced system settings**.

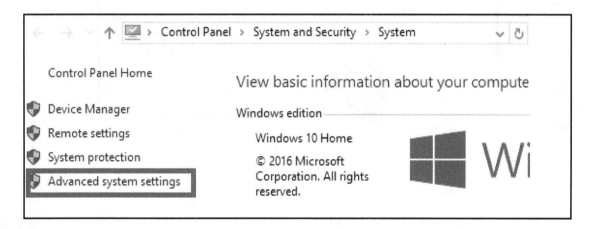

5. Now, you will see a system property window. Click on the **Environment Variables**... button:

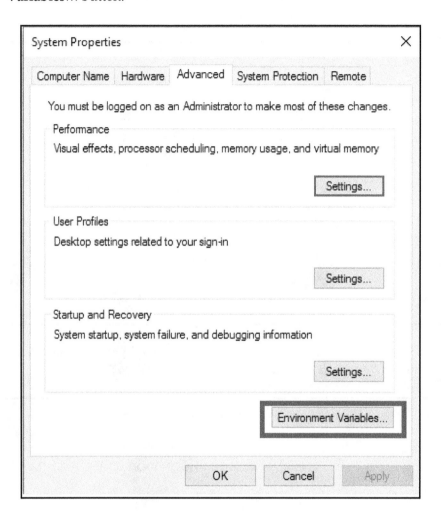

6. This will open a window for setting up environment variables. Click on **New** for system variables:

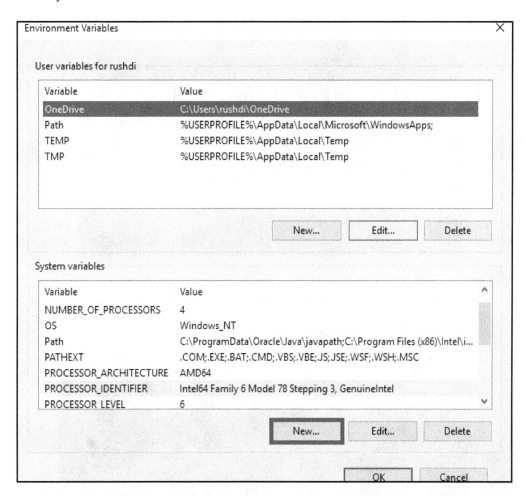

7. In the **Variable Name** textbox, type in MALLET_HOME. And in the **Variable Value** textbox, give the path C:\mallet-2.0.8RC2. Click on **OK** to close the windows.

8. To see if Mallet has been installed properly, open a command prompt window, go to the bin folder of the Mallet directory, and type in mallet. You should see all the Mallet 2.0 commands that you can use on your screen:

Now, you are ready to use Mallet. At any point, if you are not certain about the commands or parameters that you can use one of the Mallet append–help with the Mallet 2.0 command. This will list all the possible command and parameter options for a particular Mallet 2.0 command:

How to do it...

1. The Mallet distribution folder in your `c:/` drive has a directory named sample-data. This directory contains another directory named web. Inside web, you will find two more directories-the directory named en contains a few text files that are text versions of a few English web articles, and the directory named de contains a few text files that are text versions of a few German web articles. The en directory can be seen as our dataset or corpus for this recipe and you will be extracting topics from these web articles. If you have your own set of documents for which you need to extract topics, just imagine the following tasks that you are going to do by simply replacing the en directory with the directory where your documents reside.

   To do so, first transform the text files into a single file, which is of type Mallet and is not human readable, being binary. From the command line, go to `C:\mallet-2.0.8RC2/bin` and type in the following command:

   ```
   mallet import-dir --input C:\mallet-2.0.8RC2\sample-
       data\web\en --output c:/web.en.mallet --keep-sequence --
       remove-stopwords
   ```

   The command creates a Mallet file in your `C:/` drive named web.en.mallet by keeping the original sequence of data files as listed in the en directory, by removing stop-words from its standard English dictionary.

   If you want your model to consider the bi-grams of the texts during modelling, replace the command with:

   ```
   mallet import-dir --input C:\mallet-2.0.8RC2\sample-
   data\web\en --output c:/web.en.mallet --keep-sequence-
   bigrams --remove-stopwords
   ```

2. Type in the following command to run Mallet's topic modelling routing with default settings on the `we.en.mallet` file:

   ```
   mallet train-topics --input c:/web.en.mallet
   ```

The command will generate information on your command prompt as follows:

```
?        5        average equipartition theorem energy system survived law kinetic
 areas whig effects stars classical heat equilibrium thermal energies performer
dil npa
8        5        rings kehna journalist moons narrow particles relative thought w
ritten critical landing team president considered time co-owner news cinema acco
mplishments kabhi
9        5        sunderland thespis award thylacinus gods drama performances pape
r east newspaper protection run century temperature society premier asia acclaim
 success mil

<950> LL/token: -9.28624
<960> LL/token: -9.28207
<970> LL/token: -9.23096
<980> LL/token: -9.23133
<990> LL/token: -9.24076

0        5        hawes confederate kentucky war states death acted relative beaur
egard president buell carlos shiloh commonwealth virginia neutrality whig govern
or husband variety
1        5        zinta role hindi actress film indian acting top-grossing naa awa
rd female filmfare earned films drama written areas evening protection april
2        5        battle union time army gen tennessee numerous confederates debut
 newspaper line position men fighting grant's grant maj launched johnston landin
g
3        5        thylacine tasmanian back tiger extinct general king moons partic
les water devil related marsupial actors northern critical reported generally so
ciety biggest
4        5        years yard national wilderness life parks park modern world serv
ice movement independent journalist addition pouch thought early team rest onlin
e
5        5        test including cricket hill london survived american needham keh
na involved year run held original died premier ness news commercial heroine
6        5        gunnhild south gilbert thespis england mother gods greek perform
ances march productions theatre opera creating sullivan storey leading spent det
ails figure
7        5        average equipartition theorem united energy career law kinetic f
ound species thylacinus worked ended considered effects stars classical motion e
quilibrium energies
8        5        rings system dust australian number narrow ring discovered uranu
s scored batsman late saga heat received telugu helping secretary non-government
 maximum
9        5        echo sunderland norway edward record uranian december paper dail
y thomas east forced played richard orkney erik kings established markets noted

<1000> LL/token: -9.25594

Total time: 2 seconds
C:\mallet-2.0.8RC2\bin>
```

Let's examine the output. The second line of the Mallet topic modelling output contains a line:

```
1        5        zinta role hindi actress film indian acting
   top-grossing naa awa
rd female filmfare earned films drama written areas evening
   protection april
```

If you are a Hindi movie fan, then you will immediately understand that the topic is Hindi movies that involve actress Preity Zinta. For confirmation, you can look into the file named `zinta.txt` in the `C:\mallet-2.0.8RC2\sample-data\web\en` directory.

The 1 in the output indicates the paragraph number (the numbering starts from 0) and 5 is the *Dirichlet parameter* for the topic (which can be seen as the weight of the topic). As we have not set it, the number will be the default for all the paragraphs in the output.

> MALLET includes an element of randomness for topic modelling and extraction, and therefore the keyword lists will look different every time the program is run even if on the same set of data. So, don't think something went wrong in case you have a different output than that outlined in this recipe.

The command in this step is too generic, does not use any wonderful parameters from Mallet, and displays results on the console.

3. Next, we will be applying topic modelling on the same data but with more options and we will output the topics to an external file so that we can further use them. On your command prompt, type in the following:

```
mallet train-topics --input c:/web.en.mallet --num-topics 20--
    num-top-words 20 --optimize-interval 10 --xml-topic-phrase-
    report C:/web.en.xml
```

This command indicates that we will be using the `c:/web.en.mallet` file as our input, generating maximum 20 topics for the data, printing the top 20 topics, and outputting the results in `c:/web.en.xml` file. The `--optimize-interval` is used to generate better topic models by turning on hyperparameter optimization that eventually allows the model to better fit the data by prioritizing some topics over others.

After running the command, you will see that in your `C:/` drive, an XML file is generated with name `web.en.xml`. If you open the file, you will see something similar to:

```
<?xml version='1.0' ?>
<topics>
  <topic id="0" alpha="2.032473408279035" totalTokens="66" titles="test, paper,
        <word weight="0.045454545454545456" count="3">test</word>
        <word weight="0.030303030303030304" count="2">paper</word>
        <word weight="0.030303030303030304" count="2">played</word>
        <word weight="0.015151515151515152" count="1">regular</word>
        <word weight="0.015151515151515152" count="1">markets</word>
        <word weight="0.015151515151515152" count="1">commercial</word>
        <word weight="0.015151515151515152" count="1">fiction</word>
        <word weight="0.015151515151515152" count="1">kya</word>
        <word weight="0.015151515151515152" count="1">female</word>
        <word weight="0.015151515151515152" count="1">dil</word>
        <word weight="0.015151515151515152" count="1">made</word>
        <word weight="0.015151515151515152" count="1">films</word>
        <word weight="0.015151515151515152" count="1">hindi</word>
        <word weight="0.015151515151515152" count="1">actress</word>
        <word weight="0.015151515151515152" count="1">caused</word>
        <word weight="0.015151515151515152" count="1">standards</word>
        <word weight="0.015151515151515152" count="1">editor</word>
        <word weight="0.015151515151515152" count="1">graduated</word>
        <word weight="0.015151515151515152" count="1">robert</word>
        <word weight="0.015151515151515152" count="1">telescope</word>
        <phrase weight="0.25" count="1">telescope number</phrase>
        <phrase weight="0.25" count="1">australian cricketers</phrase>
        <phrase weight="0.25" count="1">hindi films</phrase>
        <phrase weight="0.25" count="1">test cricket-a</phrase>
    </topic>
```

4. There are some other options in Mallet that you can use when you use topic modelling. One of the important options is the *alpha* parameter, which is known as the smoothing parameter for the topic distribution. Try the following command:

```
mallet train-topics --input c:/web.en.mallet --num-topics 20--
   num-top-words 20 --optimize-interval 10 --alpha 2.5 --xml-
   topic-phrase-report C:/web.en.xml
```

TIP

The rule of thumb for setting the *alpha* value is set so as 50/T where T is the number of topics you choose by using the –num-topics [NUMBER] option. So, if you generate 20 topics, you should set the value of alpha to 50/20 = 2.5.

If –random-seed is not set for generating a topic model for a document, then randomness will be applied and every time a slightly/completely different xml file will be generated with the topics.

5. Mallet also generates outputs in different formats that help analyze the topics in many different ways. Type the following command in the command line:

```
mallet train-topics --input c:/web.en.mallet --num-topics 20--
    num-top-words 20 --optimize-interval 10 --output-state
        C:\web.en.gz  --output-topic-keys C:\web.en.keys.txt --
            output-doc-topics c:/web.en.composition.txt
```

This command will generate three new files in your `C:/` drive.

- `C:\web.en.gz` contains a file where every word in your corpus and the topic it belongs to. A partial look of the file can be as follows:

```
#doc source pos typeindex type topic
#alpha : 0.00529288685745327 0.005280224930316231 0.010411314990479141 0.005292639
0.005278782954717919 3.8154450835853604E-56 8.363084051683433E-65 0.01080648155617
0.005286647403862656 1.0743671245908252E-50 1.8112326797320508E-59 1.0996963864009
#beta : 0.2613020959658213
0 C:\mallet-2.0.8RC2\sample-data\web\en\elizabeth_needham.txt 0 0 elizabeth 2
0 C:\mallet-2.0.8RC2\sample-data\web\en\elizabeth_needham.txt 1 1 needham 2
0 C:\mallet-2.0.8RC2\sample-data\web\en\elizabeth_needham.txt 2 2 died 2
0 C:\mallet-2.0.8RC2\sample-data\web\en\elizabeth_needham.txt 3 3 mother 2
0 C:\mallet-2.0.8RC2\sample-data\web\en\elizabeth_needham.txt 4 1 needham 2
0 C:\mallet-2.0.8RC2\sample-data\web\en\elizabeth_needham.txt 5 4 english 2
0 C:\mallet-2.0.8RC2\sample-data\web\en\elizabeth_needham.txt 6 5 procuress 2
0 C:\mallet-2.0.8RC2\sample-data\web\en\elizabeth_needham.txt 7 6 brothel 2
0 C:\mallet-2.0.8RC2\sample-data\web\en\elizabeth_needham.txt 8 7 keeper 2
0 C:\mallet-2.0.8RC2\sample-data\web\en\elizabeth_needham.txt 9 8 century 2
0 C:\mallet-2.0.8RC2\sample-data\web\en\elizabeth_needham.txt 10 9 london 2
0 C:\mallet-2.0.8RC2\sample-data\web\en\elizabeth_needham.txt 11 10 identified 2
```

- `C:\web.en.keys.txt` contains data that we have already seen on the console in step 2, which is topic number, weight, and top keywords for each topic.

- `C:/web.en.composition.txt` contains the breakdown of each topic by percentage within each original text file you imported. The following is a partial outlook of the file. The file can be opened using any spreadsheet application such as Microsoft Excel.

#doc name topic proportion ...							
0 file:/C:/m	2	0.998723	10	2.00E-04	13	1.00E-04
1 file:/C:/m	6	0.999228	10	1.12E-04	2	1.08E-04
2 file:/C:/m	7	0.999107	10	1.30E-04	2	1.25E-04
3 file:/C:/m	1	0.827995	10	0.171402	2	9.91E-05
4 file:/C:/m	4	0.999251	10	1.09E-04	2	1.05E-04
5 file:/C:/m	10	0.999527	2	7.18E-05	13	3.73E-05
6 file:/C:/m	12	0.999228	10	1.12E-04	2	1.08E-04
7 file:/C:/m	18	0.999219	10	1.14E-04	2	1.10E-04
8 file:/C:/m	3	0.99943	10	8.31E-05	2	8.00E-05
9 file:/C:/m	14	0.999307	10	1.01E-04	2	9.72E-05
10 file:/C:/m	0	0.972324	2	0.027101	10	9.73E-05
11 file:/C:/m	5	0.704671	13	0.294834	10	7.77E-05

In most cases, these are the key commands you will be using to extract topics from article sets. The steps followed in this recipe are for extraction of topics from a collection of texts. If you have a single article for which you need to extract topics, put the article in a directory and consider that as a corpus of a single document.

Before we complete the recipe, let's take a look at the available topic modelling algorithms that can be used with Mallet:

- LDA
- Parallel LDA
- DMR LDA
- Hierarchical LDA
- Labeled LDA
- Polylingual topic model
- Hierarchical Pachinko allocation model
- Weighted topic model
- LDA with integrated phrase discovery
- Word Embeddings (word2vec) using skip-gram with negative sampling

Classifying text documents using Mallet

Our final two recipes in this chapter will be the classical machine-learning classification problem-classification of documents using language modelling. In this recipe, we will be using Mallet and its command line interface to train a model and apply the model on unseen test data.

Classification in Mallet depends on three steps:

1. Convert your training documents into Mallet's native format.
2. Train your model on the training documents.
3. Apply the model to classify unseen test documents.

When it was mentioned that you need to convert your training documents into Mallet's native format, the technical meaning of this is to convert documents into feature vectors. You do not need to extract any feature from your training or test documents as Mallet will be taking care of this. Either you can physically separate training and testing data, or you can have one flat list of documents and segment training and testing portion from command line options.

Let us consider a simple setting: you have text data that are in plain text files, one file per document. There is no need to identify the beginning or end of documents. The files will be organized in directories, where all documents with the same class label will be contained within a directory. For instance, if your text files have two classes, spam and ham, then you need to create two directories–one will contain all spam documents and the other will contain all ham documents.

Getting ready

1. The installation of Mallet has already been thoroughly outlined in the previous recipe titled Extracting Topics from text documents using Mallet and therefore we will avoid redundancy.

2. Open a web browser and paste the following URL:
   `http://www.cs.cmu.edu/afs/cs/project/theo-11/www/naive-bayes/20_newsgr`
   `oups.tar.gz`. This will download a folder containing news articles classified in 20 different directories. Save it in your Mallet installation directory:

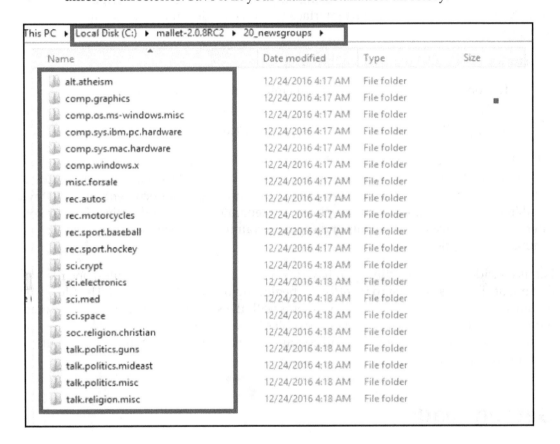

How to do it...

1. Open a command prompt window and go to the bin folder of your `Mallet` installation folder.

2. Write the following command while you are inside the bin folder:

```
mallet import-dir --input C:\mallet-2.0.8RC2\20_newsgroups\*--
    preserve-case --remove-stopwords --binary-features --gram-
        sizes 1 --output C:\20_newsgroup.classification.mallet
```

This command will take all the documents in the
`C:\mallet-2.0.8RC2\20_newsgroups` folder, remove stopwords from them,
preserve the actual cases of the words in the documents, and create binary
features with gram size 1. The output of the native file format of Mallet from the
documents will be saved as `C:\20_newsgroup.classification.mallet`.

test	9/14/2016 2:55 PM	File folder	
test_feed	12/10/2015 4:36 PM	File folder	
Users	4/1/2016 6:18 PM	File folder	
Windows	11/15/2016 3:03 PM	File folder	
WindowsAzure	12/24/2016 4:22 AM	File folder	
pdftotext	5/28/2014 3:50 PM	Application	1,152 KB
iris-test	11/2/2016 1:04 AM	ARFF Data File	1 KB
out	11/2/2016 1:09 AM	ARFF Data File	1 KB
training	10/31/2016 5:10 PM	ARFF Data File	1 KB
web.en	12/21/2016 3:19 PM	EN File	88 KB
20_newsgroup.classification.mallet	12/24/2016 4:26 AM	MALLET File	17,621 KB
web.en.mallet	12/21/2016 3:15 PM	MALLET File	36 KB
nb.model	11/3/2016 1:30 AM	MODEL File	3 KB
G_crawler.py	7/7/2016 8:49 PM	PY File	6 KB
a-r-test	12/19/2016 8:46 PM	TXT File	1 KB
iris-test	11/2/2016 1:04 AM	TXT File	0 KB
javaml-output	11/24/2016 4:46 PM	TXT File	5 KB
web.en.composition	12/21/2016 3:19 PM	TXT File	7 KB
web.en.keys	12/21/2016 3:19 PM	TXT File	3 KB
web.en	12/21/2016 3:19 PM	WinRAR archive	12 KB
web.en	12/21/2016 5:16 PM	XML File	33 KB

3. Next, create a Maximum Entropy classifier from the data using the following command. The command takes the output of the previous step as input, creates a Naïve Bayes classifier from the binary features with 1-grams and outputs the classifier as `C:\20_newsgroup.classification.classifier`:

```
mallet train-classifier --trainer NaiveBayes --input
C:\20_newsgroup.classification.mallet --output-classifier
C:\20_newsgroup.classification.classifier
```

web.en	12/21/2016 3:19 PM	EN File	88 KB
20_newsgroup.classification.mallet	12/24/2016 4:26 AM	MALLET File	17,621 KB
web.en.mallet	12/21/2016 3:15 PM	MALLET File	36 KB
nb.model	11/3/2016 1:30 AM	MODEL File	3 KB
G_crawler.py	7/7/2016 8:49 PM	PY File	6 KB
a-r-test	12/19/2016 8:46 PM	TXT File	1 KB
iris-test	11/2/2016 1:04 AM	TXT File	0 KB
javaml-output	11/24/2016 4:46 PM	TXT File	5 KB
web.en.composition	12/21/2016 3:19 PM	TXT File	7 KB
web.en.keys	12/21/2016 3:19 PM	TXT File	3 KB
web.en	12/21/2016 3:19 PM	WinRAR archive	12 KB
web.en	12/21/2016 5:16 PM	XML File	33 KB
20_newsgroup.classification.classifier	2/24/2016 4:40 AM	CLASSIFIER File	43,034 KB

Besides Naïve Bayes, there are many other algorithms supported by Mallet. The following is the complete list:

- AdaBoost
- Bagging
- Winnow
- C45 decision tree
- Ensemble trainer
- Maximum Entropy Classifier (Multinomial Logistic Regression)
- Naive bayes
- Rank Maximum Entropy Classifier
- Posterior Regularization Auxiliary Model

4. Besides training on the full dataset, you can also provide a portion of data to be used as training data and the rest as test data; and based on the test data's actual class labels, you can see the classifier's prediction performance.

Write the following command while you are in the bin folder:

```
mallet train-classifier --trainer NaiveBayes --input
    C:\20_newsgroup.classification.mallet --training-portion 0.9
```

The command randomly chooses 90% of your data and trains the Naïve Bayes classifier on them. Finally, the classifier is applied to the remaining 10% data by not seeing their actual labels; their actual classes were considered only during the classifier's evaluation.

```
NaiveBayesTrainer
Summary. train accuracy mean = 0.9678835361449131 stddev = 0.0 stderr = 0.0
Summary. test accuracy mean = 0.915 stddev = 0.0 stderr = 0.0
Summary. test precision(alt.atheism) mean = 0.7272727272727273 stddev = 0.0 stde
rr = 0.0
Summary. test precision(comp.graphics) mean = 0.89 stddev = 0.0 stderr = 0.0
Summary. test precision(comp.os.ms-windows.misc) mean = 0.975609756097561 stddev
 = 0.0 stderr = 0.0
Summary. test precision(comp.sys.ibm.pc.hardware) mean = 0.9019607843137255 stdd
ev = 0.0 stderr = 0.0
Summary. test precision(comp.sys.mac.hardware) mean = 0.9230769230769231 stddev
= 0.0 stderr = 0.0
Summary. test precision(comp.windows.x) mean = 0.968421052631579 stddev = 0.0 st
derr = 0.0
Summary. test precision(misc.forsale) mean = 0.9175257731958762 stddev = 0.0 std
err = 0.0
Summary. test precision(rec.autos) mean = 0.9702970297029703 stddev = 0.0 stderr
 = 0.0
Summary. test precision(rec.motorcycles) mean = 0.989010989010989 stddev = 0.0 s
tderr = 0.0
Summary. test precision(rec.sport.baseball) mean = 1.0 stddev = 0.0 stderr = 0.0

Summary. test precision(rec.sport.hockey) mean = 1.0 stddev = 0.0 stderr = 0.0
Summary. test precision(sci.crypt) mean = 0.9897959183673469 stddev = 0.0 stderr
 = 0.0
Summary. test precision(sci.electronics) mean = 0.9042553191489362 stddev = 0.0
stderr = 0.0
Summary. test precision(sci.med) mean = 1.0 stddev = 0.0 stderr = 0.0
Summary. test precision(sci.space) mean = 0.9711538461538461 stddev = 0.0 stderr
```

The command gives you the overall accuracy of your classifier for the 20 classes and precision, recall, and accuracy for each class with standard errors.

5. You can also run the training and testing for multiple times; each time the training and testing sets will be chosen randomly. For instance, if you want to train your classifier on 90% of your data and test the classifier on the remaining 10% of your data 10 times with random splits, use the following command:

```
mallet train-classifier --trainer NaiveBayes --input
C:\20_newsgroup.classification.mallet --training-portion 0.9--
   num-trials 10
```

6. You can also do cross-validation using Mallet where you can specify number of folds to be created during cross validation. For instance, if you want to do a 10-fold cross validation, use the following command:

```
mallet train-classifier --trainer NaiveBayes --input
   C:\20_newsgroup.classification.mallet --cross-validation 10
```

The command will give you individual results for each of the 10 trials each time with a new test portion of your original data as well as the average result for the 10 trials. Mallet also gives you a confusion matrix, which is really important for data scientists to understand their models better.

```
Trial 9 Training NaiveBayesTrainer with 17997 instances
Trial 9 Training NaiveBayesTrainer finished
Trial 9 Trainer NaiveBayesTrainer training data accuracy = 0.9671611935322554
Trial 9 Trainer NaiveBayesTrainer Test Data Confusion Matrix
Confusion Matrix, row=true, column=predicted  accuracy=0.917 most-frequent-tag b
aseline=0.0595
                        label  0   1   2   3   4   5   6   7   8   9  10  11  12
    13  14 15  16  17  18  19  |total
 0              alt.atheism  73   .   .   .   .   .   .   .   .   .   .   .   .
     .   .   .   .   .   . 24  |97
 1          comp.graphics   . 100   .   .   . 1   1   .   .   .   .   . 1
     .  1   .   .   .  1   .  |105
 2  comp.os.ms-windows.misc   .  4  83  16   .   .   . 1   .   .   . 1   .
     .   .   .   .   .   .   .  |105
 3 comp.sys.ibm.pc.hardware   . 1   2  91  3   2   .   .   .   .   .   . 2
     .   .   .   .   .   .   .  |101
 4      comp.sys.mac.hardware   . 1   .   . 92   .   .   .   .   .   .   . 1
     .   .   .   .   .   .   . |94
 5            comp.windows.x   . 2   . 2   . 96   .   .   .   .   .   .   .
     .   .   .   .   .   .   . |100
 6              misc.forsale   .   .   . 2   1   . 92   2   .   .   .   .   .
     .   . 1   1   1   . |100
 7                rec.autos   .   .   .   . 1   . 3 102   .   .   .   .   .
     .   .   .   .   .   .  |106
 8          rec.motorcycles   .   .   .   .   .   . 2 114   .   .   .   .
     .   . 1   . 2   . |119
 9        rec.sport.baseball   .   .   .   .   .   . 1   1 100   .   .   .
     . 1   .   .   .   .  |103
10        rec.sport.hockey   .   .   .   .   .   .   .   .   . 96   .   .
     .   .   .   . 1   . |97
11                sci.crypt   .   .   .   .   .   .   .   .   . . 103   .
     .   . 1   . 1   . |105
12          sci.electronics   .   .   . 2   .   .   .   .   .   .   . 1   . 112
```

7. Mallet allows you to compare the performances of multiple classifiers developed from different algorithms. For instance, the following command will give you a comparison of the two classifiers using Naïve Bayes and Maximum Entropy using 10-fold cross validation:

```
mallet train-classifier --trainer MaxEnt --trainer NaiveBayes-
    -input C:\20_newsgroup.classification.mallet --cross-
        validation 10
```

8. If you want to use your saved classifier on a set of unseen test documents (which is not our case as we have used the entire directory for training in step 2), you can use the following command:

```
mallet classify-dir --input <directory containing unseen test
    data> --output - --classifier
        C:\20_newsgroup.classification.classifier
```

This command will show you the predicted class of your unseen test documents on console. You can also save the predictions in a tab separated value file using the following command:

```
mallet classify-dir --input <directory containing unseen test
    data> --output <Your output file> --classifier
        C:\20_newsgroup.classification.classifier
```

9. Finally, it is also possible to use a saved classifier on a single unseen test document. For that purpose, use this command:

```
mallet classify-file --input <unseen test data file path> --
output - --classifier
    C:\20_newsgroup.classification.classifier
```

This command will show you the predicted class of your unseen test document on console. You can also save the predictions in a tab separated value file using the following command:

```
mallet classify-file --input <unseen test data file path> --
output <Your output file> --classifier C:\20_ne
    wsgroup.classification.classifier
```

Classifying text documents using Weka

We used Weka in `Chapter 4`, *Learn from Data – Part 1* to classify data points that are not in text format. Weka is a very useful tool to classify text documents using machine-learning models as well. In this recipe, we will demonstrate how you can use to develop document classification model using Weka 3.

Getting ready

1. To download Weka, go to `http://www.cs.waikato.ac.nz/ml/weka/downloading.html` and you will find download options for Windows, Mac, and other operating systems such as Linux. Read through the options carefully and download the appropriate version. During the writing of this book, 3.9.0 was the latest version for the developers, and as the author already had version 1.8 JVM installed in his 64-bit Windows machine, he has chosen *to download a self-extracting executable for 64-bit Windows without a Java VM.*

2. After the download is complete, double-click on the executable file and follow the on-screen instructions. You need to install the *full* version of Weka.

3. Once the installation is done, do not run the software. Instead, go to the directory where you have installed it and find the Java Archive File for Weka (weka.jar). Add this file in your Eclipse project as an external library.

4. The example document files that will be used in this recipe will be kept in directories. Each directory contains documents of similar class. To download example documents, open a web browser and copy and paste the following URL: `https://weka.wikispaces.com/file/view/text_example.zip/82917283/text_example.zip`. This will prompt you to save a file (if your browser is configured to ask you where to save files). Save the files on your `C:/` drive. Unzip the files and you will see a directory structure as follows:

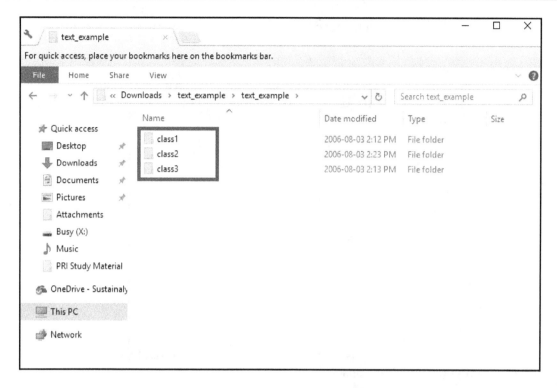

Each directory contains a few html files that belong to a particular class. The classes have labels class1, class2, and class3.

Now you are all set for classification of these documents with Weka.

How to do it...

1. Create a class and a `main()` method to put all of your codes. The main method will throw exceptions:

    ```
    public class WekaClassification {
        public static void main(String[] args) throws Exception {
    ```

2. Create a loader to load the parent directory of all of your class directories by setting the parent directory's path to the loader:

    ```
    TextDirectoryLoader loader = new TextDirectoryLoader();
    loader.setDirectory(new File("C:/text_example"));
    ```

3. Create instances from the loaded html files:

```
Instances data = loader.getDataSet();
```

4. Create word vectors from the strings of your data. To do that, first create a filter that converts string to word vectors and then set your raw data from previous step for the filter:

```
StringToWordVector filter = new StringToWordVector();
filter.setInputFormat(data);
```

5. To finalize string-to-word vector conversion, create instances from the data using this filter:

```
Instances dataFiltered = Filter.useFilter(data, filter);
```

6. Generate a Naïve Bayes classifier from this word vector:

```
NaiveBayes nb = new NaiveBayes();
nb.buildClassifier(dataFiltered);
```

7. At this point, you can also consider seeing how your model looks. To do that, print your model on console:

```
System.out.println("\n\nClassifier model:\n\n" + nb);
```

8. A partial output on your screen will look like the following:

```
smashed
  mean                                                      0       0 0.3333
  std. dev.                                            0.1667 0.1667 0.4714
  weight sum                                                3       1      3
  precision                                                1       1      1

social
  mean                                                      0       0 0.3333
  std. dev.                                            0.1667 0.1667 0.4714
  weight sum                                                3       1      3
  precision                                                1       1      1

solely
  mean                                                      0       0 0.3333
  std. dev.                                            0.1667 0.1667 0.4714
  weight sum                                                3       1      3
  precision                                                1       1      1
```

9. To evaluate the model with k-fold cross validation, write down the following
   code:

```
Evaluation eval = null;
eval = new Evaluation(dataFiltered);
eval.crossValidateModel(nb, dataFiltered, 5, new Random(1));
System.out.println(eval.toSummaryString());
```

This will print the classifier evaluation on the console:

```
Correctly Classified Instances          1              14.2857 %
Incorrectly Classified Instances        6              85.7143 %
Kappa statistic                        -0.5
Mean absolute error                     0.5714
Root mean squared error                 0.7559
Relative absolute error               126.3158 %
Root relative squared error           153.7844 %
Total Number of Instances               7
```

Note that we have used five fold cross validation and not the standard 10-fold cross
validation because the number of documents is less than 10 (to be exact, it is 7).

The complete code of the recipe is as follows:

```
import weka.core.*;
import weka.core.converters.*;
import weka.classifiers.Evaluation;
import weka.classifiers.bayes.NaiveBayes;
import weka.filters.*;
import weka.filters.unsupervised.attribute.*;

import java.io.*;
import java.util.Random;

public class WekaClassification {
    public static void main(String[] args) throws Exception {
        TextDirectoryLoader loader = new TextDirectoryLoader();
        loader.setDirectory(new File("C:/text_example"));
        Instances data = loader.getDataSet();

        StringToWordVector filter = new StringToWordVector();
        filter.setInputFormat(data);
        Instances dataFiltered = Filter.useFilter(data, filter);

        NaiveBayes nb = new NaiveBayes();
        nb.buildClassifier(dataFiltered);
        System.out.println("\n\nClassifier model:\n\n" + nb);
```

```
        Evaluation eval = null;
        eval = new Evaluation(dataFiltered);
        eval.crossValidateModel(nb, dataFiltered, 5, new Random(1));
        System.out.println(eval.toSummaryString());
    }
}
```

7
Handling Big Data

In this chapter, we will cover the following recipes:

- Training an online logistic regression model using Apache Mahout
- Applying an online logistic regression model using Apache Mahout
- Solving simple text-mining problems with Apache Spark
- Clustering using KMeans algorithm with MLib
- Creating a linear regression model with MLib
- Classifying data points with a Random Forest model using MLib

Introduction

In this chapter, you will see three key technologies used in Big Data framework, which are extremely useful for data scientists: Apache Mahout, Apache Spark, and its machine learning library named MLib.

We will start our chapter with Apache Mahout–a scalable or distributed machine learning platform for classification, regression, clustering, and collaborative filtering tasks. Mahout started as a machine learning workbench that works only on Hadoop MapReduce but eventually selected Apache Spark as its platform.

Apache Spark is a framework that brings in parallelization in Big Data processing and has similarity with MapReduce as it also distributes data across clusters. But one key difference between Spark and MapReduce is the prior attempts to keep things in memory as much as possible while the latter writes and reads continuously from the disks. Therefore, Spark is much faster than MapReduce. We will see how you, as a data scientist, can use Spark to do simple text-mining related tasks, such as counting empty lines or getting frequencies of words in a large file. Another reason to use Spark is that it can be used, not only with Java, but also with other popular languages such as Python and Scala; for MapReduce, the usual choice is Java.

MLib is a scalable machine learning library from Apache Spark, and it has a wide variety of classification, regression, clustering, collaborative filtering, and feature selection algorithms implemented. It basically sits on Spark and uses its speed to solve machine learning problems. In this chapter, you will see how to use this library to solve classification, regression, and clustering problems.

 In this book, we have used version 0.9 of Mahout, but interested readers can look at the differences between Mahout 0.10.x and MLib here: `http://www.weatheringthroughtechdays.com/2015/04/mahout-010x-first-mahout-release-as.html`.

Training an online logistic regression model using Apache Mahout

In this recipe, we will use Apache Mahout to train an online logistic regression model using Apache Mahout Java library.

Getting ready

1. In Eclipse, create a new Maven project. The author had Eclipse Mars set up. To do so, go to **File**. Then select **New** and **Other...**:

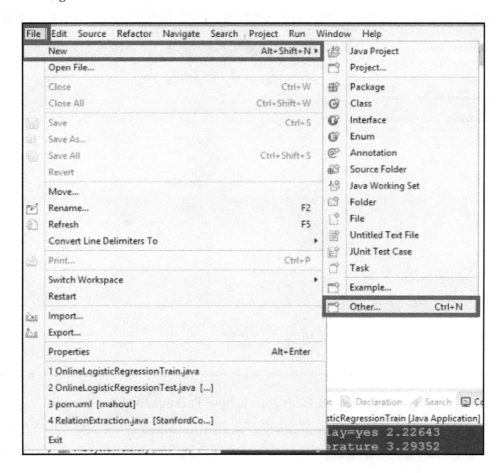

2. Then, expand Maven from the wizard and select Maven Project. Click on **Next** until you reach the window where Eclipse prompts you to provide an **Artifact Id**. Type in mahout as **Artifact Id**, and the grayed out Finish button will become visible. Click on **Finish**. This will create a Maven project for you named mahout:

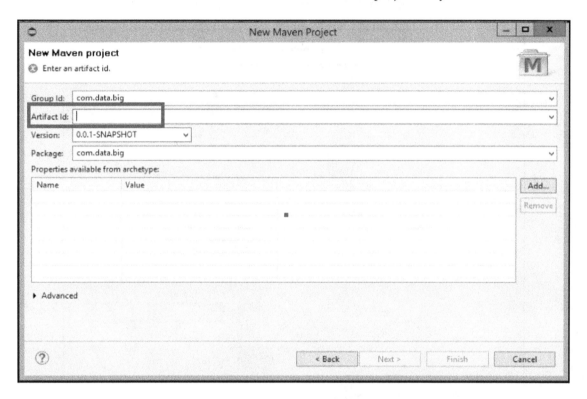

3. Double-click on pom.xml from your Eclipse Package Explorer to edit:

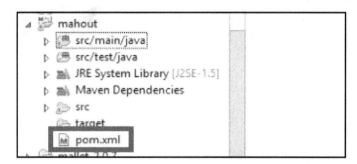

4. Click on the `pom.xml` tab. You will now see the `pom.xml` file on screen. Put the following lines in your `pom.xml` within the `<dependencies>...</dependencies>` tags and save it. This will automatically download the dependency JAR files into your project:

```
<dependency>
    <groupId>org.apache.mahout</groupId>
    <artifactId>mahout-core</artifactId>
    <version>0.9</version>
</dependency>
<dependency>
    <groupId>org.apache.mahout</groupId>
    <artifactId>mahout-examples</artifactId>
    <version>0.9</version>
</dependency>
<dependency>
    <groupId>org.apache.mahout</groupId>
    <artifactId>mahout-math</artifactId>
    <version>0.9</version>
</dependency>
```

5. Create a package named `chap7.science.data` in your project under `src/main/java` directory:

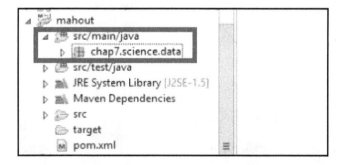

6. Right-click on the project name in Eclipse, select **New**, and then select Folder. You are going to create two folders. The first folder will contain the input dataset for which you will be creating the model, and its name will be `data`. The second folder will be named `model`, where you will be saving your model. Now enter `data` as the folder name and click on **Finish**. Repeat this step to create a folder named `model`.

7. Create a CSV file named `weather.numeric.csv` in the `data` folder with the following data:

```
outlook,temperature,humidity,windy,play
sunny,85,85,FALSE,no
sunny,80,90,TRUE,no
overcast,83,86,FALSE,yes
rainy,70,96,FALSE,yes
rainy,68,80,FALSE,yes
rainy,65,70,TRUE,no
overcast,64,65,TRUE,yes
sunny,72,95,FALSE,no
sunny,69,70,FALSE,yes
rainy,75,80,FALSE,yes
sunny,75,70,TRUE,yes
overcast,72,90,TRUE,yes
overcast,81,75,FALSE,yes
rainy,71,91,TRUE,no
```

8. Now you are ready to code.

How to do it...

1. In the package you just created, create a Java class named `OnlineLogisticRegressionTrain.java`. Double-click on the class file to write down your code. Create a class named `OnlineLogisticRegressionTrain`:

   ```
   public class OnlineLogisticRegressionTrain {
   ```

2. Start writing your `main` method:

   ```
   public static void main(String[] args) throws IOException {
   ```

3. Create two `String` variables to contain the input data file path and the path of the model file that you are going to build and save:

   ```
   String inputFile = "data/weather.numeric.csv";
   String outputFile = "model/model";
   ```

4. Now create a list to contain the features of your data file:

   ```
   List<String> features =Arrays.asList("outlook", "temperature",
     "humidity", "windy", "play");
   ```

5. This step lists all the feature names of your data file and according to their order of appearance in the data file.

6. Next, define the type of each of the features. A feature type w denotes a nominal feature, and a feature type n denotes a numeric feature type:

```
List<String> featureType = Arrays.asList("w", "n", "n", "w",
"w");
```

7. Now is the time to set the parameters of the classifier. In this step, you will be creating a parameter variable and set a few values as parameters. You will set the target variable or class variable (which is "play" in our case). If you take a look at the data, you will find that the class variable "play" takes at most two values–yes or no. Therefore, you will set the maximum target categories to 2. Next, you will set the number of features that are not class features (which in our case is 4). The next three parameters depend on the algorithm. In this recipe, you will not be using any bias for the classifier generation, and you will be using a balance learning rate of 0.5. Finally, you need to set the features and their types using a type map method:

```
LogisticModelParameters params = new
    LogisticModelParameters();
params.setTargetVariable("play");
params.setMaxTargetCategories(2);
params.setNumFeatures(4);
params.setUseBias(false);
params.setTypeMap(features, featureType);
params.setLearningRate(0.5);
```

8. You will be creating the classifier using 10 passes. This number is arbitrary and you can choose any number empirically found by you:

```
int passes = 10;
```

9. Create the online linear regression classifier:

```
OnlineLogisticRegression olr;
```

10. Create a variable to read the data from the CSV file, and start creating the regression model:

```
CsvRecordFactory csv = params.getCsvRecordFactory();
olr = params.createRegression();
```

11. Next, you will create a `for` loop to loop through each of the `10 passes`:

```
for (int pass = 0; pass < passes; pass++) {
```

12. Start reading the data file:

```
BufferedReader in = new BufferedReader(new
    FileReader(inputFile));
```

13. Get the header of your data file, which is comprised of the names of the features:

```
csv.firstLine(in.readLine());
```

14. Read the data row:

```
String row = in.readLine();
```

15. Now loop through each row that is not `null`:

```
while (row != null) {
```

16. Now for each row (or line of data), display the data point, and create an input vector:

```
System.out.println(row);
Vector input = new
    RandomAccessSparseVector(params.getNumFeatures());
```

17. Get the `targetValue` for the row:

```
int targetValue = csv.processLine(row, input);
```

18. `Train` the model with this data point:

```
olr.train(targetValue, input);
```

19. Read the next `row`:

```
row = in.readLine();
```

20. Close the loop:

```
}
```

21. Close the reader to read the input data file:

```
in.close();
```

22. Close the loop for iterating through passes:

```
}
```

23. Finally, save the `output` model to a file named `model` inside the `model` directory of your Eclipse project:

```
OutputStream modelOutput = new FileOutputStream(outputFile);
try {
    params.saveTo(modelOutput);
} finally {
    modelOutput.close();
}
```

24. Close the `main` method and the class:

```
}
}
```

25. If you run the code, you will see the data rows of your input data file on your console as your output, and in the learned model, it will be saved in the model directory of your Eclipse project.

The complete code for the recipe is as follows:

```
package chap7.science.data;

import java.io.BufferedReader;
import java.io.FileOutputStream;
import java.io.FileReader;
import java.io.IOException;
import java.io.OutputStream;
import java.util.Arrays;
import java.util.List;
import org.apache.mahout.classifier.sgd.CsvRecordFactory;
import org.apache.mahout.classifier.sgd.LogisticModelParameters;
import org.apache.mahout.classifier.sgd.OnlineLogisticRegression;
import org.apache.mahout.math.RandomAccessSparseVector;
import org.apache.mahout.math.Vector;

public class OnlineLogisticRegressionTrain {
    public static void main(String[] args) throws IOException {
        String inputFile = "data/weather.numeric.csv";
```

```
String outputFile = "model/model";

List<String> features =Arrays.asList("outlook", "temperature",
  "humidity", "windy", "play");
List<String> featureType = Arrays.asList("w", "n", "n", "w",
  "w");
LogisticModelParameters params = new LogisticModelParameters();
params.setTargetVariable("play");
params.setMaxTargetCategories(2);
params.setNumFeatures(4);
params.setUseBias(false);
params.setTypeMap(features,featureType);
params.setLearningRate(0.5);


int passes = 10;
OnlineLogisticRegression olr;

CsvRecordFactory csv = params.getCsvRecordFactory();
olr = params.createRegression();

for (int pass = 0; pass < passes; pass++) {
   BufferedReader in = new BufferedReader(new
     FileReader(inputFile));
   csv.firstLine(in.readLine());
   String row = in.readLine();
   while (row != null) {
      System.out.println(row);
      Vector input = new
        RandomAccessSparseVector(params.getNumFeatures());
      int targetValue = csv.processLine(row, input);
      olr.train(targetValue, input);
      row = in.readLine();
   }
   in.close();
}

OutputStream modelOutput = new FileOutputStream(outputFile);
try {
   params.saveTo(modelOutput);
} finally {
   modelOutput.close();
}
 }
}
```

Applying an online logistic regression model using Apache Mahout

In this recipe, we will demonstrate how you can apply an online logistic regression model on unseen, unlabeled test data using Apache Mahout. Note that this recipe is very closely related to the previous recipe and requires you to build a model using training data. This requirement is demonstrated in the previous recipe.

Getting ready

1. After completing the previous recipe, go to the project folder that you created, and go inside the directory named `model` that you created in the last recipe. You should see a `model` file there.

2. Next, create a test file. Go to the `data` folder that you created in your project folder in the last recipe. Create a test file named `weather.numeric.test.csv` with the following data:

   ```
   outlook,temperature,humidity,windy,play
   overcast,90,80,TRUE,yes
   overcast,95,88,FALSE,yes
   rainy,67,78,TRUE,no
   rainy,90,97,FALSE,no
   sunny,50,67,FALSE,yes
   sunny,67,75,TRUE,no
   ```

3. In your Eclipse project named mahout, you should see a package named `chap7.science.data` inside `src/main/java folder`. This package was created in the previous recipe. Create a Java class named `OnlineLogisticRegressionTest.java` in this package. Double-click on the Java class file to edit.

How to do it...

1. Create the `class`:

   ```
   public class OnlineLogisticRegressionTest {
   ```

2. Declare a few class variables. First, create two variables to hold the path of your test `data` file and `model` file (that you created in the last recipe):

```
private static String inputFile =
   "data/weather.numeric.test.csv";
private static String modelFile = "model/model";
```

3. Start creating your `main` method:

```
public static void main(String[] args) throws Exception {
```

4. Create a variable of class type AUC as you will be calculating the **Area Under Curve (AUC)** measurement of your classifier as a performance indicator:

```
Auc auc = new Auc();
```

5. Next, read and load the parameters of the online logistic regression algorithm from the `model` file:

```
LogisticModelParameters params =
   LogisticModelParameters.loadFrom(new File(modelFile));
```

6. Create a variable to read the test data file:

```
CsvRecordFactory csv = params.getCsvRecordFactory();
```

7. Create an `onlinelogisticregression` classifier:

```
OnlineLogisticRegression olr = params.createRegression();
```

8. Now read the test data file:

```
InputStream in = new FileInputStream(new File(inputFile));
BufferedReader reader = new BufferedReader(new
   InputStreamReader(in, Charsets.UTF_8));
```

9. The first line of the test data file is the header of the file or the list of features. So, you will ignore this line from classification and read the next line (or row or data point):

```
String line = reader.readLine();
csv.firstLine(line);
line = reader.readLine();
```

10. You will likely want to display the classification results on console. Create a `PrintWriter` variable for that purpose:

```
PrintWriter output=new PrintWriter(new
    OutputStreamWriter(System.out, Charsets.UTF_8), true);
```

11. You will be printing the predicted class, `model's output`, and `log likelihood`. Create the header and print them on console:

```
output.println(""class","model-output","log-likelihood"");
```

12. Now iterate through each line that is not null:

```
while (line != null) {
```

13. Create the feature `vector` for your test data:

```
Vector vector = new
    SequentialAccessSparseVector(params.getNumFeatures());
```

14. Create a variable to hold the actual `classvalue` of each row/data point:

```
int classValue = csv.processLine(line, vector);
```

15. Classify the test data point and get the `score` from the classifier:

```
double score = olr.classifyScalarNoLink(vector);
```

16. Print on console the following–the `classValue`, `score`, and `log likelihood`:

```
output.printf(Locale.ENGLISH, "%d,%.3f,%.6f%n", classValue,
    score, olr.logLikelihood(classValue, vector));
```

17. Add the `score` and the `classvalue` to the AUC variable:

```
auc.add(classValue, score);
```

18. Read the next line and close the loop:

```
line = reader.readLine();
}
```

19. Close the `reader`:

    ```
    reader.close();
    ```

20. Now let's print the output of your classification. First, print the AUC:

    ```
    output.printf(Locale.ENGLISH, "AUC = %.2f%n", auc.auc());
    ```

21. Next, you will be printing the confusion `matrix` of your classification. Create a confusion `matrix` for that. As the training/test data has two classes, you will have a 2×2 confusion `matrix`:

    ```
    Matrix matrix = auc.confusion();
    output.printf(Locale.ENGLISH, "confusion: [[%.1f, %.1f], [%.1f,
        %.1f]]%n", matrix.get(0, 0), matrix.get(1, 0), matrix.get(0,
        1), matrix.get(1, 1));
    ```

22. Hold the entropy values in the `matrix`. You do not need to create a new `matrix` variable for this, but you can do if you want to:

    ```
    matrix = auc.entropy();
    output.printf(Locale.ENGLISH, "entropy: [[%.1f, %.1f], [%.1f,
        %.1f]]%n", matrix.get(0, 0), matrix.get(1, 0), matrix.get(0,
        1), matrix.get(1, 1));
    ```

23. Close the `main` method and the class:

    ```
    }
    }
    ```

The complete code for the recipe is as follows:

```
package chap7.science.data;

import com.google.common.base.Charsets;
import org.apache.mahout.math.Matrix;
import org.apache.mahout.math.SequentialAccessSparseVector;
import org.apache.mahout.math.Vector;
import org.apache.mahout.classifier.evaluation.Auc;
import org.apache.mahout.classifier.sgd.CsvRecordFactory;
import org.apache.mahout.classifier.sgd.LogisticModelParameters;
import org.apache.mahout.classifier.sgd.OnlineLogisticRegression;
import java.io.BufferedReader;
import java.io.File;
import java.io.FileInputStream;
import java.io.InputStream;
import java.io.InputStreamReader;
```

```java
import java.io.OutputStreamWriter;
import java.io.PrintWriter;
import java.util.Locale;

public class OnlineLogisticRegressionTest {

    private static String inputFile = "data/weather.numeric.test.csv";
    private static String modelFile = "model/model";

    public static void main(String[] args) throws Exception {
        Auc auc = new Auc();
        LogisticModelParameters params =
            LogisticModelParameters.loadFrom(new File(modelFile));
        CsvRecordFactory csv = params.getCsvRecordFactory();
        OnlineLogisticRegression olr = params.createRegression();
        InputStream in = new FileInputStream(new File(inputFile));
        BufferedReader reader = new BufferedReader(new
            InputStreamReader(in, Charsets.UTF_8));
        String line = reader.readLine();
        csv.firstLine(line);
        line = reader.readLine();
        PrintWriter output=new PrintWriter(new
            OutputStreamWriter(System.out, Charsets.UTF_8), true);
        output.println(""class","model-output","log-likelihood"");
        while (line != null) {
            Vector vector = new
                SequentialAccessSparseVector(params.getNumFeatures());
            int classValue = csv.processLine(line, vector);
            double score = olr.classifyScalarNoLink(vector);
            output.printf(Locale.ENGLISH, "%d,%.3f,%.6f%n", classValue,
                score, olr.logLikelihood(classValue, vector));
            auc.add(classValue, score);
            line = reader.readLine();
        }
        reader.close();
        output.printf(Locale.ENGLISH, "AUC = %.2f%n", auc.auc());
        Matrix matrix = auc.confusion();
        output.printf(Locale.ENGLISH, "confusion: [[%.1f, %.1f], [%.1f,
            %.1f]]%n", matrix.get(0, 0), matrix.get(1, 0), matrix.get(0,
                1), matrix.get(1, 1));
        matrix = auc.entropy();
        output.printf(Locale.ENGLISH, "entropy: [[%.1f, %.1f], [%.1f,
            %.1f]]%n", matrix.get(0, 0), matrix.get(1, 0), matrix.get(0,
                1), matrix.get(1, 1));
    }
}
```

If you run the code, the output will be as follows:

```
"class","model-output","log-likelihood"
1,119.133,0.000000
1,123.028,0.000000
0,15.888,-15.887942
0,63.213,-100.000000
1,-6.692,-6.693089
0,24.286,-24.286465
AUC = 0.67
confusion: [[0.0, 1.0], [3.0, 2.0]]
entropy: [[NaN, NaN], [0.0, -9.2]]
```

Solving simple text mining problems with Apache Spark

According to the Apache Spark website, Spark runs programs up to 100x faster than Hadoop MapReduce in memory, or 10x faster on disk. Generally speaking, Apache Spark is an open-source cluster-computing framework. Its processing engine provides good speed with ease of use, and it offers sophisticated analytics to data scientists.

In this recipe, we will demonstrate how you can use Apache Spark to solve very simple data problems. Of course, the data problems are merely dummy problems and not real-world problems, but this can be a starting point for you to understand intuitively the use of Apache Spark for using it on a large scale.

Getting ready

1. In Eclipse, create a new Maven project. The author had Eclipse Mars set up. To do so, go to **File**. Then select **New** and **Other...**:

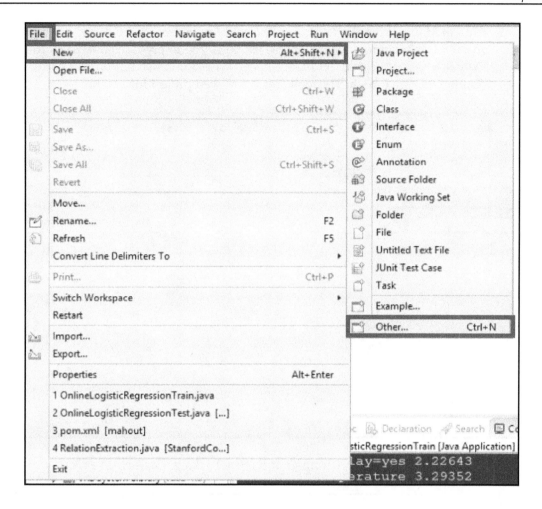

2. Expand Maven from the wizard and select **Maven Project**. Click on **Next** until you reach the window where Eclipse prompts you to provide an **Artifact Id**. Type in `mlib` as the **Artifact Id**, and the grayed-out Finish button will become visible. Click on **Finish**. This will create a Maven project for you named `mlib`:

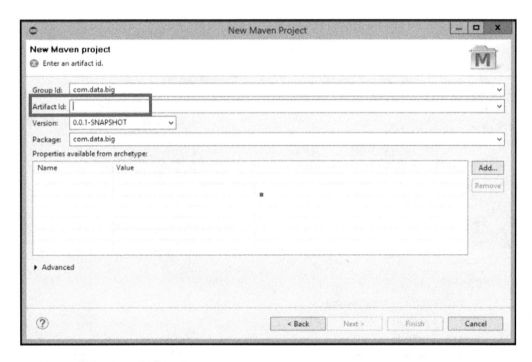

3. Double-click on `pom.xml` from your Eclipse Package Explorer to edit:

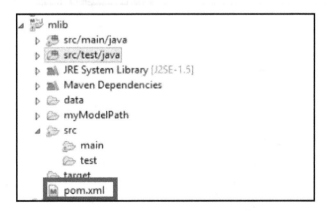

4. Click on `pom.xml` tab. You will now see the `pom.xml` file on screen. Put the following lines in your `pom.xml` within the `<dependencies>...</dependencies>` tags and save it. This will automatically download the dependency JAR files into your project:

```
<dependency>
  <groupId>org.apache.spark</groupId>
  <artifactId>spark-mllib_2.10</artifactId>
  <version>1.3.1</version>
</dependency>
```

5. Create a package named `com.data.big.mlib` in your project under `src/main/java directory`:

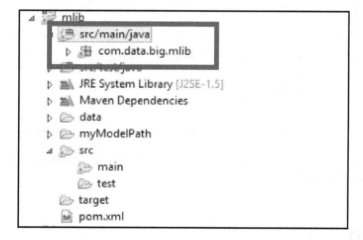

6. Right-click on the project name in Eclipse, and select **New**, then select Folder. You are going to create a folder named `data` where you are going to put your input data file for this recipe.

7. You will be using the literature of William Shakespeare in text format. Open a browser and put the link `http://norvig.com/ngrams/`. This will open a page named Natural Language Corpus Data: Beautiful Data. In the Files for Download section, you will find a .txt file named `shakespeare`. Download this file anywhere in your system:

6.5 MB big.txt	File of running text used in my spell correction article.	
1.0 MB smaller.txt	Excerpt of file of running text from my spell correction article. Smaller; faster
0.3 MB count_big.txt	A word count file (29,136 words) for big.txt.
1.5 MB count_1w100k.txt	A word count file with 100,000 most popular words, all uppercase.
.02 MB words4.txt	4360 words of length 4 (for word games)
.04 MB sgb-words.txt	5757 words of length 5 (for word games) from Knuth's Stanford GraphBase
.03 MB words.js	1000 most common words of English from xkcd Simple Writer (more than 1.0
4.3 MB shakespeare.txt	The complete works of Shakespeare, tokenized so that there is a space betwee
3.0 MB sowpods.txt	The SOWPODS word list (267,750 words) -- used by Scrabble players (excep
1.9 MB TWL06.txt	The Tournament Word List (178,690 words) -- used by North American Scrab
1.9 MB enable1.txt	The ENABLE word list (172,819 words) -- also used by word game players.
2.7 MB word.list	The YAWL (Yet Another Word List) word list (263,533 words) -- formed by c
	(See Internet Scrabble Club for more lists.)

8. In the package that you created, create a Java class file named `SparkTest`. Double-click to start writing your code in it.

How to do it...

1. Create your class:

```
public class SparkTest {
```

2. Start writing your `main` method:

```
public static void main( String[] args ){
```

3. First, get the path of your input data file. This is the file that you have downloaded with Shakespeare literature and saved in the data folder in your project:

```
String inputFile = "data/shakespeare.txt";
```

4. Spark properties are used to control application settings and are configured separately for each application. One way to set these properties is using a `SparkConf` passed to your SparkContext. `SparkConf` allows you to configure some of the common properties:

```
SparkConf configuration = new
    SparkConf().setMaster("local[4]").setAppName("My App");
JavaSparkContext sparkContext = new
    JavaSparkContext(configuration);
```

5. Note that if we used `local[2]`, it would achieve a minimal parallelism. The preceding syntax enables an application to run four threads.

6. JavaRDD is a distributed collection of objects. Create an RDD object. The main purpose of this object in this recipe will be to collect lines in the `shakespeare.txt` file that are empty:

```
JavaRDD<String> rdd =
    sparkContext.textFile(inputFile).cache();
```

If we use `local[*]`, Spark will use all the cores of the system.

7. Count the lines in the input data file that are empty lines:

```
long emptyLines = rdd.filter(new Function<String,Boolean>(){
    private static final long serialVersionUID = 1L;
    public Boolean call(String s){
    return s.length() == 0;
    }
}).count();
```

8. Print on console the number of `emptylines` in the file:

```
System.out.println("Empty Lines: " + emptyLines);
```

9. Next, create the following code snippet to retrieve the word frequencies from the input data file:

```
JavaPairRDD<String, Integer> wordCounts = rdd
    .flatMap(s -> Arrays.asList(s.toLowerCase().split(" ")))
    .mapToPair(word -> new Tuple2<>(word, 1))
    .reduceByKey((a, b) -> a + b);
```

One of the reasons to choose Apache Spark over MapReduce is it takes less code to achieve the same thing. For instance, the lines of code in this step retrieve words and their frequencies from a text document. The same can be achieved using MapReduce with over 100 lines of codes as depicted here: `https://hadoop.apache.org/docs/r1.2.1/mapred_tutor ial.html#Example%3A+WordCount+v2.0`.

10. Using the `wordCounts` RDD, you can collect the words and their frequencies as maps and then iterate over the map and print the word–frequency pair:

```
Map<String, Integer> wordMap = wordCounts.collectAsMap();
for (Entry<String, Integer> entry : wordMap.entrySet()) {
    System.out.println("Word = " + entry.getKey() + ", Frequency
        = " + entry.getValue());
}
```

11. Close the `sparkContext` that you created:

```
sparkContext.close();
```

12. Close the `main` method and the class:

```
}
}
```

The complete code for the recipe is as follows:

```
package com.data.big.mlib;

import java.util.Arrays;
import java.util.Map;
import java.util.Map.Entry;
import org.apache.spark.SparkConf;
import org.apache.spark.api.java.JavaPairRDD;
import org.apache.spark.api.java.JavaRDD;
import org.apache.spark.api.java.JavaSparkContext;
import org.apache.spark.api.java.function.Function;
import scala.Tuple2;
public class SparkTest {
    public static void main( String[] args ){
        String inputFile = "data/shakespeare.txt";
        SparkConf configuration = new
            SparkConf().setMaster("local[4]").setAppName("My App");
        JavaSparkContext sparkContext = new
            JavaSparkContext(configuration);
        JavaRDD<String> rdd = sparkContext.textFile(inputFile).cache();
```

```
long emptyLines = rdd.filter(new Function<String,Boolean>(){
    private static final long serialVersionUID = 1L;
    public Boolean call(String s){
        return s.length() == 0;
    }
}).count();
System.out.println("Empty Lines: " + emptyLines);
JavaPairRDD<String, Integer> wordCounts = rdd
    .flatMap(s -> Arrays.asList(s.toLowerCase().split(" ")))
    .mapToPair(word -> new Tuple2<>(word, 1))
    .reduceByKey((a, b) -> a + b);
Map<String, Integer> wordMap = wordCounts.collectAsMap();
for (Entry<String, Integer> entry : wordMap.entrySet()) {
    System.out.println("Word = " + entry.getKey() + ", Frequency
        = " + entry.getValue());
}
sparkContext.close();
    }
}
```

If you run the code, the partial output will be as follows:

```
Empty Lines: 35941
.....................................................................
.............................

Word = augustus, Frequency = 4
Word = bucklers, Frequency = 3
Word = guilty, Frequency = 66
Word = thunder'st, Frequency = 1
Word = hermia's, Frequency = 7
Word = sink, Frequency = 37
Word = burn, Frequency = 76
Word = relapse, Frequency = 2
Word = boar, Frequency = 16
Word = cop'd, Frequency = 2


.....................................................................
.............................
```

A good article that can encourage users to use Apache Spark instead of MapReduce can be found here: https://www.mapr.com/blog/5-minute-g uide-understanding-significance-apache-spark.

Clustering using KMeans algorithm with MLib

In this recipe, we will demonstrate how you can cluster data points without labels using KMeans algorithm with MLib. As discussed in the introduction of this chapter, MLib is the machine learning component of Apache Spark and is a competitive (even better) alternative to Apache Mahout.

Getting ready

1. You will be using the Maven project you created in the previous recipe (solving simple text mining problems with Apache Spark). If you have not done so yet, follow steps 1-6 in the *Getting ready* section of that recipe.

2. Go to `https://github.com/apache/spark/blob/master/data/mllib/kmeans_data.txt`, and download the data and save as `km-data.txt` in the data folder of your project that you created by following the instruction in step 1. Alternatively, you can create a text file named `km-data.txt` in the data folder of your project and copy-paste the data from the aforementioned URL.

3. In the package that you created, create a Java class file named `KMeansClusteringMlib.java`. Double-click to start writing your code in it.

   Now you are ready to do some coding.

How to do it...

1. Create a class named `KMeansClusteringMlib`:

   ```
   public class KMeansClusteringMlib {
   ```

2. Start writing your `main` method:

   ```
   public static void main( String[] args ){
   ```

3. Create a Spark configuration, and using the configuration, create a Spark context. Note that if we used `local[2]`, it would achieve a minimal parallelism. The following syntax enables an application to run four threads:

```
SparkConf configuration = new
  SparkConf().setMaster("local[4]").setAppName("K-means
    Clustering");
JavaSparkContext sparkContext = new
  JavaSparkContext(configuration);
```

4. Now you will be loading and parsing your input data:

```
String path = "data/km-data.txt";
```

5. `JavaRDD` is a distributed collection of objects. Create an RDD object to read the data file:

```
JavaRDD<String> data = sparkContext.textFile(path);
```

6. Now, you need to read the data values from the preceding RDD where the values are separated by a white space. Parse and read these data values to another RDD:

```
JavaRDD<Vector> parsedData = data.map(
    new Function<String, Vector>() {
        private static final long serialVersionUID = 1L;

        public Vector call(String s) {
            String[] sarray = s.split(" ");
            double[] values = new double[sarray.length];
            for (int i = 0; i < sarray.length; i++)
                values[i] = Double.parseDouble(sarray[i]);
            return Vectors.dense(values);
        }
    }
);
parsedData.cache();
```

7. Now define a few parameters for the KMeans clustering algorithm. We will be using only two clusters to separate the data points with 10 iterations at best. Along with the parsed data, use the parameter values to create a clusterer:

```
int numClusters = 2;
int iterations = 10;
KMeansModel clusters = KMeans.train(parsedData.rdd(),
    numClusters, iterations);
```

8. Calculate the sum of squared errors within set of the clusterer:

```
double sse = clusters.computeCost(parsedData.rdd());
    System.out.println("Sum of Squared Errors within set = " +
        sse);
```

9. Finally, close the `sparkContext`, the `main` method, and the class:

```
        sparkContext.close();
    }
}
```

The complete code for the recipe is as follows:

```
package com.data.big.mlib;

import org.apache.spark.api.java.*;
import org.apache.spark.api.java.function.Function;
import org.apache.spark.mllib.clustering.KMeans;
import org.apache.spark.mllib.clustering.KMeansModel;
import org.apache.spark.mllib.linalg.Vector;
import org.apache.spark.mllib.linalg.Vectors;
import org.apache.spark.SparkConf;

public class KMeansClusteringMlib {
    public static void main( String[] args ){
        SparkConf configuration = new
            SparkConf().setMaster("local[4]").setAppName("K-means
                Clustering");
        JavaSparkContext sparkContext = new
            JavaSparkContext(configuration);

        // Load and parse data
        String path = "data/km-data.txt";
        JavaRDD<String> data = sparkContext.textFile(path);
        JavaRDD<Vector> parsedData = data.map(
                new Function<String, Vector>() {
```

```
        private static final long serialVersionUID = 1L;

        public Vector call(String s) {
            String[] sarray = s.split(" ");
            double[] values = new double[sarray.length];
            for (int i = 0; i < sarray.length; i++)
                values[i] = Double.parseDouble(sarray[i]);
            return Vectors.dense(values);
        }
    }
    );
parsedData.cache();

// Cluster the data into two classes using KMeans
int numClusters = 2;
int iterations = 10;
KMeansModel clusters = KMeans.train(parsedData.rdd(),
    numClusters, iterations);

// Evaluate clustering by computing Within Set Sum of Squared
    Errors
double sse = clusters.computeCost(parsedData.rdd());
System.out.println("Sum of Squared Errors within set = " + sse);
sparkContext.close();
    }
}
```

If you run the code, the output will be as follows:

```
Sum of Squared Errors within set = 0.11999999999994547
```

Creating a linear regression model with MLib

In this recipe, you will see how you can use a linear regression model to model with MLib.

Getting ready

1. You will be using the Maven project you created in the recipe named *Solving simple text mining problems with Apache Spark*. If you have not done so yet, then follow steps 1-6 in the *Getting ready* section of that recipe.

2. Go to `https://github.com/apache/spark/blob/master/data/mllib/ridge-data/lpsa.data`, download the data, and save as `lr-data.txt` in the data folder of your project that you created by following the instruction in step 1. Alternatively, you can create a text file named `lr-data.txt` in the data folder of your project and copy-paste the data from the aforementioned URL.

3. In the package that you created, create a Java class file named `LinearRegressionMlib.java`. Double-click to start writing your code in it.

   Now, you are ready to do some coding.

How to do it...

1. Create a class named `LinearRegressionMlib`:

   ```
   public class LinearRegressionMlib {
   ```

2. Start writing your `main` method:

   ```
   public static void main(String[] args) {
   ```

3. Create a Spark configuration, and using the configuration, create a Spark context. Note that if we used `local[2]`, it would achieve a minimal parallelism. The following syntax enables an application to run four threads:

   ```
   SparkConf configuration = new
     SparkConf().setMaster("local[4]").setAppName("Linear
       Regression");
   JavaSparkContext sparkContext = new
     JavaSparkContext(configuration);
   ```

4. Now you will be loading and parsing your input data:

   ```
   String inputData = "data/lr-data.txt";
   ```

5. `JavaRDD` is a distributed collection of objects. Create an RDD object to read the data file:

```
JavaRDD<String> data = sparkContext.textFile(inputData);
```

6. Now, you need to read the data values from the above RDD. The input data has two parts or sections that are separated by commas. The features are separated by white spaces in the second part. The labeled points are the first part of each row in the input data. Parse and read these data values to another RDD. Create a feature vector with the features. Put the feature vector along with the labeled points:

```
JavaRDD<LabeledPoint> parsedData = data.map(
    new Function<String, LabeledPoint>() {
        private static final long serialVersionUID = 1L;

        public LabeledPoint call(String line) {
            String[] parts = line.split(",");
            String[] features = parts[1].split(" ");
            double[] featureVector = new
                double[features.length];
            for (int i = 0; i < features.length - 1; i++){
                featureVector[i] =
                    Double.parseDouble(features[i]);
            }
          return new LabeledPoint(Double.parseDouble(parts[0]),
                Vectors.dense(featureVector));
        }
    }
);
parsedData.cache();
```

7. Next, you will be building the linear regression model using 10 iterations. Create a model with the feature vector, labelled points, and information on number of iterations:

```
int iterations = 10;
final LinearRegressionModel model =
  LinearRegressionWithSGD.train(JavaRDD.toRDD(parsedData),
    iterations);
```

8. Then, you will use the model to get the predictions and put them to another RDD variable named predictions. The model will predict a value given the set of features and return the prediction and the actual label. Note that the predictions you will be getting at this point are predictions for the data points in your training set (`lr-data.txt`). Tuple2 contains both the predicted value through regression and the actual value:

```
JavaRDD<Tuple2<Double, Double>> predictions = parsedData.map(
    new Function<LabeledPoint, Tuple2<Double, Double>>() {
        private static final long serialVersionUID = 1L;

        public Tuple2<Double, Double> call(LabeledPoint point)
    {
            double prediction = model.predict(point.features());
            return new Tuple2<Double, Double>(prediction,
                point.label());
        }
    }
);
```

9. Finally, calculate the mean squared error for your linear regression model on the training data. The error is the square of the difference of the value predicted by your model and actual value mentioned in the dataset for each data point. Finally, the error for each data point is averaged:

```
double mse = new JavaDoubleRDD(predictions.map(
    new Function<Tuple2<Double, Double>, Object>() {
        private static final long serialVersionUID = 1L;

        public Object call(Tuple2<Double, Double> pair) {
            return Math.pow(pair._1() - pair._2(), 2.0);
        }
    }
).rdd()).mean();
System.out.println("training Mean Squared Error = " + mse);
```

10. Finally, close the `sparkContext`, the `main` method, and the class:

```
sparkContext.close();
    }
}
```

The complete code for the recipe will be:

```
package com.data.big.mlib;

import scala.Tuple2;
import org.apache.spark.api.java.*;
import org.apache.spark.api.java.function.Function;
import org.apache.spark.mllib.linalg.Vectors;
import org.apache.spark.mllib.regression.LabeledPoint;
import org.apache.spark.mllib.regression.LinearRegressionModel;
import org.apache.spark.mllib.regression.LinearRegressionWithSGD;
import org.apache.spark.SparkConf;

public class LinearRegressionMlib {

    public static void main(String[] args) {
        SparkConf configuration = new
          SparkConf().setMaster("local[4]").setAppName("Linear
            Regression");
        JavaSparkContext sparkContext = new
          JavaSparkContext(configuration);

        // Load and parse the data
        String inputData = "data/lr-data.txt";
        JavaRDD<String> data = sparkContext.textFile(inputData);
        JavaRDD<LabeledPoint> parsedData = data.map(
            new Function<String, LabeledPoint>() {
                private static final long serialVersionUID = 1L;

                public LabeledPoint call(String line) {
                    String[] parts = line.split(",");
                    String[] features = parts[1].split(" ");
                    double[] featureVector = new
                      double[features.length];
                    for (int i = 0; i < features.length - 1; i++){
                      featureVector[i] =
                          Double.parseDouble(features[i]);
                    }
                  return new LabeledPoint(Double.parseDouble(parts[0]),
                      Vectors.dense(featureVector));
                }
            }
            );
        parsedData.cache();

        // Building the model
        int iterations = 10;
        final LinearRegressionModel model =
```

```
        LinearRegressionWithSGD.train(JavaRDD.toRDD(parsedData),
            iterations);

    // Evaluate model on training examples and compute training
        error
    JavaRDD<Tuple2<Double, Double>> predictions = parsedData.map(
        new Function<LabeledPoint, Tuple2<Double, Double>>() {
            private static final long serialVersionUID = 1L;

            public Tuple2<Double, Double> call(LabeledPoint point) {
                double prediction = model.predict(point.features());
                return new Tuple2<Double, Double>(prediction,
                  point.label());
            }
        }
        );
    double mse = new JavaDoubleRDD(predictions.map(
        new Function<Tuple2<Double, Double>, Object>() {
            private static final long serialVersionUID = 1L;

            public Object call(Tuple2<Double, Double> pair) {
                return Math.pow(pair._1() - pair._2(), 2.0);
            }
        }
        ).rdd()).mean();
    System.out.println("training Mean Squared Error = " + mse);
    sparkContext.close();
    }
}
```

The output of the code when you run it will be as follows:

```
training Mean Squared Error = 6.487093790021849
```

Classifying data points with Random Forest model using MLib

In this recipe, we will demonstrate how you can classify data points using Random Forest algorithm with MLib.

Getting ready

1. You will be using the Maven project you created in the recipe named *Solving simple text mining problems with Apache Spark*. If you have not done so yet, then follow steps 1-6 in the *Getting ready* section of that recipe.

2. Go to `https://github.com/apache/spark/blob/master/data/mllib/sample_b inary_classification_data.txt`, download the data, and save as `rf-data.txt` in the data folder of your project that you created by following the instruction in step 1. Alternatively, you can create a text file named `rf-data.txt` in the data folder of your project and copy-paste the data from the aforementioned URL.

3. In the package that you created, create a Java class file named `RandomForestMlib.java`. Double-click to start writing your code in it.

How to do it...

1. Create a class named `RandomForestMlib`:

   ```
   public class RandomForestMlib {
   ```

2. Start writing your `main` method.

   ```
   public static void main(String args[]){
   ```

3. Create a Spark configuration, and using the configuration, create a Spark context. Note that if we used `local[2]`, it would achieve a minimal parallelism. The following syntax enables an application to run four threads:

   ```
   SparkConf configuration = new
     SparkConf().setMaster("local[4]").setAppName("Random
       Forest");
   JavaSparkContext sparkContext = new
     JavaSparkContext(configuration);
   ```

4. Now you will be loading and parsing your input data:

```
String input = "data/rf-data.txt";
```

5. Read the data by loading the input file as LibSVM file and putting it into an RDD.

```
JavaRDD<LabeledPoint> data =
   MLUtils.loadLibSVMFile(sparkContext.sc(),
      input).toJavaRDD();
```

6. You will be using 70% of the data to train the model and 30% of the data as test data for the model. The selection of the data will be random.

```
JavaRDD<LabeledPoint>[] dataSplits = data.randomSplit(new
   double[]{0.7, 0.3});
JavaRDD<LabeledPoint> trainingData = dataSplits[0];
JavaRDD<LabeledPoint> testData = dataSplits[1];
```

7. Now, you will be configuring a few parameters to set up Random Forest to generate the model from training data. You need to define number classes that your data points can have. You will also need to create a map for the nominal features. You can define the number of trees in the forest. If you do not know what to select as the feature subset selection process for the classifier, you can select "auto". The remaining four parameters are required for the forest structure.

```
Integer classes = 2;
HashMap<Integer, Integer> nominalFeatures = new
 HashMap<Integer, nteger>();
Integer trees = 3;
String featureSubsetProcess = "auto";
String impurity = "gini";
Integer maxDepth = 3;
Integer maxBins = 20;
Integer seed = 12345;
```

8. Using these parameters, create a RandomForest classifier.

```
final RandomForestModel rf =
   RandomForest.trainClassifier(trainingData, classes,
      nominalFeatures, trees, featureSubsetProcess, impurity,
         maxDepth, maxBins, seed);
```

9. As a next step, use the model to predict the class labels of data points given their feature vector. `Tuple2<Double,Double>` contains the predicted value and the actual class value for each data point:

```
JavaPairRDD<Double, Double> label =
    testData.mapToPair(new PairFunction<LabeledPoint, Double,
        Double>() {
            private static final long serialVersionUID = 1L;

            public Tuple2<Double, Double> call(LabeledPoint p) {
                return new Tuple2<Double, Double>
                    (rf.predict(p.features()), p.label());
            }
    });
```

10. Finally, calculate the error for the prediction. You simply count the number of times the predicted value mismatches with the actual value, and then take the average by dividing by total number of test instances:

```
Double error =
    1.0 * label.filter(new Function<Tuple2<Double, Double>,
        Boolean>() {
            private static final long serialVersionUID = 1L;

            public Boolean call(Tuple2<Double, Double> p1) {
                return !p1._1().equals(p1._2());
            }
    }).count() / testData.count();
```

11. Print out the test error on the console. You might also like to see the actual `RandomForest` model learned from the training data:

```
System.out.println("Test Error: " + error);
System.out.println("Learned classification forest model:\n" +
    rf.toDebugString());
```

12. Close the `sparkContext`, the `main` method, and the class:

```
sparkContext.close();
    }
}
```

The complete code for the recipe is as follows:

```
package com.data.big.mlib;

import scala.Tuple2;
import java.util.HashMap;
import org.apache.spark.SparkConf;
import org.apache.spark.api.java.JavaPairRDD;
import org.apache.spark.api.java.JavaRDD;
import org.apache.spark.api.java.JavaSparkContext;
import org.apache.spark.api.java.function.Function;
import org.apache.spark.api.java.function.PairFunction;
import org.apache.spark.mllib.regression.LabeledPoint;
import org.apache.spark.mllib.tree.RandomForest;
import org.apache.spark.mllib.tree.model.RandomForestModel;
import org.apache.spark.mllib.util.MLUtils;

public class RandomForestMlib {
    public static void main(String args[]){

        SparkConf configuration = new
            SparkConf().setMaster("local[4]").setAppName("Random Forest");
        JavaSparkContext sparkContext = new
            JavaSparkContext(configuration);

        // Load and parse the data file.
        String input = "data/rf-data.txt";
        JavaRDD<LabeledPoint> data =
            MLUtils.loadLibSVMFile(sparkContext.sc(), input).toJavaRDD();
        // Split the data into training and test sets (30% held out for
            testing)
        JavaRDD<LabeledPoint>[] dataSplits = data.randomSplit(new
            double[]{0.7, 0.3});
        JavaRDD<LabeledPoint> trainingData = dataSplits[0];
        JavaRDD<LabeledPoint> testData = dataSplits[1];

        // Train a RandomForest model.
        Integer classes = 2;
        HashMap<Integer, Integer> nominalFeatures = new HashMap<Integer,
            Integer>();//  Empty categoricalFeaturesInfo indicates all
                features are continuous.
        Integer trees = 3; // Use more in practice.
        String featureSubsetProcess = "auto"; // Let the algorithm
            choose.
        String impurity = "gini";
        Integer maxDepth = 3;
        Integer maxBins = 20;
        Integer seed = 12345;
```

```
final RandomForestModel rf =
    RandomForest.trainClassifier(trainingData, classes,
        nominalFeatures, trees, featureSubsetProcess, impurity,
        maxDepth, maxBins, seed);

// Evaluate model on test instances and compute test error
JavaPairRDD<Double, Double> label =
    testData.mapToPair(new PairFunction<LabeledPoint, Double,
        Double>() {
        private static final long serialVersionUID = 1L;

        public Tuple2<Double, Double> call(LabeledPoint p) {
            return new Tuple2<Double, Double>
                (rf.predict(p.features()), p.label());
        }
    });

Double error =
    1.0 * label.filter(new Function<Tuple2<Double, Double>,
        Boolean>() {
        private static final long serialVersionUID = 1L;

        public Boolean call(Tuple2<Double, Double> pl) {
            return !pl._1().equals(pl._2());
        }
    }).count() / testData.count();
System.out.println("Test Error: " + error);
System.out.println("Learned classification forest model:\n" +
    rf.toDebugString());
sparkContext.close();
    }
}
```

If you run the code, the output will be as follows:

```
Test Error: 0.034482758620689655
Learned classification forest model:
TreeEnsembleModel classifier with 3 trees

  Tree 0:
    If (feature 427 <= 0.0)
     If (feature 407 <= 0.0)
      Predict: 0.0
     Else (feature 407 > 0.0)
      Predict: 1.0
    Else (feature 427 > 0.0)
      Predict: 0.0
  Tree 1:
```

```
If (feature 405 <= 0.0)
 If (feature 624 <= 253.0)
  Predict: 0.0
 Else (feature 624 > 253.0)
  If (feature 650 <= 0.0)
   Predict: 0.0
  Else (feature 650 > 0.0)
   Predict: 1.0
Else (feature 405 > 0.0)
 If (feature 435 <= 0.0)
  If (feature 541 <= 0.0)
   Predict: 1.0
  Else (feature 541 > 0.0)
   Predict: 0.0
 Else (feature 435 > 0.0)
  Predict: 1.0
Tree 2:
 If (feature 271 <= 72.0)
  If (feature 323 <= 0.0)
   Predict: 0.0
  Else (feature 323 > 0.0)
   Predict: 1.0
 Else (feature 271 > 72.0)
  If (feature 414 <= 0.0)
   If (feature 159 <= 124.0)
    Predict: 0.0
   Else (feature 159 > 124.0)
    Predict: 1.0
  Else (feature 414 > 0.0)
   Predict: 0.0
```

8
Learn Deeply from Data

In this chapter, we will cover the following recipes:

- Creating a Word2vec neural net using Deep Learning for Java (DL4j)
- Creating a deep belief neural net using Deep Learning for Java (DL4j)
- Creating a deep autoencoder using Deep Learning for Java (DL4j)

Introduction

Deep learning is simply neural networks with multiple layers. It is also known as deep neural network learning or unsupervised feature learning. The author believes that deep learning will become the next accomplice of machine learning practitioners and data scientists because of its ability to solve real-world data problems.

Deep Learning for Java (DL4j) is an open-source, distributed Java library for deep learning for JVM. It comes with other libraries, as follows:

- Deeplearning4J: Neural Net Platform
- ND4J: NumPy for the JVM
- DataVec: Tool for machine learning ETL operations
- JavaCPP: The bridge between Java and native C++
- Arbiter: Evaluation tool for machine learning algorithms
- RL4J: Deep reinforcement learning for the JVM

However, we will be focusing on a few key recipes for DL4j only, given the scope of this book. To be specific, we will be discussing recipes to use Word2vec algorithm and their use for real-world NLP and information retrieval problem, deep belief neural networks and deep autoencoders and their usage. Curious readers are highly encouraged to visit `https://github.com/deeplearning4j/dl4j-examples` to get more examples. Note that the codes in the recipes of the chapter are based on these examples on GitHub.

Also note that in this chapter, a big portion is dedicated to showing how the DL4j library is set up because the procedure is very complex, and the readers need to pay attention in order to successfully execute of the code in this book and code of their own.

There are two prerequisites for all the recipes in this chapter: Java Developer version 1.7 or higher (the author had 1.8) and Apache Maven. The recipes in this chapter are implemented using the Eclipse Java IDE (the author had Eclipse Mars). Although `https://deeplearning4j.org/quickstart` contains an impressive amount of material on setting up DL4j with Java, most of them are focused on another IDE, named IntelliJ.

To perform the recipes in this chapter, we will require the following:

1. To use DL4j, you will need Apache Maven installed, which is a software project management and comprehension tool. At the time of writing this book, version 3.3.9 of Apache Maven was the latest one and the readers are encouraged to use this version.
2. Go to `https://maven.apache.org/download.cgi` and download a binary zip archive into your system:

System Requirements

Java Development Kit (JDK)	Maven 3.3 requires JDK 1.7 or above to execute - it still allows you to build against 1.3 and other JDK versions by Using
Memory	No minimum requirement
Disk	Approximately 10MB is required for the Maven installation itself. In addition to that, additional disk space will be used for depending on usage but expect at least 500MB.
Operating System	No minimum requirement. Start up scripts are included as shell scripts and Windows batch files.

Files

Maven is distributed in several formats for your convenience. Simply pick a ready-made binary distribution archive and follow the installation instruc

In order to guard against corrupted downloads/installations, it is highly recommended to verify the signature of the release bundles against the publi

	Link	Checksum
Binary tar.gz archive	apache-maven-3.3.9-bin.tar.gz	apache-maven-3.3.9-bin.tar.gz.md5
Binary zip archive	apache-maven-3.3.9-bin.zip	apache-maven-3.3.9-bin.zip.md5
Source tar.gz archive	apache-maven-3.3.9-src.tar.gz	apache-maven-3.3.9-src.tar.gz.md5
Source zip archive	apache-maven-3.3.9-src.zip	apache-maven-3.3.9-src.zip.md5

3. Once you download, unzip the file archive, and you will find a folder structure as follows:

bin	2017-02-06 1:51 PM	File folder	
boot	2017-02-06 1:51 PM	File folder	
conf	2017-02-06 1:51 PM	File folder	
lib	2017-02-06 1:51 PM	File folder	
LICENSE	2015-11-10 11:44 ...	File	19 KB
NOTICE	2015-11-10 11:44 ...	File	1 KB
README.txt	2015-11-10 11:38 ...	Text Document	3 KB

4. Now you need to put the path of `bin` folder in this distribution in your class path. To do so, right-click on your My Computer icon and click on **properties**. Click on **Advanced system settings** and then on **Environmental variables…**:

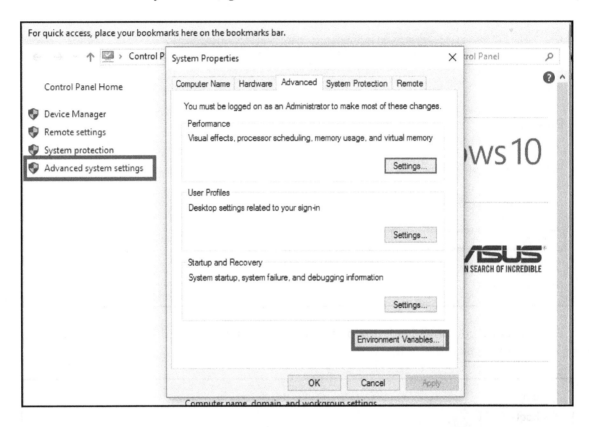

5. When the **Environment Variables** window appears, go to **System variables** and select the variable named `Path`. Click on the **Edit...** button:

6. When the **Edit environment variable** window appears, click on the **New** button and add the path to the `bin` folder of the Maven distribution. Click on **OK** to complete this action:

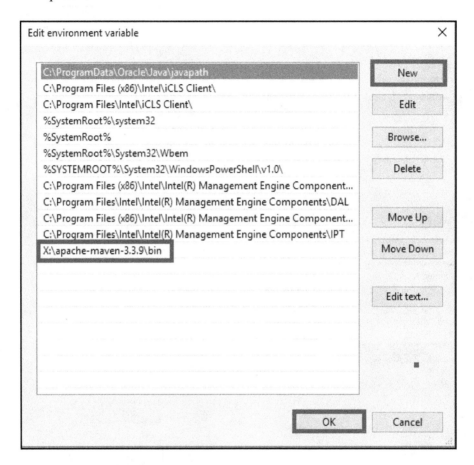

7. Now that you are back to **Environment Variables** window, set up the JAVA_HOME system variable. In the **System variables** section, click on the **New** button:

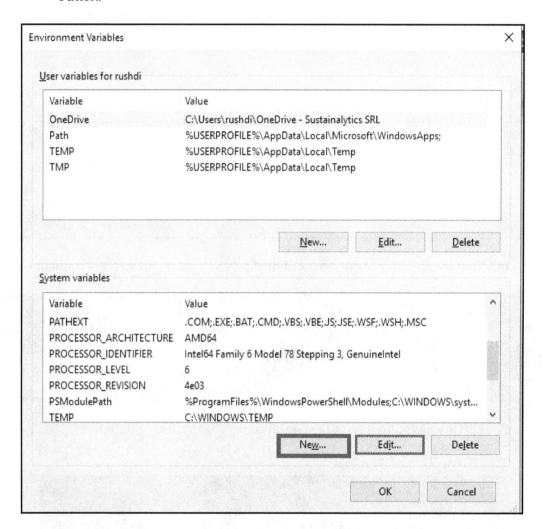

8. Name the variable `JAVA_HOME` and put the path of your **Java Development Kit** (**JDK**) folder (remember, not the `bin` folder).

 Please note that you need a Java version of at least 7 installed on your system to run the recipes in this chapter.

9. Click on **OK** to complete the command. Close windows opened along the way:

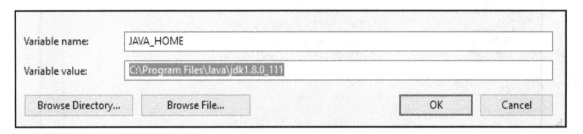

10. Now check if Maven has been installed properly using the `mvn -v` command:

```
C:\Users\rushdi>mvn -v
Apache Maven 3.3.9 (bb52d8502b132ec0a5a3f4c09453c07478323dc5; 2015-11-10T11:41:47-05:00)
Maven home: X:\apache-maven-3.3.9\bin\..
Java version: 1.8.0_111, vendor: Oracle Corporation
Java home: C:\Program Files\Java\jdk1.8.0_111\jre
Default locale: en_CA, platform encoding: Cp1252
OS name: "windows 10", version: "10.0", arch: "amd64", family: "dos"
```

11. Also, check the version of Java installed on your system with the `java -version` command:

```
C:\Users\rushdi>java -version
java version "1.8.0_111"
Java(TM) SE Runtime Environment (build 1.8.0_111-b14)
Java HotSpot(TM) 64-Bit Server VM (build 25.111-b14, mixed mode)

C:\Users\rushdi>
```

12. Now open the Eclipse IDE. The author has the Mars version installed. Go to **File**, then click on **New,** then click on **Other**…:

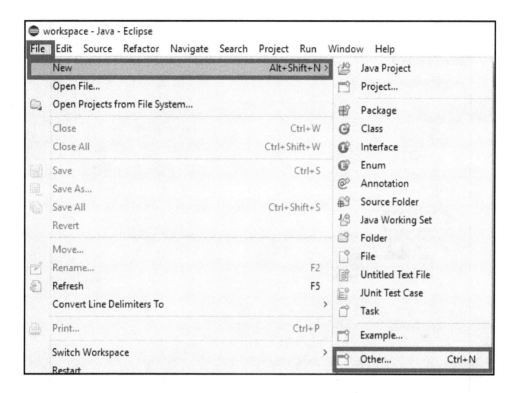

13. In the Wizard, expand the Maven option and select the Maven Project. Click on **Next**:

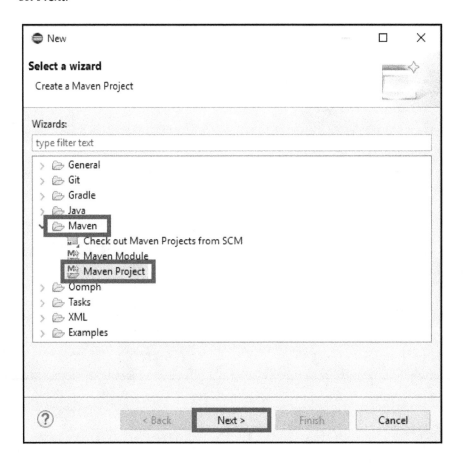

14. Keep clicking on **Next** until you reach the following window. In this window, fill out the **Group Id** and **Artifact Id** as follows or with anything you like. Click on **Finish**:

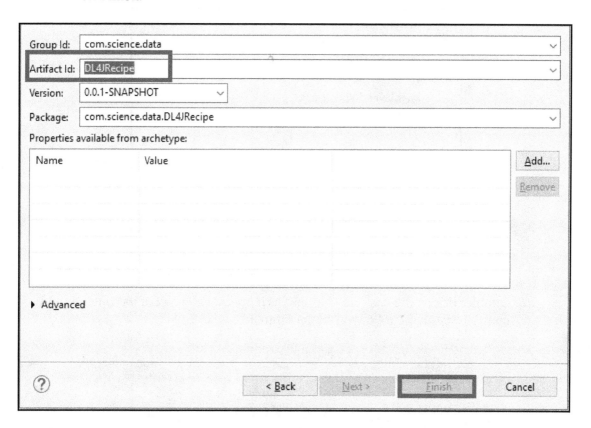

15. This will create a project as follows. If you expand your project by double-clicking on its name, you will see an xml file named POM.xml:

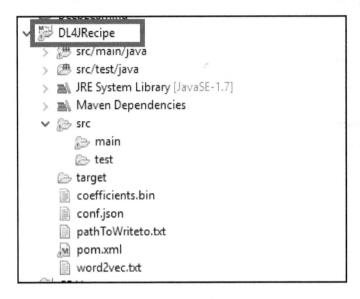

16. Double click on the pom.xml file, and as it opens, delete all of its contents, and copy and paste the following content into it:

```
<project xmlns="http://maven.apache.org/POM/4.0.0"
    xmlns:xsi="http://www.w3.org/2001/XMLSchema-instance"
  xsi:schemaLocation="http://maven.apache.org/POM/4.0.0
 http://maven.apache.org/xsd/maven-4.0.0.xsd">
<modelVersion>4.0.0</modelVersion>

 <groupId>org.deeplearning4j</groupId>
 <artifactId>deeplearning4j-examples</artifactId>
 <version>0.4-rc0-SNAPSHOT</version>

 <name>DeepLearning4j Examples</name>
<description>Examples of training different data
    sets</description>
<properties>
 <nd4j.version>0.4-rc3.7</nd4j.version>
 <dl4j.version>  0.4-rc3.7</dl4j.version>
 <canova.version>0.0.0.13</canova.version>
 <jackson.version>2.5.1</jackson.version>
</properties>
```

```
<distributionManagement>
  <snapshotRepository>
      <id>sonatype-nexus-snapshots</id>
      <name>Sonatype Nexus snapshot repository</name>
<url>https://oss.sonatype.org/content/repositories/snapshots</url>
  </snapshotRepository>
  <repository>
      <id>nexus-releases</id>
      <name>Nexus Release Repository</name>
  <url>http://oss.sonatype.org/service/local/
      staging/deploy/maven2/</url>
  </repository>
   </distributionManagement>
  <dependencyManagement>
   <dependencies>
      <dependency>
          <groupId>org.nd4j</groupId>
          <artifactId>nd4j-x86</artifactId>
          <version>${nd4j.version}</version>
      </dependency>
    </dependencies>
   </dependencyManagement>
  <dependencies>
  <dependency>
      <groupId>org.deeplearning4j</groupId>
      <artifactId>deeplearning4j-nlp</artifactId>
      <version>${dl4j.version}</version>
  </dependency>

  <dependency>
      <groupId>org.deeplearning4j</groupId>
      <artifactId>deeplearning4j-core</artifactId>
      <version>${dl4j.version}</version>
  </dependency>
  <dependency>
      <groupId>org.deeplearning4j</groupId>
      <artifactId>deeplearning4j-ui</artifactId>
      <version>${dl4j.version}</version>
  </dependency>
  <dependency>
      <groupId>org.nd4j</groupId>
      <artifactId>nd4j-x86</artifactId>
      <version>${nd4j.version}</version>
  </dependency>
  <dependency>
      <artifactId>canova-nd4j-image</artifactId>
      <groupId>org.nd4j</groupId>
      <version>${canova.version}</version>
```

```xml
        </dependency>
        <dependency>
            <artifactId>canova-nd4j-codec</artifactId>
            <groupId>org.nd4j</groupId>
            <version>${canova.version}</version>
        </dependency>
        <dependency>
            <groupId>com.fasterxml.jackson.dataformat</groupId>
            <artifactId>jackson-dataformat-yaml</artifactId>
            <version>${jackson.version}</version>
        </dependency>
    </dependencies>
    <build>
      <plugins>
        <plugin>
            <groupId>org.codehaus.mojo</groupId>
            <artifactId>exec-maven-plugin</artifactId>
            <version>1.4.0</version>
            <executions>
                <execution>
                    <goals>
                        <goal>exec</goal>
                    </goals>
                </execution>
            </executions>
            <configuration>
                <executable>java</executable>
            </configuration>
        </plugin>
        <plugin>
            <groupId>org.apache.maven.plugins</groupId>
            <artifactId>maven-shade-plugin</artifactId>
            <version>1.6</version>
            <configuration>
  <createDependencyReducedPom>true</createDependencyReducedPom>
        <filters>
        <filter>
        <artifact>*:*</artifact>
        <excludes>
           <exclude>org/datanucleus/**</exclude>
            <exclude>META-INF/*.SF</exclude>
            <exclude>META-INF/*.DSA</exclude>
            <exclude>META-INF/*.RSA</exclude>
        </excludes>
                </filter>
            </filters>
        </configuration>
        <executions>
```

```xml
            <execution>
                <phase>package</phase>
                <goals>
                    <goal>shade</goal>
                </goals>
                <configuration>
                    <transformers>
<transformer implementation="org.apache.maven.plugins.
   shade.resource.AppendingTransformer">
<resource>reference.conf</resource>
                    </transformer>
<transformer implementation="org.apache.maven.plugins.
        shade.resource.ServicesResourceTransformer"/>
<transformer implementation="org.apache.maven.plugins.
        shade.resource.ManifestResourceTransformer">
                    </transformer>
                </transformers>
            </configuration>
        </execution>
    </executions>
</plugin>

<plugin>
    <groupId>org.apache.maven.plugins</groupId>
    <artifactId>maven-compiler-plugin</artifactId>
    <configuration>
        <source>1.7</source>
        <target>1.7</target>
    </configuration>
 </plugin>
</plugins>
</build>
</project>
```

17. This will download all the necessary dependencies (see the following screenshot for a partial picture), and you are ready to create some code:

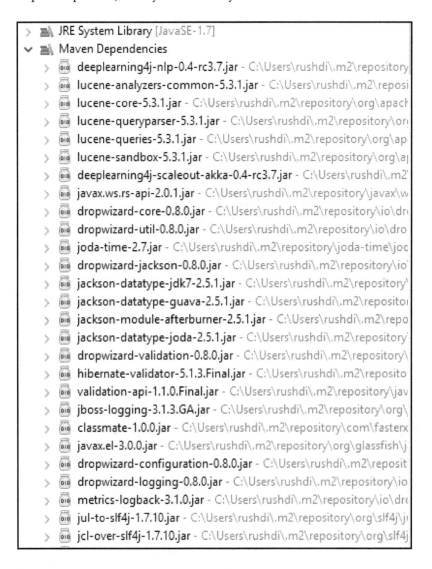

18. Go to
    `https://github.com/deeplearning4j/dl4j-examples/tree/master/dl4j-examp`
    `les/src/main/resources` and download the `raw_sentences.txt` file to your
    `C:/` drive:

Branch: master ▼	dl4j-examples / dl4j-examples / src / main / **resources** /
🖼 agibsonccc committed on **GitHub** Merge pull request #339 from gks141270/master ...	
..	
📁 DataExamples	Add files via upload
📁 NewsData	Done changes as suggested by Adam, Gibson mentioned in pull request a...
📁 PredictGender	Changes based on Adam's suggestions
📁 animals	Moving animals examples into main example repo.
📁 classification	Refactor project structure into modules for dl4j, dl4j-spark, datavec
📁 paravec	paravec inference example
📁 rnnRegression	Removed files that are generated when running example
📄 dropwizard.yml	Refactor project structure into modules for dl4j, dl4j-spark, datavec
📄 iris.txt	Refactor project structure into modules for dl4j, dl4j-spark, datavec
📄 log4j.properties	Final Canova->DataVec changes; update pom files + add comments to poms
📄 logback.xml	Final Canova->DataVec changes; update pom files + add comments to poms
📄 oneline.txt	Refactor project structure into modules for dl4j, dl4j-spark, datavec
📄 raw_sentences.txt	Refactor project structure into modules for dl4j, dl4j-spark, datavec
📄 words.txt	Refactor project structure into modules for dl4j, dl4j-spark, datavec

Creating a Word2vec neural net using Deep Learning for Java (DL4j)

Word2vec can be seen as a two-layer neural net that works with natural text. With its typical usage, the input for the algorithm can be a text corpus, and its output is a set of feature vectors for words in that corpus. Note that Word2vec is not, strictly speaking, a deep neural network as it translates text into a numerical form that deep neural nets can read and understand. In this recipe, we will see how we can use the popular deep learning Java library named deep learning for Java (from this point on, DL4j) to apply Word2vec to raw text.

How to do it...

1. Create a class named `Word2VecRawTextExample`:

   ```
   public class Word2VecRawTextExample {
   ```

2. Create a logger for this class. The logger facility has already been included in your project, as you have used Maven to build your project:

   ```
   private static Logger log =
      LoggerFactory.getLogger(Word2VecRawTextExample.class);
   ```

3. Start creating your main method:

   ```
   <dependency><groupId>org.nd4j</groupId><artifactId>nd4j-
   native</artifactId><version>0.7.2</version></dependency>

      public static void main(String[] args) throws Exception {
   ```

4. The first thing you will do is to get the file path for the sample raw sentences text file that you have downloaded:

   ```
   String filePath = "c:/raw_sentences.txt";
   ```

5. Now take the raw sentences in your `.txt` file, traverse them with your iterator, and preprocess them (for example, converting everything to lower case, strip white space before and after for each line):

```
log.info("Load & Vectorize Sentences....");
SentenceIterator iter =
    UimaSentenceIterator.createWithPath(filePath);
```

6. Word2vec uses words or tokens rather than sentences. Therefore, your next task will be to tokenize the raw text:

```
TokenizerFactory t = new DefaultTokenizerFactory();
t.setTokenPreProcessor(new CommonPreprocessor());
```

7. Vocabulary cache or Vocab cache is a mechanism in DL4j for handling general purpose natural language tasks such as TF-IDF. `InMemoryLookupCache` is the reference implementation:

```
InMemoryLookupCache cache = new InMemoryLookupCache();
    WeightLookupTable table = new InMemoryLookupTable.Builder()
            .vectorLength(100)
            .useAdaGrad(false)
            .cache(cache)
        .lr(0.025f).build();
```

8. Now that the data is ready, you are also ready to configure the `Word2vec` neural network:

```
log.info("Building model....");
Word2Vec vec = new Word2Vec.Builder()
        .minWordFrequency(5).iterations(1)
        .layerSize(100).lookupTable(table)
        .stopWords(new ArrayList<String>())
        .vocabCache(cache).seed(42)
        .windowSize(5).iterate(iter).tokenizerFactory(t).build();
```

minWordFrequency is the minimum number of times a word must appear in the corpus. In this recipe, if it appears less than five times, a word is not learned. Words must appear in multiple contexts to learn useful features about them. If you have a very large corpus, it is reasonable to raise the minimum. LayerSize denotes the number of features in the word vector or the number of dimensions in the feature space. Next, fit the model by starting the neural net training:

```
log.info("Fitting Word2Vec model....");
vec.fit();
```

9. Write the word vectors created from the neural net into an output file. In our case, the output is written to a file named c:/word2vec.txt:

```
<dependency><groupId>org.nd4j</groupId><artifactId>nd4j-
    native</artifactId><version>0.7.2</version></dependency>
log.info("Writing word vectors to text file....");
WordVectorSerializer.writeWordVectors(vec, "c:/word2vec.txt");
```

10. You also can evaluate the quality of the feature vectors. vec.wordsNearest("word1", numWordsNearest) provides us with the words that are clustered as semantically similar words by the neural net. You can set the number of nearest words you want with the second parameter of wordsNearest. vec.similarity("word1","word2") will return the cosine similarity of the two words you enter. The closer it is to 1, the more similar the net perceives those words to be:

```
log.info("Closest Words:");
Collection<String> lst = vec.wordsNearest("man", 5);
System.out.println(lst);
double cosSim = vec.similarity("cruise", "voyage");
System.out.println(cosSim);
```

11. The output of the preceding lines will be as follows:

```
[family, part, house, program, business]
1.0000001192092896
```

12. Close the main method and the class:

```
}
}
```

How it works...

1. Right-click on your project name in Eclipse, select **New,** and then select Package.
   Give the following as your package name: word2vec.chap8.science.data.
   Click on **Finish**:

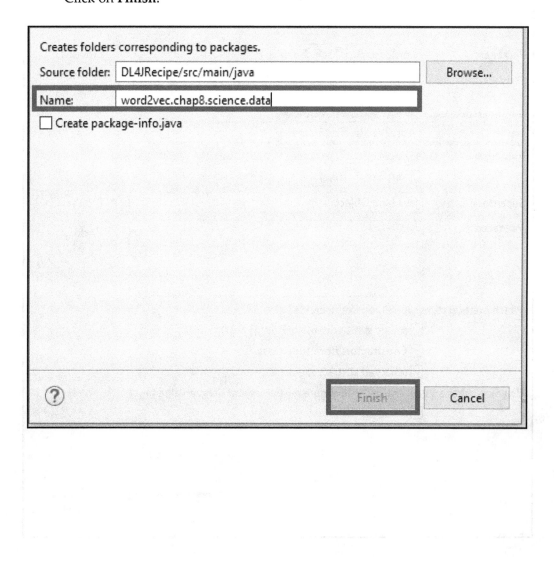

2. Now that you have a package, right-click on the package name, select **New**, and then select **Class**. The name of the class should be `Word2VecRawTextExample`. Click on **Finish**:

Source folder:	DL4JRecipe/src/main/java Browse...
Package:	word2vec.chap8.science.data Browse...
☐ Enclosing type:	Browse...

Name:	Word2VecRawTextExample
Modifiers:	⦿ public ○ package ○ private ○ protected
	☐ abstract ☐ final ☐ static
Superclass:	java.lang.Object Browse...
Interfaces:	Add... Remove

Which method stubs would you like to create?

   ☐ public static void main(String[] args)

   ☐ Constructors from superclass

   ☑ Inherited abstract methods

Do you want to add comments? (Configure templates and default value here)

   ☐ Generate comments

⑦   Finish   Cancel

In the editor, copy and paste the following code:

```
package word2vec.chap8.science.data;

import org.deeplearning4j.models.embeddings.WeightLookupTable;
import org.deeplearning4j.models.embeddings.inmemory.InMemoryLookupTable;
import org.deeplearning4j.models.embeddings.loader.WordVectorSerializer;
import org.deeplearning4j.models.word2vec.Word2Vec;
import
org.deeplearning4j.models.word2vec.wordstore.inmemory.InMemoryLookupCache;
import org.deeplearning4j.text.sentenceiterator.SentenceIterator;
import org.deeplearning4j.text.sentenceiterator.UimaSentenceIterator;
import
org.deeplearning4j.text.tokenization.tokenizer.preprocessor.CommonPreproces
sor;
import
org.deeplearning4j.text.tokenization.tokenizerfactory.DefaultTokenizerFacto
ry;
import
org.deeplearning4j.text.tokenization.tokenizerfactory.TokenizerFactory;

import org.slf4j.Logger;
import org.slf4j.LoggerFactory;

import java.util.ArrayList;
import java.util.Collection;

public class Word2VecRawTextExample {

    private static Logger log =
LoggerFactory.getLogger(Word2VecRawTextExample.class);

    public static void main(String[] args) throws Exception {

        // Gets Path to Text file
        String filePath = "c:/raw_sentences.txt";

        log.info("Load & Vectorize Sentences....");
        // Strip white space before and after for each line
        SentenceIterator iter =
            UimaSentenceIterator.createWithPath(filePath);
        // Split on white spaces in the line to get words
        TokenizerFactory t = new DefaultTokenizerFactory();
        t.setTokenPreProcessor(new CommonPreprocessor());

        InMemoryLookupCache cache = new InMemoryLookupCache();
        WeightLookupTable table = new InMemoryLookupTable.Builder()
                .vectorLength(100)
```

```
                    .useAdaGrad(false)
                    .cache(cache)
                    .lr(0.025f).build();

            log.info("Building model....");
            Word2Vec vec = new Word2Vec.Builder()
                .minWordFrequency(5).iterations(1)
                .layerSize(100).lookupTable(table)
                .stopWords(new ArrayList<String>())
                .vocabCache(cache).seed(42)
                .windowSize(5).iterate(iter).tokenizerFactory(t).build();

            log.info("Fitting Word2Vec model....");
            vec.fit();

            log.info("Writing word vectors to text file....");
            // Write word
            WordVectorSerializer.writeWordVectors(vec, "word2vec.txt");

            log.info("Closest Words:");
            Collection<String> lst = vec.wordsNearest("man", 5);
            System.out.println(lst);
            double cosSim = vec.similarity("cruise", "voyage");
            System.out.println(cosSim);
        }
    }
```

There's more

- `minWordFrequency`: Is the minimum number of times a word must appear in the corpus. In this recipe, if it appears less than five times, a word is not learned. Words must appear in multiple contexts to learn useful features about them. If you have very large corpora, it is reasonable to raise the minimum.
- `iterations`: This is the number of times you allow the neural net to update its coefficients for one batch of the data. Too few iterations can cause insufficient learning, and too many will make the net's training longer.
- `layerSize`: Denotes the number of features in the word vector or the number of dimensions in the feature space.
- iterate tells the net what batch of the dataset it is getting its training on.
- `tokenizer`: Feeds it the words from the current batch.

Creating a Deep Belief neural net using Deep Learning for Java (DL4j)

A deep-belief network can be defined as a stack of restricted Boltzmann machines where each RBM layer communicates with both the previous and subsequent layers. In this recipe, we will see how we can create such a network. For simplicity's sake, in this recipe, we have limited ourselves to a single hidden layer for our neural nets. So the net we develop in this recipe is not strictly speaking a deep belief neural net, but the readers are encouraged to add more hidden layers.

How to do it...

1. Create a class named `DBNIrisExample`:

   ```
   public class DBNIrisExample {
   ```

2. Create a logger for the class to log messages:

   ```
   private static Logger log =
      LoggerFactory.getLogger(DBNIrisExample.class);
   ```

3. Start writing your main method:

   ```
   public static void main(String[] args) throws Exception {
   ```

4. First, customize two parameters of the Nd4j class: the maximum number of slices to print and the maximum number elements per slice. Set them to −1:

   ```
   Nd4j.MAX_SLICES_TO_PRINT = -1;
   Nd4j.MAX_ELEMENTS_PER_SLICE = -1;
   ```

5. Next, customize other parameters:

```
final int numRows = 4;
 final int numColumns = 1;
  int outputNum = 3;
  int numSamples = 150;
  int batchSize = 150;
  int iterations = 5;
  int splitTrainNum = (int) (batchSize * .8);
  int seed = 123;
  int listenerFreq = 1;
```

- In DL4j, input data can be a two-dimensional data, and therefore, you need to assign the number of rows and columns of the data. The number of columns is set to 1 as the Iris dataset is one-dimensional.
- In the code, numSamples is the total data and batchSize is the amount of data in each batch.
- splitTrainNum is the variable to allocate data for training and testing. Here, 80% of all the dataset is training data, and the rest is treated as test data.
- listenerFreq decides how often we see loss function's value for logging in the process. This value is set to 1 here, which means the value is logged after each epoch.

6. Use the following piece of code to load the Iris dataset automatically with the batch size and number of samples information:

```
log.info("Load data....");
DataSetIterator iter = new IrisDataSetIterator(batchSize,
    numSamples);
```

7. Format the data:

```
DataSet next = iter.next();
    next.normalizeZeroMeanZeroUnitVariance();
```

8. Next, split the data into training and testing. For splitting, use random seeds and enforce numerical stability for training:

```
log.info("Split data....");
 SplitTestAndTrain testAndTrain =
     next.splitTestAndTrain(splitTrainNum, new Random(seed));
 DataSet train = testAndTrain.getTrain();
 DataSet test = testAndTrain.getTest();
 Nd4j.ENFORCE_NUMERICAL_STABILITY = true;
```

9. Now, write down the following chunk of code to build your model:

```
MultiLayerConfiguration conf = new
    NeuralNetConfiguration.Builder()
    .seed(seed)
    .iterations(iterations)
    .learningRate(1e-6f)
   .optimizationAlgo(OptimizationAlgorithm.CONJUGATE_GRADIENT)
    .l1(1e-1).regularization(true).l2(2e-4)
    .useDropConnect(true)
    .list(2)
```

10. Let's examine this piece of code:
    - With the seed method, you lock in weight initialization for tuning
    - Then you set the number of training iterations for prediction or classification
    - You then define the optimization step size and select the Back Propagation algorithm to calculate gradients
    - Finally, in the list() method, supply 2 as a parameter for the number of neural net layers (besides input layer)

11. Then add the following method calls to the code in the preceding step. This code is to set up the first layer for your neural net:

```
.layer(0, new RBM.Builder(RBM.HiddenUnit.RECTIFIED,
    RBM.VisibleUnit.GAUSSIAN)

    .nIn(numRows * numColumns)

    .nOut(3)
    .weightInit(WeightInit.XAVIER)
    .k(1)
    .activation("relu")
    .lossFunction(LossFunctions.LossFunction.RMSE_XENT)
    .updater(Updater.ADAGRAD)
    .dropOut(0.5)
    .build()
)
```

- The value of 0 in the first line is the layer's index
- k() is for contrastive divergence
- Instead of binary RBM, which we cannot use in this case as the Iris data is of float values, we have RBM.VisibleUnit.GAUSSIAN here, enabling the model to handle continuous values
- Updater.ADAGRAD is used to optimize the learning rate

12. Then add the following method calls to the code in the preceding step. This piece of code is to set up layer 1 for your neural net:

```
.layer(1, new
    OutputLayer.Builder(LossFunctions.LossFunction.MCXENT)

    .nIn(3)

    .nOut(outputNum)
    .activation("softmax")
    .build()
)   .build();
```

13. Finalize the model building:

```
MultiLayerNetwork model = new MultiLayerNetwork(conf);
model.init();
```

14. Once the model is configured, finalize its training:

```
model.setListeners(Arrays.asList((IterationListener) new
    ScoreIterationListener(listenerFreq)));
log.info("Train model....");
model.fit(train);
```

15. You can evaluate the weights with the following piece of code:

```
log.info("Evaluate weights....");
for(org.deeplearning4j.nn.api.Layer layer : model.getLayers())
{
    INDArray w =
     layer.getParam(DefaultParamInitializer.WEIGHT_KEY);
    log.info("Weights: " + w);
}
```

16. Finally, evaluate your model:

```
log.info("Evaluate model....");
Evaluation eval = new Evaluation(outputNum);
INDArray output = model.output(test.getFeatureMatrix());
for (int i = 0; i < output.rows(); i++) {
    String actual =
        test.getLabels().getRow(i).toString().trim();
    String predicted = output.getRow(i).toString().trim();
    log.info("actual " + actual + " vs predicted " +
        predicted);
}

eval.eval(test.getLabels(), output);
log.info(eval.stats());
```

17. The output of this segment of code will be as follows:

```
==========================Scores====================================
Accuracy:   0.8333
Precision: 1
Recall:     0.8333
F1 Score:   0.9090909090909091
```

18. Finally, close the main method and your class:

```
    }
}
```

How it works...

1. Right-click on your project name in Eclipse, select New, and then select Package. Give the following as your package name: `deepbelief.chap8.science.data.` Click on **Finish**.

2. Now that you have a package, right-click on the package name, select New, and then select Class. The name of the class should be `DBNIrisExample`. Click on **Finish**.

In the editor, copy and paste the following code:

```
package deepbelief.chap8.science.data;


import org.deeplearning4j.datasets.iterator.DataSetIterator;
import org.deeplearning4j.datasets.iterator.impl.IrisDataSetIterator;
import org.deeplearning4j.eval.Evaluation;
import org.deeplearning4j.nn.api.OptimizationAlgorithm;
import org.deeplearning4j.nn.conf.MultiLayerConfiguration;
import org.deeplearning4j.nn.conf.NeuralNetConfiguration;
import org.deeplearning4j.nn.conf.Updater;
import org.deeplearning4j.nn.conf.layers.OutputLayer;
import org.deeplearning4j.nn.conf.layers.RBM;
import org.deeplearning4j.nn.multilayer.MultiLayerNetwork;
import org.deeplearning4j.nn.params.DefaultParamInitializer;
import org.deeplearning4j.nn.weights.WeightInit;
import org.deeplearning4j.optimize.api.IterationListener;
import org.deeplearning4j.optimize.listeners.ScoreIterationListener;
import org.nd4j.linalg.api.ndarray.INDArray;
import org.nd4j.linalg.dataset.DataSet;
import org.nd4j.linalg.dataset.SplitTestAndTrain;
import org.nd4j.linalg.factory.Nd4j;
import org.nd4j.linalg.lossfunctions.LossFunctions;
import org.slf4j.Logger;
import org.slf4j.LoggerFactory;
import java.util.Arrays;
import java.util.Random;

public class DBNIrisExample {

    private static Logger log =
      LoggerFactory.getLogger(DBNIrisExample.class);

    public static void main(String[] args) throws Exception {
        Nd4j.MAX_SLICES_TO_PRINT = -1;
        Nd4j.MAX_ELEMENTS_PER_SLICE = -1;

        final int numRows = 4;
        final int numColumns = 1;
        int outputNum = 3;
        int numSamples = 150;
        int batchSize = 150;
        int iterations = 5;
        int splitTrainNum = (int) (batchSize * .8);
        int seed = 123;
        int listenerFreq = 1;
```

```
log.info("Load data....");
DataSetIterator iter = new IrisDataSetIterator(batchSize,
  numSamples);
DataSet next = iter.next();
next.normalizeZeroMeanZeroUnitVariance();

log.info("Split data....");
SplitTestAndTrain testAndTrain =
    next.splitTestAndTrain(splitTrainNum, new Random(seed));
DataSet train = testAndTrain.getTrain();
DataSet test = testAndTrain.getTest();
Nd4j.ENFORCE_NUMERICAL_STABILITY = true;

log.info("Build model....");
MultiLayerConfiguration conf = new
  NeuralNetConfiguration.Builder()
    .seed(seed)
    .iterations(iterations)
    .learningRate(1e-6f)
    .optimizationAlgo(OptimizationAlgorithm.CONJUGATE_GRADIENT)
    .l1(1e-1).regularization(true).l2(2e-4)
    .useDropConnect(true)
    .list(2)
    .layer(0, new RBM.Builder(RBM.HiddenUnit.RECTIFIED,
     RBM.VisibleUnit.GAUSSIAN)
     .nIn(numRows * numColumns)
     .nOut(3)
     .weightInit(WeightInit.XAVIER)
     .k(1)
     .activation("relu")
     .lossFunction(LossFunctions.LossFunction.RMSE_XENT)
     .updater(Updater.ADAGRAD)
     .dropOut(0.5)
     .build()
   )
   .layer(1, new
      OutputLayer.Builder(LossFunctions.LossFunction.MCXENT)
     .nIn(3)
     .nOut(outputNum)
     .activation("softmax")
     .build()
 )
.build();
MultiLayerNetwork model = new MultiLayerNetwork(conf);
model.init();

model.setListeners(Arrays.asList((IterationListener) new
    ScoreIterationListener(listenerFreq)));
```

```
log.info("Train model....");
model.fit(train);

log.info("Evaluate weights....");
for(org.deeplearning4j.nn.api.Layer layer : model.getLayers())
{
    INDArray w =
    layer.getParam(DefaultParamInitializer.WEIGHT_KEY);
    log.info("Weights: " + w);
}

log.info("Evaluate model....");
Evaluation eval = new Evaluation(outputNum);
INDArray output = model.output(test.getFeatureMatrix());

for (int i = 0; i < output.rows(); i++) {
    String actual =
        test.getLabels().getRow(i).toString().trim();
    String predicted = output.getRow(i).toString().trim();
    log.info("actual " + actual + " vs predicted " +
        predicted);
}

eval.eval(test.getLabels(), output);
log.info(eval.stats());
    }
}
```

Creating a deep autoencoder using Deep Learning for Java (DL4j)

A deep autoencoder is a deep neural network that is composed of two deep-belief networks that are symmetrical. The networks usually have two separate four or five shallow layers (restricted Boltzmann machines) representing the encoding and decoding half of the net. In this recipe, you will be developing a deep autoencoder consisting of one input layer, four decoding layers, four encoding layers, and one output layer. In doing so, we will be using a very popular dataset named MNIST.

To learn more about MNIST, visit `http://yann.lecun.com/exdb/mnist/`. If you want to know more about deep autoencoders, visit `https://deeple arning4j.org/deepautoencoder.` to complete the command. Close windows opened along the way. command. command. and click **Other**... until you reach the following window. In this window, fill out the **Group Id** and **Artifact Id** as follows or with anything you like. Click on **Finish**.

How to do it...

1. Start by creating a class named `DeepAutoEncoderExample`:

   ```
   public class DeepAutoEncoderExample {
   ```

2. Throughout the code, you will be logging messages. So, create a logger for your class:

   ```
   private static Logger log =
       LoggerFactory.getLogger(DeepAutoEncoderExample.class);
   ```

3. Start writing your `main` method:

   ```
   public static void main(String[] args) throws Exception {
   ```

4. At the very beginning of your main method, define some parameters that will be required to change or configure:

   ```
   final int numRows = 28;
   final int numColumns = 28;
   int seed = 123;
   int numSamples = MnistDataFetcher.NUM_EXAMPLES;
   int batchSize = 1000;
   int iterations = 1;
   int listenerFreq = iterations/5;
   ```

   - The rows and columns are set to 28 because the image size in the MNIST database is 28×28 pixels
   - A random seed of 123 is chosen
   - numSamples is the total number of samples in the example dataset
   - batchSize is set to 1000 so that 1000 data samples are used each time
   - `listenerFreq` decides how often we see the loss function's value for logging in the process

5. Then, load the MNIST data points with the batch size and the number of samples information:

```
log.info("Load data....");
DataSetIterator iter = new
    MnistDataSetIterator(batchSize,numSamples,true);
```

6. Next, you will be configuring the neural net. First, you build a multilayer neural net with the seed, iterations, and by setting line gradient descent as the optimization algorithm. You also set that there will be 10 layers in total: one input layer, four encoding layers, a decoding layer, and one output layer:

```
log.info("Build model....");
MultiLayerConfiguration conf = new
 NeuralNetConfiguration.Builder()
.seed(seed)
.iterations(iterations)
.optimizationAlgo(OptimizationAlgorithm.LINE_GRADIENT_DESCENT)
.list(10)
```

7. Then add the following code to the code in the previous step. This is where you create all 10 layers with back propagation set:

```
.layer(0, new RBM.Builder().nIn(numRows *
    numColumns).nOut(1000).lossFunction
      (LossFunctions.LossFunction.RMSE_XENT).build())
.layer(1, new RBM.Builder().nIn(1000).nOut(500).lossFunction
      (LossFunctions.LossFunction.RMSE_XENT).build())
.layer(2, new RBM.Builder().nIn(500).nOut(250).lossFunction
      (LossFunctions.LossFunction.RMSE_XENT).build())
.layer(3, new RBM.Builder().nIn(250).nOut(100).lossFunction
      (LossFunctions.LossFunction.RMSE_XENT).build())
.layer(4, new RBM.Builder().nIn(100).nOut(30).lossFunction
      (LossFunctions.LossFunction.RMSE_XENT).build())
      //encoding
        stops
.layer(5, new RBM.Builder().nIn(30).nOut(100).lossFunction
      (LossFunctions.LossFunction.RMSE_XENT).build())
      //decoding
        starts
.layer(6, new RBM.Builder().nIn(100).nOut(250).lossFunction
      (LossFunctions.LossFunction.RMSE_XENT).build())
.layer(7, new RBM.Builder().nIn(250).nOut(500).lossFunction
      (LossFunctions.LossFunction.RMSE_XENT).build())
.layer(8, new RBM.Builder().nIn(500).nOut(1000).lossFunction
      (LossFunctions.LossFunction.RMSE_XENT).build())
.layer(9, new OutputLayer.Builder(LossFunctions.
```

```
        LossFunction.RMSE_XENT).nIn(1000).nOut(numRows*numColumns).
            build())
    .pretrain(true).backprop(true) .build();
```

8. Now that you have configured the model, initialize it:

```
MultiLayerNetwork model = new MultiLayerNetwork(conf);
model.init();
```

9. Finalize the training:

```
model.setListeners(Arrays.asList((IterationListener) new
ScoreIterationListener(listenerFreq)));
  log.info("Train model....");
   while(iter.hasNext()) {
 DataSet next = iter.next();
  model.fit(new
    DataSet(next.getFeatureMatrix(),next.getFeatureMatrix()));
}
```

10. Finally, close the `main` method and class:

```
}
}
```

How it works...

1. Right-click on your project name in Eclipse, select New, and then select Package. Give the following as your package name: `deepbelief.chap8.science.data`. Click on **Finish**.

2. Now that you have a package, right-click on the package name, select **New**, and then select Class. The name of the class should be `DeepAutoEncoderExample`. Click on **Finish**.

In the editor, copy and paste the following code:

```
package deepbelief.chap8.science.data;
import org.deeplearning4j.datasets.fetchers.MnistDataFetcher;
import org.deeplearning4j.datasets.iterator.impl.MnistDataSetIterator;
import org.deeplearning4j.nn.api.OptimizationAlgorithm;
import org.deeplearning4j.nn.conf.MultiLayerConfiguration;
import org.deeplearning4j.nn.conf.NeuralNetConfiguration;
import org.deeplearning4j.nn.conf.layers.OutputLayer;
import org.deeplearning4j.nn.conf.layers.RBM;
```

```java
import org.deeplearning4j.nn.multilayer.MultiLayerNetwork;
import org.deeplearning4j.optimize.api.IterationListener;
import org.deeplearning4j.optimize.listeners.ScoreIterationListener;
import org.nd4j.linalg.dataset.DataSet;
import org.nd4j.linalg.dataset.api.iterator.DataSetIterator;
import org.nd4j.linalg.lossfunctions.LossFunctions;
import org.slf4j.Logger;
import org.slf4j.LoggerFactory;
import java.util.Arrays;

public class DeepAutoEncoderExample {
    private static Logger log =
      LoggerFactory.getLogger(DeepAutoEncoderExample.class);

    public static void main(String[] args) throws Exception {
        final int numRows = 28;
        final int numColumns = 28;
        int seed = 123;
        int numSamples = MnistDataFetcher.NUM_EXAMPLES;
        int batchSize = 1000;
        int iterations = 1;
        int listenerFreq = iterations/5;

        log.info("Load data....");
        DataSetIterator iter = new
          MnistDataSetIterator(batchSize,numSamples,true);

        log.info("Build model....");
        MultiLayerConfiguration conf = new
          NeuralNetConfiguration.Builder()
                .seed(seed)
                .iterations(iterations)
        .optimizationAlgo(OptimizationAlgorithm.LINE_GRADIENT_DESCENT)
                .list(10)
        .layer(0, new RBM.Builder().nIn(numRows *
          numColumns).nOut(1000).lossFunction
            (LossFunctions.LossFunction.RMSE_XENT).build())
        .layer(1, new RBM.Builder().nIn(1000).nOut(500).lossFunction
            (LossFunctions.LossFunction.RMSE_XENT).build())
        .layer(2, new RBM.Builder().nIn(500).nOut(250).lossFunction
            (LossFunctions.LossFunction.RMSE_XENT).build())
        .layer(3, new RBM.Builder().nIn(250).nOut(100).lossFunction
            (LossFunctions.LossFunction.RMSE_XENT).build())
        .layer(4, new RBM.Builder().nIn(100).nOut(30).lossFunction
            (LossFunctions.LossFunction.RMSE_XENT).build())
                //encoding
                    stops
        .layer(5, new RBM.Builder().nIn(30).nOut(100).lossFunction
```

```
                (LossFunctions.LossFunction.RMSE_XENT).build())
                //decoding
                  starts
        .layer(6, new RBM.Builder().nIn(100).nOut(250).lossFunction
                (LossFunctions.LossFunction.RMSE_XENT).build())
        .layer(7, new RBM.Builder().nIn(250).nOut(500).lossFunction
                (LossFunctions.LossFunction.RMSE_XENT).build())
        .layer(8, new RBM.Builder().nIn(500).nOut(1000).lossFunction
                (LossFunctions.LossFunction.RMSE_XENT).build())
        .layer(9, new OutputLayer.Builder(LossFunctions.
            LossFunction.RMSE_XENT).nIn(1000).nOut(numRows*numColumns).
                build())
        .pretrain(true).backprop(true) .build();

        MultiLayerNetwork model = new MultiLayerNetwork(conf);
        model.init();

        model.setListeners(Arrays.asList((IterationListener) new
            ScoreIterationListener(listenerFreq)));

        log.info("Train model....");
        while(iter.hasNext()) {
            DataSet next = iter.next();
            model.fit(new
           DataSet(next.getFeatureMatrix(),next.getFeatureMatrix()));
        }
    }
}
```

9
Visualizing Data

In this chapter, we will cover the following recipes:

- Plotting a 2D sine graph
- Plotting histograms
- Plotting a bar chart
- Plotting box plots or whisker diagrams
- Plotting scatter plots
- Plotting donut plots
- Plotting area graphs

Introduction

Data visualization is becoming increasingly popular in the data science community because it is the visual communication of information using the underlying data with the help of dots, lines, or bars. Visualization not only communicates information to the data scientist, but also presents it to an audience with no or little knowledge of the underlying data distribution or the nature of the data. On many occasions, data visualization is used by management, stakeholders, and business executives to make decisions or to understand trends.

In this chapter, we present seven recipes to visualize data using sine graphs, histograms, bar charts, box plots, scatter plots, donut or pie plots, and area graphs. This being a cookbook, we do not give enough background on these plots, their advantages, and the area of usage except a very short introduction on them. Rather, we focus on the technicalities of the Java library that can accomplish the visualizations.

In this chapter, we will be using a Java library for graphical presentation of data named GRAL–shorthand for GRAphing Library. There are a few reasons to consider GRAL for data visualization recipes in this chapter:

- A comprehensive collection of classes
- Availability of data processing features such as smoothing, rescaling, statistics, and histograms
- Availability of plots popular among data scientists. The plots include the following:
  - xy/scatter plot
  - bubble plot
  - line plot
  - area plot
  - bar plot
  - pie plot
  - donut plot
  - box-and-whisker plot
  - raster plot
- Features for displaying legends
- Several file formats are supported as data sources or data sinks (CSV, bitmap image data, audio file data)
- Exporting plots in bitmap and vector file formats (PNG, GIF, JPEG, EPS, PDF, SVG)
- Small memory footprint (about 300 kilobytes)

Interested readers are encouraged to check out a comparison of various Java data visualization libraries: `https://github.com/eseifert/gral/wiki/comparison`.

Plotting a 2D sine graph

In this recipe, we will use a free Java graph library named **GRAphing Library** (**GRAL**) to plot a 2D sine graph. On many occasions, sine graphs can be particularly useful for data scientists since they are a trigonometric graph that can be used to model fluctuations in data (for example, using temperature data to create a model that predicts the times during the year that a location would be pleasant to visit).

Getting ready

1. To use GRAL in your project, you need to download the GRAL JAR file and include it in your project as an external Java library. To download the Jar file, go to `http://trac.erichseifert.de/gral/wiki/Download` and download GRAL JAR file version 0.10 from the legacy version section. The file that you are going to download is a zip file named `gral-core-0.10.zip`:

Download

Here, you will find packaged archives for the core library of GRAL and example applications in various formats.
⇨ LGPL license.

To use GRAL in your project just add the JARs for `gral-core` and `VectorGraphics2D` to the class path of your pr‹

To use the example applications execute the JAR with `gral-core` in the classpath:

```
$ java -cp gral-core-0.11.jar gral-examples-0.11-jar
```

Stable version

Version 0.11		
GRAL	⇨ gral-core-0.11.jar (273 KiB)	
Source code	⇨ gral-core-0.11-sources.jar (290 KiB)	
JavaDoc API documentation	⇨ gral-core-0.11-javadoc.jar (771 KiB)	⇨ browse online
Example applications	⇨ gral-examples-0.11.jar (46 KiB)	

Warning: This version will break legacy code that was written for GRAL 0.10 or earlier.

Legacy versions

Version 0.10		
GRAL	⇨ gral-core-0.10.zip (1503 KiB)	⇨ gral-core-0.10.tar.bz2 (633 KiB)
Example applications	⇨ gral-examples-0.10.zip (350 KiB)	⇨ gral-examples-0.10.tar.bz2 (329 KiB)
JavaDoc API documentation	⇨ browse online	
Version 0.9		
Ready-to-include binary JAR files	⇨ GRAL-0.9-bin.zip (313 KiB)	⇨ GRAL-0.9-bin.tar.bz2 (312 KiB)
Complete source code	⇨ GRAL-0.9-src.zip (542 KiB)	⇨ GRAL-0.9-src.tar.bz2 (165 KiB)
JavaDoc API documentation	⇨ GRAL-0.9-doc.zip (1194 KiB)	⇨ GRAL-0.9-doc.tar.bz2 (266 KiB)
Version 0.8		

Once you download the file, extract the files and you will see the files and folders in the distributions. Among them, you will find a folder named `lib`, which is the folder of interest.

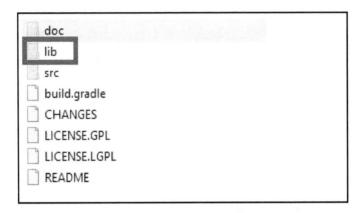

2. Go to the `lib` folder. There will be two Jar files there: `gral-core-0.10` and `VectorGraphics2D-0.9.1`. For this tutorial, you will only need to consider `gral-core-0.10.jar`:

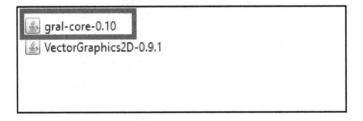

3. In our Eclipse project, we add this JAR file as an external library file:

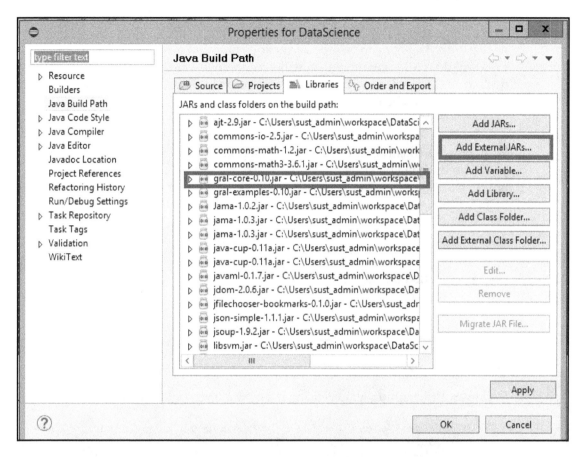

4. Now you are ready to do some coding to plot a sine graph.

How to do it...

1. First, we create a Java class named `SineGraph` that extends `JFrame`, because we are going to plot the output graph from our data onto a `JFrame`:

```
public class SineGraph extends JFrame {
```

2. Next, declare a serial version UID as a class variable:

```
private static final long serialVersionUID = 1L;
```

3. serialVersionUID can be seen as version control in a Serializable class. JVM will do it for you automatically if you do not explicitly declare serialVersionUID. More details regarding this are beyond the scope of this book and can be found at http://docs.oracle.com/javase/1.5.0/docs/api/java/io/Serializable.html .

4. Next, create a constructor for the class. The constructor will define the behavior of your frame when you close it, define the size of the frame for plotting the sine graph, and also create a data table based on the values in a for loop. Therefore, in this example, we will see a true sine graph. Your actual data might not be a perfect sine graph:

```
public SineGraph() throws FileNotFoundException, IOException {
```

5. Set default action on closing the frame:

```
setDefaultCloseOperation(EXIT_ON_CLOSE);
```

6. Set the size of the frame:

```
setSize(1600, 1400);
```

7. Create artificial x and y values using a loop and then put them in a data table:

```
DataTable data = new DataTable(Double.class, Double.class);
  for (double x = -5.0; x <= 5.0; x+=0.25) {
  double y = 5.0*Math.sin(x);
  data.add(x, y);
}
```

8. To plot a sine graph, we will be using the XYPlot class of GRAL. Create an XYPlot object by sending the data that you have created as a parameter:

```
XYPlot plot = new XYPlot(data);
```

9. Set the `plot` to interactive panel:

```
XYPlot plot = new XYPlot(data);
```

10. To render the plot, create a 2D line `renderer`. Add this line render and the data to the `XYPlot` object:

```
LineRenderer lines = new DefaultLineRenderer2D();
plot.setLineRenderer(data, lines);
```

11. With GRAL, it is possible to plot `color` graphs using its `Color` class:

```
Color color = new Color(0.0f, 0.0f, 0.0f);
```

12. As the argument for the constructor of the `Color` class, you need to send out the values of Red, Green, and Blue. In the preceding case, you are plotting a black-and-white graph since you have sent 0 as the Red, Green, and Blue values.

13. Set the color for the points and for the lines:

```
plot.getPointRenderer(data).setColor(color);
plot.getLineRenderer(data).setColor(color);
```

14. Close the constructor:

```
}
```

15. To run the program, write down the following `main()` method:

```
public static void main(String[] args) {
SineGraph frame = null;
try {
 frame = new SineGraph();
} catch (IOException e) {
}
frame.setVisible(true);
}
```

The complete code for the recipe will be as follows:

```java
import java.awt.Color;
import java.io.FileNotFoundException;
import java.io.IOException;
import javax.swing.JFrame;
import de.erichseifert.gral.data.DataTable;
import de.erichseifert.gral.plots.XYPlot;
import de.erichseifert.gral.plots.lines.DefaultLineRenderer2D;
import de.erichseifert.gral.plots.lines.LineRenderer;
import de.erichseifert.gral.ui.InteractivePanel;

public class SineGraph extends JFrame {
    private static final long serialVersionUID = 1L;

    public SineGraph() throws FileNotFoundException, IOException {
        setDefaultCloseOperation(EXIT_ON_CLOSE);
        setSize(1600, 1400);

        DataTable data = new DataTable(Double.class, Double.class);
        for (double x = -5.0; x <= 5.0; x+=0.25) {
            double y = 5.0*Math.sin(x);
            data.add(x, y);
        }

        XYPlot plot = new XYPlot(data);
        getContentPane().add(new InteractivePanel(plot));
        LineRenderer lines = new DefaultLineRenderer2D();
        plot.setLineRenderer(data, lines);
        Color color = new Color(0.0f, 0.3f, 1.0f);
        plot.getPointRenderer(data).setColor(color);
        plot.getLineRenderer(data).setColor(color);
    }

    public static void main(String[] args) {
        SineGraph frame = null;
        try {
            frame = new SineGraph();
        } catch (IOException e) {
        }
        frame.setVisible(true);
    }
}
```

The output of the program will be a nicely laid out sine graph:

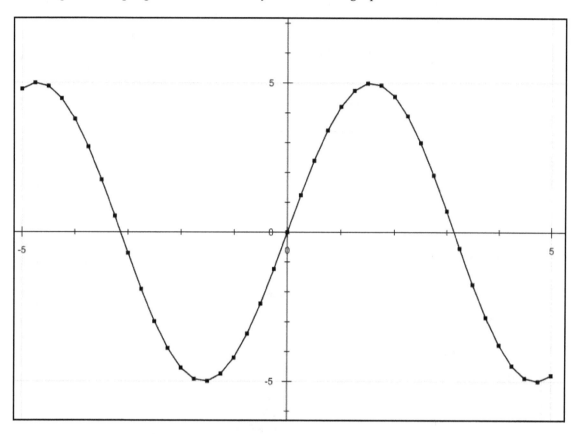

Plotting histograms

Histograms are a very popular method of discovering the frequency distribution of a set of continuous data. In a histogram, data scientists usually show the quantitative variable along the x axis and frequency of that variable along the y axis. A few key features of histograms that make it very useful are as follows:

- Only numerical data can be plotted
- Huge datasets can easily be plotted
- The x axis is usually used as bins or intervals of quantitative variables
- In this recipe, we will see how to plot histograms using **GRAL**

Getting ready

1. To use GRAL to plot histograms, we need the example applications provided with the library in the form of Jar files. These example applications can be downloaded from `http://trac.erichseifert.de/gral/wiki/Download`. Download the `gral-examples-0.10.zip` file from the download location to your local disk. Extract the files:

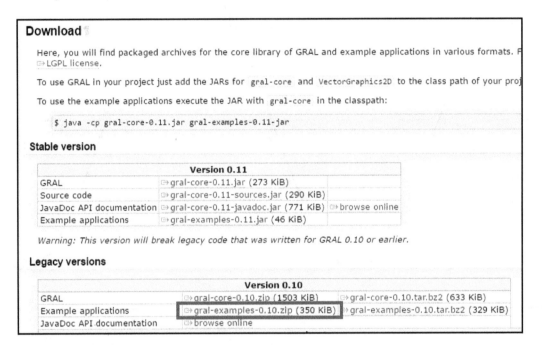

2. Once you download the Zip file and extract it, you will see a directory structure as follows, where our folder of interest is the `lib` folder:

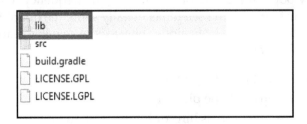

3. Inside `lib`, you will find three Jar files: `gral-core-0.10`, `gral-examples-0.10`, and `VectorGraphics2D-0.9.1`. The first one was used in the first recipe of this chapter. In this recipe, you will use the second one as well:

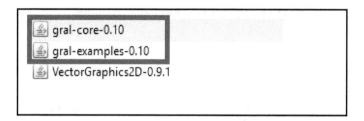

4. Include these two Jar files in your project as an external library:

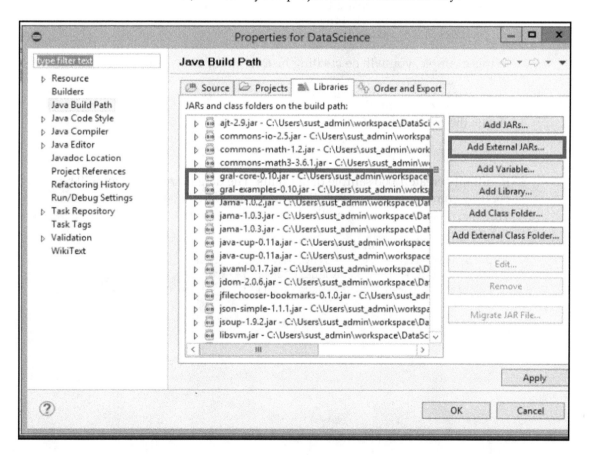

5. Now you are ready to use the program included in the GRAL example package to plot histograms. The recipe that we will see in the next section can be found at the `gral-examples-0.10\gral-examples-0.10\src\main\java\de\erichseifert\gral\examples\barplot` of the example package that you have downloaded.

How to do it...

1. Create a class named `HistogramPlot` that will extend the `ExamplePanel` class. Create a serial version UID:

```
public class HistogramPlot extends ExamplePanel {
private static final long serialVersionUID =
    4458280577519421950L;
```

2. In this example, you will be creating histogram for `1000` sample data point:

```
private static final int SAMPLE_COUNT = 1000;
```

3. Create the constructor of the class:

```
public HistogramPlot() {
```

4. Randomly create 1,000 sample data points. The data points that you will be creating come from a Gaussian distribution as you will be using `random.nextGaussian()` method of Java `Random` class:

```
Random random = new Random();
DataTable data = new DataTable(Double.class);
 for (int i = 0; i < SAMPLE_COUNT; i++) {
    data.add(random.nextGaussian());
 }
```

5. Create a `histogram` from the data and the create a second dimension for plotting:

```
Histogram1D histogram = new Histogram1D(data,
    Orientation.VERTICAL,new Number[] {-4.0, -3.2, -2.4, -1.6,
       -0.8, 0.0, 0.8, 1.6, 2.4, 3.2, 4.0});
DataSource histogram2d = new EnumeratedData(histogram, (-4.0 +
    -3.2)/2.0, 0.8);
```

6. The values in the array are the intervals or bins on the *x* axis of your histogram:

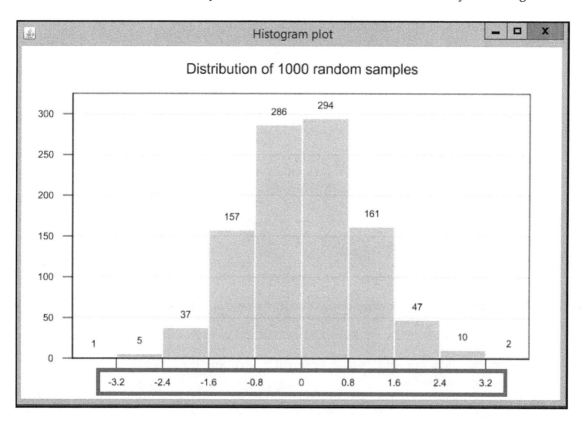

7. As you see that histograms are `Barplot`, create a bar plot and provide your histogram information to the bar plot:

```
BarPlot plot = new BarPlot(histogram2d);
```

8. Now, format the plot area.

9. Set the co-ordinates of the histogram inside the frame:

```
plot.setInsets(new Insets2D.Double(20.0, 65.0, 50.0, 40.0));
```

10. Set the title of the histogram:

```
plot.getTitle().setText(
String.format("Distribution of %d random samples",
  data.getRowCount()));
```

11. Set the width of the histogram bars:

```
plot.setBarWidth(0.78);
```

12. Format the x axis. If you are familiar with Microsoft Excel, then you must know that there are options for tick alignment and spacing for a given axis as well. Users can select if they want to see the minor ticks on the axis. GRAL, fortunately, gives you this facility, which makes your graphing more appealing to the scientific community.

13. Configure the tick alignment for *x* axis. Note the argument for the `getAxisRenderer()` method, which is for *x* axis:

```
plot.getAxisRenderer(BarPlot.AXIS_X).setTickAlignment(0.0);
```

14. Configure the tick spacing:

```
plot.getAxisRenderer(BarPlot.AXIS_X).setTickSpacing(0.8);
```

15. Finally, configure the minor ticks so that they are not visible:

```
plot.getAxisRenderer(BarPlot.AXIS_X).setMinorTicksVisible(false);
```

16. Format the *y* axis. In this case, you will be defining the range of height that the bars can extend to:

```
plot.getAxis(BarPlot.AXIS_Y).setRange(0.0,
MathUtils.ceil(histogram.getStatistics().get(Statistics.MAX)*1.1,
  25.0));
```

17. Also set the tick alignment, spacing, and visibility of minor ticks as you did for the *x* axis:

```
plot.getAxisRenderer(BarPlot.AXIS_Y).setTickAlignment(0.0);
plot.getAxisRenderer(BarPlot.AXIS_Y).setMinorTicksVisible(false);
plot.getAxisRenderer(BarPlot.AXIS_Y).setIntersection(-4.4);
```

18. Next, format the bars. Set the colors of the bars and configure your histogram to display the frequency values at the top of the bars:

```
plot.getPointRenderer(histogram2d).setColor(
GraphicsUtils.deriveWithAlpha(COLOR1, 128));
plot.getPointRenderer(histogram2d).setValueVisible(true);
```

19. Finally, add the plot to swing components:

```
InteractivePanel panel = new InteractivePanel(plot);
panel.setPannable(false);
panel.setZoomable(false);
add(panel);
```

20. Close the constructor:

```
}
```

21. You also need to implement all the methods in the ExamplePanel class. To make it simple, override the getTitle() and getDescription() methods as follows:

```
@Override
 public String getTitle() {
    return "Histogram plot";
 }
@Override
   public String getDescription() {
     return String.format("Histogram of %d samples",
      SAMPLE_COUNT);
   }
```

22. The main method of the class will be as follows:

```
public static void main(String[] args) {
new HistogramPlot().showInFrame();
}
```

23. Finally, close the class:

```
}
```

24. The complete code for the recipe is as follows:

```java
import java.util.Random;
import de.erichseifert.gral.data.DataSource;
import de.erichseifert.gral.data.DataTable;
import de.erichseifert.gral.data.EnumeratedData;
import de.erichseifert.gral.data.statistics.Histogram1D;
import de.erichseifert.gral.data.statistics.Statistics;
import de.erichseifert.gral.examples.ExamplePanel;
import de.erichseifert.gral.plots.BarPlot;
import de.erichseifert.gral.ui.InteractivePanel;
import de.erichseifert.gral.util.GraphicsUtils;
import de.erichseifert.gral.util.Insets2D;
import de.erichseifert.gral.util.MathUtils;
import de.erichseifert.gral.util.Orientation;


public class HistogramPlot extends ExamplePanel {
    /** Version id for serialization. */
    private static final long serialVersionUID = 4458280577519421950L;

    private static final int SAMPLE_COUNT = 1000;

    //@SuppressWarnings("unchecked")
    public HistogramPlot() {
        // Create example data
        Random random = new Random();
        DataTable data = new DataTable(Double.class);
        for (int i = 0; i < SAMPLE_COUNT; i++) {
            data.add(random.nextGaussian());
        }

        // Create histogram from data
        Histogram1D histogram = new Histogram1D(data,
         Orientation.VERTICAL, new Number[] {-4.0, -3.2, -2.4, -1.6,
            -0.8, 0.0, 0.8, 1.6, 2.4, 3.2, 4.0});
        // Create a second dimension (x axis) for plotting
        DataSource histogram2d = new EnumeratedData(histogram, (-4.0 +
            -3.2)/2.0, 0.8);

        // Create new bar plot
        BarPlot plot = new BarPlot(histogram2d);

        // Format plot
```

```
        plot.setInsets(new Insets2D.Double(20.0, 65.0, 50.0, 40.0));
        plot.getTitle().setText(
                String.format("Distribution of %d random samples",
                    data.getRowCount())));
        plot.setBarWidth(0.78);

        // Format x axis
        plot.getAxisRenderer(BarPlot.AXIS_X).setTickAlignment(0.0);
        plot.getAxisRenderer(BarPlot.AXIS_X).setTickSpacing(0.8);
        plot.getAxisRenderer(BarPlot.AXIS_X).setMinorTicksVisible(false);
        // Format y axis
        plot.getAxis(BarPlot.AXIS_Y).setRange(0.0,
            MathUtils.ceil(histogram.getStatistics().
                get(Statistics.MAX)*1.1, 25.0));
        plot.getAxisRenderer(BarPlot.AXIS_Y).setTickAlignment(0.0);
        plot.getAxisRenderer(BarPlot.AXIS_Y).setMinorTicksVisible(false);
        plot.getAxisRenderer(BarPlot.AXIS_Y).setIntersection(-4.4);

        // Format bars
        plot.getPointRenderer(histogram2d).setColor(
            GraphicsUtils.deriveWithAlpha(COLOR1, 128));
        plot.getPointRenderer(histogram2d).setValueVisible(true);

        // Add plot to Swing component
        InteractivePanel panel = new InteractivePanel(plot);
        panel.setPannable(false);
        panel.setZoomable(false);
        add(panel);
    }

    @Override
    public String getTitle() {
        return "Histogram plot";
    }

    @Override
    public String getDescription() {
        return String.format("Histogram of %d samples", SAMPLE_COUNT);
    }

    public static void main(String[] args) {
        new HistogramPlot().showInFrame();
    }
}
```

Plotting a bar chart

Bar plots are the most common graph types used by data scientists. It is simple to draw a bar chart using GRAL. In this recipe, we will be using GRAL to plot the following bar chart:

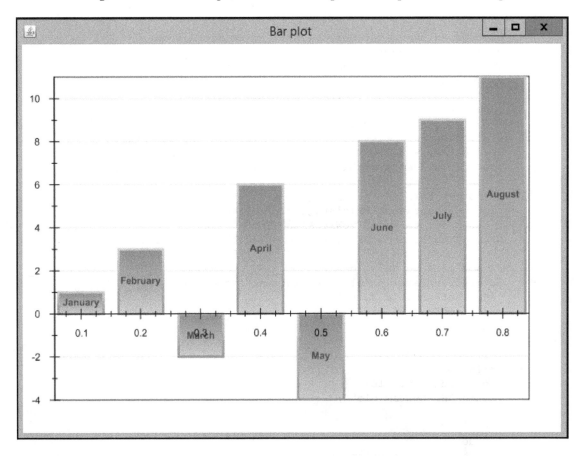

Getting ready

1. To use GRAL to plot bar charts, we need the example applications provided with the library in the form of Jar files. These example applications can be downloaded from `http://trac.erichseifert.de/gral/wiki/Download`. Download the `gral-examples-0.10.zip` file from the download location into your local disk. Extract the files.

2. Once you download the ZIP files, and extract them, you will see a directory structure as shown in the *Getting ready* section of the *Plotting a 2D sine graph* recipe, where our folder of interest is the `lib` folder.

3. Inside the `lib` folder, you will find three Jar files: `gral-core-0.10`, `gral-examples-0.10`, and `VectorGraphics2D-0.9.1`. In this recipe, you will be using the first two of the aforementioned Jar files.

4. Include these two JAR files in your project as external libraries.

Now you are ready to use the program included in the GRAL example package to plot histograms. The recipe that we will see in the next section can be found at the `gral-examples-0.10\gral-examples-0.10\src\main\java\de\erichseifert\gral\examples\barplot` of the example package that you have downloaded.

How to do it...

1. Create a class named `SimpleBarPlot`. Like the previous recipe, this class will extend the `ExamplePanel` class of the GRAL library:

   ```
   publicclassSimpleBarPlotextendsExamplePanel {
   ```

2. Create a serial version UID:

   ```
   privatestaticfinallong serialVersionUID =-2793954497895054530L;
   ```

3. Start developing the constructor:

   ```
   publicSimpleBarPlot() {
   ```

4. First, you will create example data. In the bar chart shown at the beginning of this recipe, each bar has three values: the value of the x axis, the value of the y axis, and the name of the bar. For example, the first bar has an x axis value of 0.1, a y axis value of 1 and the name January. You will create data points for all the bars in the following way:

```
DataTable data = new DataTable(Double.class, Integer.class,
    String.class);
data.add(0.1, 1, "January");
data.add(0.2, 3, "February");
data.add(0.3, -2, "March");
data.add(0.4, 6, "April");
data.add(0.5, -4, "May");
data.add(0.6, 8, "June");
data.add(0.7, 9, "July");
data.add(0.8, 11, "August");
```

5. The constructor of the DataTable class takes three values here: x axis (double), y axis (integer), and finally, the name of the bar (String).

6. The rest of the coding will be used to format your bar chart.

7. Create a new bar chart:

```
BarPlot plot = newBarPlot(data);
```

8. Set the dimension of the bar chart thickness of the bars in your chart:

```
plot.setInsets(new Insets2D.Double(40.0, 40.0, 40.0, 40.0));
plot.setBarWidth(0.075);
```

9. Now, you will be formatting your bars. To do so, first you need to create a BarRenderer using your data:

```
BarRenderer pointRenderer = (BarRenderer)
    plot.getPointRenderer(data);
```

10. Next, set the color of the bars:

```
pointRenderer.setColor(
  new LinearGradientPaint(0f,0f, 0f,1f,
  new float[] { 0.0f, 1.0f },
  new Color[] { COLOR1, GraphicsUtils.deriveBrighter(COLOR1) }
  )
);
```

11. Next, set the properties of the bar chart:

    To show the values on the bar chart, use this code:

    ```
    pointRenderer.setValueVisible(true);
    ```

    Set the third value (name of the month) in your data as the value column:

    ```
    pointRenderer.setValueColumn(2);
    ```

    Set the position of the values to center:

    ```
    pointRenderer.setValueLocation(Location.CENTER);
    ```

    Set the color of the values:

    ```
    pointRenderer.setValueColor(GraphicsUtils.deriveDarker(COLOR1));
    ```

    Turn on the boldface feature of the value font:

    ```
    pointRenderer.setValueFont(Font.decode
        (null).deriveFont(Font.BOLD));
    ```

12. Add the bar chart to the `Swing` component:

    ```
    add(newInteractivePanel(plot));
    ```

13. Close the constructor:

    ```
    }
    ```

14. You need to implement two more methods that are in the `ExamplePanel` class of the GRAL library:

    ```
    @Override
    public String getTitle() {
     return "Bar plot";
    }
    @Override
     public String getDescription() {
        return "Bar plot with example data and color gradients";
     }
    ```

15. The `main` method to run the code so far will look like this:

```
public static void main(String[] args) {
new SimpleBarPlot().showInFrame();
}
```

16. Close the class:

```
}
```

The complete source code for the recipe is as follows:

```
import java.awt.Color;
import java.awt.Font;
import java.awt.LinearGradientPaint;
import de.erichseifert.gral.data.DataTable;
import de.erichseifert.gral.examples.ExamplePanel;
import de.erichseifert.gral.plots.BarPlot;
import de.erichseifert.gral.plots.BarPlot.BarRenderer;
import de.erichseifert.gral.ui.InteractivePanel;
import de.erichseifert.gral.util.GraphicsUtils;
import de.erichseifert.gral.util.Insets2D;
import de.erichseifert.gral.util.Location;

public class SimpleBarPlot extends ExamplePanel {
    /** Version id for serialization. */
    private static final long serialVersionUID = -2793954497895054530L;

    @SuppressWarnings("unchecked")
    public SimpleBarPlot() {
        // Create example data
        DataTable data = new DataTable(Double.class, Integer.class,
            String.class);
        data.add(0.1,  1, "January");
        data.add(0.2,  3, "February");
        data.add(0.3, -2, "March");
        data.add(0.4,  6, "April");
        data.add(0.5, -4, "May");
        data.add(0.6,  8, "June");
        data.add(0.7,  9, "July");
        data.add(0.8, 11, "August");

        // Create new bar plot
        BarPlot plot = new BarPlot(data);

        // Format plot
        plot.setInsets(new Insets2D.Double(40.0, 40.0, 40.0, 40.0));
        plot.setBarWidth(0.075);
```

```
    // Format bars
    BarRenderer pointRenderer = (BarRenderer)
      plot.getPointRenderer(data);
    pointRenderer.setColor(
        new LinearGradientPaint(0f,0f, 0f,1f,
            new float[] { 0.0f, 1.0f },
            new Color[] { COLOR1,
                GraphicsUtils.deriveBrighter(COLOR1) }
        )
    );
    /*pointRenderer.setBorderStroke(new BasicStroke(3f));
    pointRenderer.setBorderColor(
        new LinearGradientPaint(0f,0f, 0f,1f,
            new float[] { 0.0f, 1.0f },
            new Color[] { GraphicsUtils.deriveBrighter(COLOR1),
             COLOR1 }
        )
    );*/
    pointRenderer.setValueVisible(true);
    pointRenderer.setValueColumn(2);
    pointRenderer.setValueLocation(Location.CENTER);
    pointRenderer.setValueColor(GraphicsUtils.deriveDarker(COLOR1));
pointRenderer.setValueFont(Font.decode(null).deriveFont(Font.BOLD));

    // Add plot to Swing component
    add(new InteractivePanel(plot));
  }

  @Override
  public String getTitle() {
    return "Bar plot";
  }

  @Override
  public String getDescription() {
    return "Bar plot with example data and color gradients";
  }

  public static void main(String[] args) {
    new SimpleBarPlot().showInFrame();
  }
}
```

Plotting box plots or whisker diagrams

Box plots are another effective visualization tool for data scientists. They give important descriptive statistics of a data distribution. A typical box plot will contain the following information about a data distribution:

- Minimum value
- First quartile
- Median
- Third quartile
- Maximum value

Other values such as inter-quartile range can also be derived from these statistics by getting the difference between the third and first quartiles.

In this recipe, you will be using GRAL to draw box plots for data distributions.

Getting ready

1. To use GRAL to plot bar charts, we need the example applications provided with the library in the form of Jar files. These example applications can be downloaded from `http://trac.erichseifert.de/gral/wiki/Download`. Download the `gral-examples-0.10.zip` file from the download location into your local disk. Extract the files.
2. Once you download the ZIP files and extract them, you will see a directory structure as shown in the *Getting ready* section of the *Plotting a 2D sine graph* recipe. Our folder of interest is the `lib` folder.
3. Inside `lib`, you will find three Jar files: `gral-core-0.10`, `gral-examples-0.10`, and `VectorGraphics2D-0.9.1`. In this recipe, you will be using the first two of the aforementioned Jar files.
4. Include these two JAR files in your project as external libraries.

Now you are ready to use the program included in the GRAL example package to plot box plots. The recipe that we will see in the next section can be found at the `gral-examples-0.10\gral-examples-0.10\src\main\java\de\erichseifert\gral\examples\boxplot` of the example package that you have downloaded. When you successfully run the code in this recipe, you will see box plots like this:

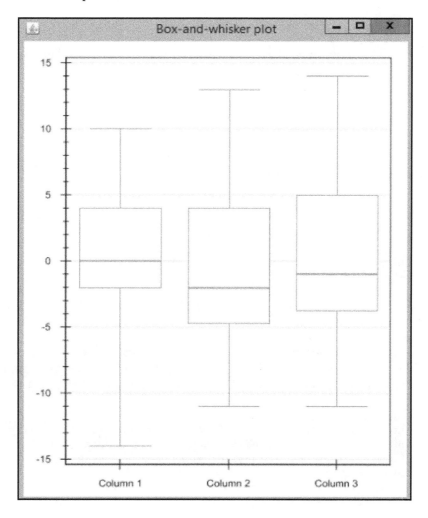

How to do it...

1. First, create a class named `SimpleBoxPlot` that extends the class `ExamplePanel` in the GRAL library. Provide a serial version UID:

```
public class SimpleBoxPlot extends ExamplePanel {
private static final long serialVersionUID =
    5228891435595348789L;
```

2. You will be generating 50 random samples for the box plots that you will be creating and rendering. Create the following class variables:

```
private static final int SAMPLE_COUNT = 50;
private static final Random random = new Random();
```

3. Create the constructor for the class:

```
public SimpleBoxPlot() {
```

4. Set the dimensions of your box plot window:

```
setPreferredSize(new Dimension(400, 600));
```

5. Create a data table where each row will contain three column values and all of them are integers:

```
DataTable data = new DataTable(Integer.class, Integer.class,
    Integer.class);
```

6. Generate 50 data samples with three integer values (the column values in the data table). The data samples will contain values from a Gaussian distribution (you won't necessarily need to draw them from a Gaussian distribution):

```
for (int i = 0; i < SAMPLE_COUNT; i++) {
int x = (int) Math.round(5.0*random.nextGaussian());
int y = (int) Math.round(5.0*random.nextGaussian());
int z = (int) Math.round(5.0*random.nextGaussian());
data.add(x, y, z);
}
```

7. Create a new box plot with the data:

```
DataSource boxData = BoxPlot.createBoxData(data);
BoxPlot plot = new BoxPlot(boxData);
```

8. Set the dimension of the inset of your window where you are going to plot the Boxplot:

```
plot.setInsets(newInsets2D.Double(20.0, 50.0, 40.0, 20.0));
```

9. Format the values in the *x* axis:

```
plot.getAxisRenderer(BoxPlot.AXIS_X).setCustomTicks(
DataUtils.map(
new Double[] {1.0, 2.0, 3.0},
new String[] {"Column 1", "Column 2", "Column 3"}
)
);
```

10. The rest of the code will be rendering the box plots. First, create a point renderer with the data:

```
BoxWhiskerRenderer pointRenderer =
    (BoxWhiskerRenderer) plot.getPointRenderer(boxData);
```

11. Next, set the box plot's border colors, the colors of the whiskers (third quartile to maximum and minimum to first quartile) and center bar (median bar):

```
pointRenderer.setBoxBorderColor(COLOR1);
pointRenderer.setWhiskerColor(COLOR1);
pointRenderer.setCenterBarColor(COLOR1);
```

12. For box pots, use vertical navigation:

```
plot.getNavigator().setDirection(XYNavigationDirection.VERTICAL);
```

13. Send the box plot to the swing component for rendering:

```
InteractivePanel panel = new InteractivePanel(plot);
add(panel);
```

14. Close the constructor:

```
}
```

15. You need to implement the following two methods in the ExamplePanel class by overriding them:

```
@Override
public String getTitle() {
return "Box-and-whisker plot";
}
@Override
public String getDescription() {
return String.format("Three box-and-whisker plots created from
%d random samples", SAMPLE_COUNT);
}
```

16. Then, add the `main` method and close the class:

```
public static void main(String[] args) {
new SimpleBoxPlot().showInFrame();
}
}
```

17. The complete source code is given here:

```
import java.awt.Dimension;
import java.util.Random;
import de.erichseifert.gral.data.DataSource;
import de.erichseifert.gral.data.DataTable;
import de.erichseifert.gral.examples.ExamplePanel;
import de.erichseifert.gral.plots.BoxPlot;
import de.erichseifert.gral.plots.BoxPlot.BoxWhiskerRenderer;
import de.erichseifert.gral.plots.XYPlot.XYNavigationDirection;
import de.erichseifert.gral.ui.InteractivePanel;
import de.erichseifert.gral.util.DataUtils;
import de.erichseifert.gral.util.Insets2D;

public class SimpleBoxPlot extends ExamplePanel {
    /** Version id for serialization. */
    private static final long serialVersionUID = 5228891435595348789L;
    private static final int SAMPLE_COUNT = 50;
    private static final Random random = new Random();

    @SuppressWarnings("unchecked")
    public SimpleBoxPlot() {
        setPreferredSize(new Dimension(400, 600));

        // Create example data
        DataTable data = new DataTable(Integer.class, Integer.class,
            Integer.class);
```

```
    for (int i = 0; i < SAMPLE_COUNT; i++) {
        int x = (int) Math.round(5.0*random.nextGaussian());
        int y = (int) Math.round(5.0*random.nextGaussian());
        int z = (int) Math.round(5.0*random.nextGaussian());
        data.add(x, y, z);
    }

    // Create new box-and-whisker plot
    DataSource boxData = BoxPlot.createBoxData(data);
    BoxPlot plot = new BoxPlot(boxData);

    // Format plot
    plot.setInsets(new Insets2D.Double(20.0, 50.0, 40.0, 20.0));

    // Format axes
    plot.getAxisRenderer(BoxPlot.AXIS_X).setCustomTicks(
        DataUtils.map(
            new Double[] {1.0, 2.0, 3.0},
            new String[] {"Column 1", "Column 2", "Column 3"}
        )
    );

    // Format boxes
    /*Stroke stroke = new BasicStroke(2f);
    ScaledContinuousColorMapper colors =
        new LinearGradient(GraphicsUtils.deriveBrighter(COLOR1),
            Color.WHITE);
    colors.setRange(1.0, 3.0);*/

    BoxWhiskerRenderer pointRenderer =
            (BoxWhiskerRenderer) plot.getPointRenderer(boxData);
    /*pointRenderer.setWhiskerStroke(stroke);
    pointRenderer.setBoxBorderStroke(stroke);
    pointRenderer.setBoxBackground(colors);*/
    pointRenderer.setBoxBorderColor(COLOR1);
    pointRenderer.setWhiskerColor(COLOR1);
    pointRenderer.setCenterBarColor(COLOR1);

    plot.getNavigator().setDirection(XYNavigationDirection.VERTICAL);

    // Add plot to Swing component
    InteractivePanel panel = new InteractivePanel(plot);
    add(panel);
}

@Override
public String getTitle() {
    return "Box-and-whisker plot";
```

```
    }

    @Override
    public String getDescription() {
        return String.format("Three box-and-whisker plots created from %d
            random samples", SAMPLE_COUNT);
    }

    public static void main(String[] args) {
        new SimpleBoxPlot().showInFrame();
    }
}
```

Plotting scatter plots

This recipe demonstrates how to use GRAL to draw scatter plots for 100,000 random data points. Scatter plots use both the *x* and *y* axes to plot data points and are a good means to demonstrate the correlation between variables.

Getting ready

1. To use GRAL for plotting bar charts, we need the example applications provided with the library in the form of Jar files. These example applications can be downloaded from http://trac.erichseifert.de/gral/wiki/Download. Download the gral-examples-0.10.zip file from the download location into your local disk. Extract the files.

2. Once you've downloaded the ZIP files and extracted them, you will see a directory structure as shown in the *Getting ready* section of the *Plotting a 2D sine graph* recipe. Our folder of interest is the lib folder.

3. Inside lib, you will find three Jar files: gral-core-0.10, gral-examples-0.10, and VectorGraphics2D-0.9.1. In this recipe, you will be using the first two of the aforementioned Jar files.

4. Include these two Jar files in your project as external libraries.

Now you are ready to use the program included in the GRAL example package to plot scatter plots. The recipe that we will see in the next section can be found at `gral-examples-0.10\gral-examples-0.10\src\main\java\de\erichseifert\gral\examples\xyplot` in the example package that you have downloaded. When you successfully run the code in this recipe, you will see a scatter plot of 100,000 random data points, as follows:

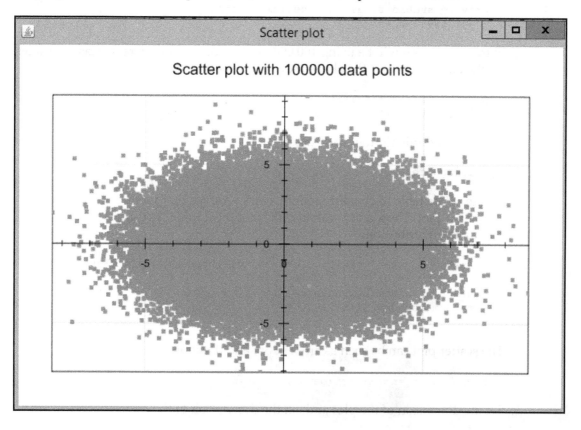

How to do it...

1. First, create a class named `ScatterPlot` that extends the `ExamplePanel` class of the GRAL library. Add the serial version UID in the class:

    ```
    public class ScatterPlot extends ExamplePanel {
    private static final long serialVersionUID =
      -412699430625953887L;
    ```

2. In the recipe, you will be using 100,000 random data points. Create class variables for the data points and the element of randomness in them:

    ```
    private static final int SAMPLE_COUNT = 100000;
    private static final Random random = new Random();
    ```

3. Start writing code for the constructor:

    ```
    publicScatterPlot() {
    ```

4. Create a data table to contain random x and y values that you will be plotting in the scatter plot. The x and y values will be of the double type and are drawn from a Gaussian distribution:

    ```
    DataTable data = new DataTable(Double.class, Double.class);
    for (int i = 0; i <= SAMPLE_COUNT; i++) {
    data.add(random.nextGaussian()*2.0,
     random.nextGaussian()*2.0);
     }
    ```

5. The scatter plot can be seen as an `XYplot`, and therefore, we create one:

    ```
    XYPlot plot =newXYPlot(data);
    ```

6. Set the dimension of the plot and get the description of the plot:

    ```
    plot.setInsets(new Insets2D.Double(20.0, 40.0, 40.0, 40.0));
    plot.getTitle().setText(getDescription());
    ```

7. Format the data points and add some color to them:

    ```
    plot.getPointRenderer(data).setColor(COLOR1);
    ```

8. Finally, send the plot to the Java Swing component and close the constructor:

```
add(new InteractivePanel(plot), BorderLayout.CENTER);
}
```

9. You also need to implement the following two methods as you are extending the ExamplePanel class:

```
@Override
public String getTitle() {
return "Scatter plot";
}
@Override
public String getDescription() {
return String.format("Scatter plot with %d data points",
SAMPLE_COUNT);
}
```

10. Finally, put the main method block to run the code and close the class:

```
public static void main(String[] args) {
new ScatterPlot().showInFrame();
}
}
```

The source code for the recipe is as follows:

```
import java.awt.BorderLayout;
import java.util.Random;
import de.erichseifert.gral.data.DataTable;
import de.erichseifert.gral.examples.ExamplePanel;
import de.erichseifert.gral.plots.XYPlot;
import de.erichseifert.gral.ui.InteractivePanel;
import de.erichseifert.gral.util.Insets2D;

public class ScatterPlot extends ExamplePanel {
    /** Version id for serialization. */
    private static final long serialVersionUID = -4126994306259538887L;

    private static final int SAMPLE_COUNT = 100000;
    /** Instance to generate random data values. */
    private static final Random random = new Random();

    @SuppressWarnings("unchecked")
    public ScatterPlot() {
        // Generate 100,000 data points
        DataTable data = new DataTable(Double.class, Double.class);
        for (int i = 0; i <= SAMPLE_COUNT; i++) {
```

```
        data.add(random.nextGaussian()*2.0,
          random.nextGaussian()*2.0);
    }

    // Create a new xy-plot
    XYPlot plot = new XYPlot(data);

    // Format plot
    plot.setInsets(new Insets2D.Double(20.0, 40.0, 40.0, 40.0));
    plot.getTitle().setText(getDescription());

    // Format points
    plot.getPointRenderer(data).setColor(COLOR1);

    // Add plot to Swing component
    add(new InteractivePanel(plot), BorderLayout.CENTER);
    }

    @Override
    public String getTitle() {
        return "Scatter plot";
    }

    @Override
    public String getDescription() {
        return String.format("Scatter plot with %d data points",
          SAMPLE_COUNT);
    }

    public static void main(String[] args) {
        new ScatterPlot().showInFrame();
    }
}
```

Plotting donut plots

Donut plots a version of pie chart, are a popular data visualization technique that give visuals for proportions in your data. In this recipe, we will see how we can use the GRAL Java library to plot donut plots for 10 random variables.

Getting ready

1. To use GRAL for plotting bar charts, we need the example applications provided with the library in the form of Jar files. These example applications can be downloaded from `http://trac.erichseifert.de/gral/wiki/Download`. Download the `gral-examples-0.10.zip` file from the download location into your local disk. Extract the files.

2. You will see a directory structure as in the *Getting ready* section of the *Plotting a 2D sine graph* recipe. Our folder of interest is the `lib` folder.

3. Inside `lib`, you will find three Jar files: `gral-core-0.10`, `gral-examples-0.10`, and `VectorGraphics2D-0.9.1`. In this recipe, you will be using the first two of the aforementioned Jar files.

4. Include these two Jar files in your project as external library.

Now you are ready to use the program included in the GRAL example package to plot donut plots. The recipe that we will see in the next section can be found at `gral-examples-0.10\gral-examples-0.10\src\main\java\de\erichseifert\gral\examples\pieplot` in the example package that you have downloaded. When you successfully run the code in this recipe, you will see a **Donut plot of 10 random data values** similar to this:

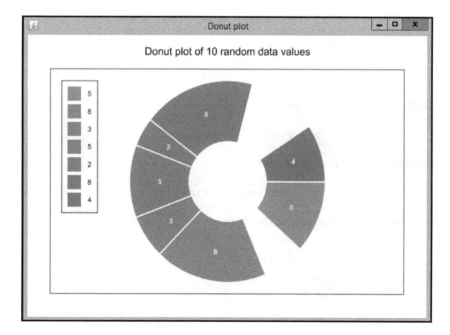

How to do it…

1. Create a class named `SimplePiePlot` that extends the `ExamplePanel` class of the GRAL library. Provide a serial version UID:

   ```
   public class SimplePiePlot extends ExamplePanel {
   ```

2. Next, declare two class variables for generating 10 random data points:

   ```
   privatestaticfinalintSAMPLE_COUNT = 10;
   privatestatic Random random = new Random();
   ```

3. Start writing the code for your constructor:

   ```
   public SimplePiePlot() {
   ```

4. Create a data table and put 10 random numbers in it. In this example, you will be generating a random integer with seed value 8 and add 2 always with the random number generated by the Random class. Then, when you will be adding the value to your data table, you check whether the generated value is less than or equal to 0.15. If the value satisfies this condition, then add the negative of the generated value; otherwise, add the value as it is to your data table:

   ```
   DataTable data = new DataTable(Integer.class);
   for (int i = 0; i < SAMPLE_COUNT; i++) {
   int val = random.nextInt(8) + 2;
   data.add((random.nextDouble() <= 0.15) ? -val : val);
   }
   ```

5. Create a `PiePlot` with your data:

   ```
   PiePlot plot = new PiePlot(data);
   ```

6. Get the title of your donut plot:

   ```
   plot.getTitle().setText(getDescription());
   ```

7. Now, set the relative size of the donut:

   ```
   plot.setRadius(0.9);
   ```

8. If you want to see the legends visible on your plot, set the legend visible to `true`; set it to `false` otherwise:

```
plot.setLegendVisible(true);
```

9. Provide the dimension of your plot:

```
plot.setInsets(new Insets2D.Double(20.0, 40.0, 40.0, 40.0));
```

10. Create a point render for your donut plot:

```
PieSliceRenderer pointRenderer =
    (PieSliceRenderer) plot.getPointRenderer(data);
```

11. Set the relative size of the inner region:

```
pointRenderer.setInnerRadius(0.4);
```

12. Set a reasonable gap between slices:

```
pointRenderer.setGap(0.2);
```

13. Change the color of the slices:

```
LinearGradient colors = new LinearGradient(COLOR1, COLOR2);
pointRenderer.setColor(colors);
```

14. Format the labels and how you want to display them. In this example, you are displaying the values in white and in bold font:

```
pointRenderer.setValueVisible(true);
pointRenderer.setValueColor(Color.WHITE);
pointRenderer.setValueFont(Font.decode(null)
.deriveFont(Font.BOLD));
```

15. Finally, add the plot to Swing component:

```
add(new InteractivePanel(plot), BorderLayout.CENTER);
```

16. Close the constructor:

```
}
```

17. You need to implement two more methods in your code as you have extended your class from the `ExamplePanel` class:

```
@Override
public String getTitle() {
return "Donut plot";
}
 @Override
  public String getDescription() {
  return String.format("Donut plot of %d random data values",
    SAMPLE_COUNT);
  }
```

18. Add the main method to run the code:

```
publicstaticvoid main(String[] args) {
new SimplePiePlot().showInFrame();
}
```

19. Close your class:

```
}
```

20. The code for the recipe is as follows:

```
import java.awt.BorderLayout;
import java.awt.Color;
import java.awt.Font;
import java.util.Random;
import de.erichseifert.gral.data.DataTable;
import de.erichseifert.gral.examples.ExamplePanel;
import de.erichseifert.gral.plots.PiePlot;
import de.erichseifert.gral.plots.PiePlot.PieSliceRenderer;
import de.erichseifert.gral.plots.colors.LinearGradient;
import de.erichseifert.gral.ui.InteractivePanel;
import de.erichseifert.gral.util.Insets2D;

public class SimplePiePlot extends ExamplePanel {
    /** Version id for serialization. */
    private static final long serialVersionUID = -3039317265508932299L;

    private static final int SAMPLE_COUNT = 10;
    /** Instance to generate random data values. */
    private static Random random = new Random();

    @SuppressWarnings("unchecked")
    public SimplePiePlot() {
```

```
    // Create data
    DataTable data = new DataTable(Integer.class);
    for (int i = 0; i < SAMPLE_COUNT; i++) {
        int val = random.nextInt(8) + 2;
        data.add((random.nextDouble() <= 0.15) ? -val : val);
    }

    // Create new pie plot
    PiePlot plot = new PiePlot(data);

    // Format plot
    plot.getTitle().setText(getDescription());
    // Change relative size of pie
    plot.setRadius(0.9);
    // Display a legend
    plot.setLegendVisible(true);
    // Add some margin to the plot area
    plot.setInsets(new Insets2D.Double(20.0, 40.0, 40.0, 40.0));

    PieSliceRenderer pointRenderer =
            (PieSliceRenderer) plot.getPointRenderer(data);
    // Change relative size of inner region
    pointRenderer.setInnerRadius(0.4);
    // Change the width of gaps between segments
    pointRenderer.setGap(0.2);
    // Change the colors
    LinearGradient colors = new LinearGradient(COLOR1, COLOR2);
    pointRenderer.setColor(colors);
    // Show labels
    pointRenderer.setValueVisible(true);
    pointRenderer.setValueColor(Color.WHITE);
    pointRenderer.setValueFont(Font.decode(null).deriveFont(Font.BOLD));

    // Add plot to Swing component
    add(new InteractivePanel(plot), BorderLayout.CENTER);
}

@Override
public String getTitle() {
    return "Donut plot";
}

@Override
public String getDescription() {
    return String.format("Donut plot of %d random data values",
        SAMPLE_COUNT);
}
```

```
        public static void main(String[] args) {
            new SimplePiePlot().showInFrame();
        }
    }
```

Plotting area graphs

Area graphs are useful tools to display how quantitative values develop over a given interval. For data scientists, they are an effective means of understanding trends. They are based on line graphs, but the area beneath the line drawn based on the values in the axes is filled with a certain color or texture. In this recipe, you will be using the GRAL Java library to plot area graphs.

Getting ready

1. To use GRAL to plot bar charts, we need the example applications provided with the library in the form of Jar files. These example applications can be downloaded from `http://trac.erichseifert.de/gral/wiki/Download`. Download the `gral-examples-0.10.zip` file from the download location into your local disk. Extract the files.

2. Then you will see a directory structure as in the *Getting ready* section of the *Plotting a 2D sine graph* recipe. Our folder of interest is the `lib` folder.

3. Inside `lib`, you will find three Jar files: `gral-core-0.10`, `gral-examples-0.10`, and `VectorGraphics2D-0.9.1`. In this recipe, you will be using the first two of the aforementioned Jar files.

4. Include these two Jar files in your project as external libraries.

Now you are ready to use the program included in the GRAL example package to plot area graphs. When you successfully run the code in this recipe, you will see an area plot similar to the following:

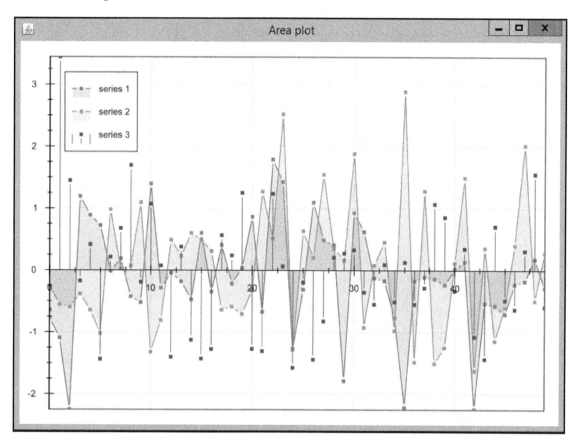

How to do it...

1. First, create a class named `AreaPlot` that extends GRAL's `ExamplePanel`. Provide a serial version UID for your class:

```
public class AreaPlot extends ExamplePanel {
private static final long serialVersionUID =
    3287044991898775949L;
```

2. You will be using random values for plotting the area graph. Therefore, create a class variable for this randomization:

```
private static final Random random = new Random();
```

3. Next, start creating the constructor for the class:

```
public AreaPlot() {
```

4. Create a data table that will hold four data points: one x value and three y values. All the values of your data points for this example will be of the double type:

```
DataTable data = new DataTable(Double.class, Double.class,
    Double.class, Double.class);
```

5. Create a for loop that runs 50 times, starting from the 0.0 value of x and incrementing each time by 1:

```
for (double x = 0.0; x < 50; x ++) {
```

6. Create three y variables to hold the y values. The y values will be randomly generated in the next step from a Gaussian data distribution:

```
y1 = random.nextGaussian();
y2 = random.nextGaussian();
y3 = random.nextGaussian();
```

7. Finally, add the (x, y1, y2, y3) values to your data table and close the for loop:

```
data.add(x, y1, y2, y3);
}
```

For a better graph, you can replace the for loop in steps 5 to 7 with the following code:

```
for (double x=0.0; x<.5*Math.PI; x+=Math.PI/15.0) {
  double y1 = Double.NaN, y2 = Double.NaN, y3 = Double.NaN;
  if (x>=0.00*Math.PI && x<2.25*Math.PI) {
     y1 = 4.0*Math.sin(x + 0.5*Math.PI) +
          0.1*random.nextGaussian();
  }
  if (x>=0.25*Math.PI && x<2.50*Math.PI) {
     y2 = 4.0*Math.cos(x + 0.5*Math.PI) +
          0.1*random.nextGaussian();
  }
  if (x>=0.00*Math.PI && x<2.50*Math.PI) {
```

```
        y3 = 2.0*Math.sin(2.0*x/2.5)          +
            0.1*random.nextGaussian();
    }
        data.add(x, y1, y2, y3);
    }
```

8. Then, add the three sets of data series using GRAL's `DataSeries` class. The class has a constructor that takes the following form:

```
    public DataSeries(DataSource data, int... cols)
```

9. Here, according to GRAL's Java API documentation at http://www.erichseifert.de/dev/gral/0.9/apidocs/de/erichseifert/gral/data/DataSeries.html, the first column will be column 0, the second column 1, and so on, whereas the values of the specified columns is the column number in the data source:

```
    DataSeries data1 = new DataSeries("series 1", data, 0, 1);
    DataSeries data2 = new DataSeries("series 2", data, 0, 2);
    DataSeries data3 = new DataSeries("series 3", data, 0, 3);
```

10. Create an `XYPlot` with three data series. You will be interested in displaying the legends on the graph. Also, set the dimensions of your graph:

```
    XYPlot plot = new XYPlot(data1, data2, data3);
    plot.setLegendVisible(true);
    plot.setInsets(new Insets2D.Double(20.0, 40.0, 20.0, 20.0));
```

11. An added task for area graphs is to fill out the plot area with colors. You will be calling a static method named `formatFilledArea` and `formatLineArea` for this task. See the area graph for the difference between the first two series and the third series:

```
    formatFilledArea(plot, data1, COLOR2);
    formatFilledArea(plot, data2, COLOR1);
    formatLineArea(plot, data3, GraphicsUtils.deriveDarker(COLOR1));
```

12. Add the plot to the Swing component and close the constructor:

```
    add(new InteractivePanel(plot));
    }
```

13. Create a static method to fill the area with a certain color. The method will take the XY plot you have created, the data series, and the color as parameters:

```
private static void formatFilledArea(XYPlot plot, DataSource
    data, Color color) {
```

14. Create a point renderer. Remember that you will be rendering 2D images, and therefore, use the appropriate class. Set the color for the point renderer and set the point renderer with the data series:

```
PointRenderer point = new DefaultPointRenderer2D();
point.setColor(color);
plot.setPointRenderer(data, point);
```

15. Likewise, create a 2D line renderer using GRAL's appropriate class, set the color for the line renderer, and set the gap between the lines to 3.0 points. Next, format the gap to be rounded. Finally, set the line renderer with the data series:

```
LineRenderer line = new DefaultLineRenderer2D();
line.setColor(color);
line.setGap(3.0);
line.setGapRounded(true);
plot.setLineRenderer(data, line);
```

16. After the point and line renderer, you are left with the area renderer. Create a 2D area renderer and set its color. Set the renderer with the data series. Close the method:

```
AreaRenderer area = new DefaultAreaRenderer2D();
area.setColor(GraphicsUtils.deriveWithAlpha(color, 64));
plot.setAreaRenderer(data, area);
}
```

17. Similarly, create a static method to format the line area. The method will take three parameters: the XYPlot that you have created in the constructor, the data series, and the color:

```
private static void formatLineArea(XYPlot plot, DataSource
    data, Color color) {
```

18. Create a 2D point renderer, set the color, and set the renderer with the data series:

```
PointRenderer point = new DefaultPointRenderer2D();
point.setColor(color);
plot.setPointRenderer(data, point);
```

19. You will not be using a line renderer in this method. It will make the third data series look different from the first two data series:

```
plot.setLineRenderer(data, null);
```

20. Just like the previous step, create a 2D area renderer, set the gap of areas, set its color, and set the renderer with the data series:

```
AreaRenderer area = new LineAreaRenderer2D();
area.setGap(3.0);
area.setColor(color);
plot.setAreaRenderer(data, area);
}
```

21. You need to override two methods of the `ExamplePanel` class as follows:

```
@Override
public String getTitle() {
return "Area plot";
}
@Override
public String getDescription() {
return "Area plot of three series with different styling";
}
```

22. To run the preceding code, you need a main method as follows. Close the class afterwards:

```
public static void main(String[] args) {
new AreaPlot().showInFrame();
}
}
```

The complete code for this recipe is as follows:

```
import java.awt.Color;
import java.util.Random;
import de.erichseifert.gral.data.DataSeries;
import de.erichseifert.gral.data.DataSource;
import de.erichseifert.gral.data.DataTable;
import de.erichseifert.gral.examples.ExamplePanel;
import de.erichseifert.gral.plots.XYPlot;
import de.erichseifert.gral.plots.areas.AreaRenderer;
import de.erichseifert.gral.plots.areas.DefaultAreaRenderer2D;
import de.erichseifert.gral.plots.areas.LineAreaRenderer2D;
import de.erichseifert.gral.plots.lines.DefaultLineRenderer2D;
import de.erichseifert.gral.plots.lines.LineRenderer;
```

```java
import de.erichseifert.gral.plots.points.DefaultPointRenderer2D;
import de.erichseifert.gral.plots.points.PointRenderer;
import de.erichseifert.gral.ui.InteractivePanel;
import de.erichseifert.gral.util.GraphicsUtils;
import de.erichseifert.gral.util.Insets2D;

public class AreaPlot extends ExamplePanel {
    /** Version id for serialization. */
    private static final long serialVersionUID = 3287044991898775949L;

    /** Instance to generate random data values. */
    private static final Random random = new Random();

    public AreaPlot() {
        // Generate data
        DataTable data = new DataTable(Double.class, Double.class,
          Double.class, Double.class);
        for (double x = 0.0; x < 50; x ++) {
            double y1 = Double.NaN, y2 = Double.NaN, y3 = Double.NaN;
            y1 = random.nextGaussian();
            y2 = random.nextGaussian();
            y3 = random.nextGaussian();
            data.add(x, y1, y2, y3);
        }

        // Create data series
        DataSeries data1 = new DataSeries("series 1", data, 0, 1);
        DataSeries data2 = new DataSeries("series 2", data, 0, 2);
        DataSeries data3 = new DataSeries("series 3", data, 0, 3);

        // Create new xy-plot
        XYPlot plot = new XYPlot(data1, data2, data3);
        plot.setLegendVisible(true);
        plot.setInsets(new Insets2D.Double(20.0, 40.0, 20.0, 20.0));

        // Format data series
        formatFilledArea(plot, data1, COLOR2);
        formatFilledArea(plot, data2, COLOR1);
        formatLineArea(plot, data3, GraphicsUtils.deriveDarker(COLOR1));

        // Add plot to Swing component
        add(new InteractivePanel(plot));
    }

    private static void formatFilledArea(XYPlot plot, DataSource data,
        Color color) {
        PointRenderer point = new DefaultPointRenderer2D();
        point.setColor(color);
```

```
        plot.setPointRenderer(data, point);
        LineRenderer line = new DefaultLineRenderer2D();
        line.setColor(color);
        line.setGap(3.0);
        line.setGapRounded(true);
        plot.setLineRenderer(data, line);
        AreaRenderer area = new DefaultAreaRenderer2D();
        area.setColor(GraphicsUtils.deriveWithAlpha(color, 64));
        plot.setAreaRenderer(data, area);
    }

    private static void formatLineArea(XYPlot plot, DataSource data,
        Color color) {
        PointRenderer point = new DefaultPointRenderer2D();
        point.setColor(color);
        plot.setPointRenderer(data, point);
        plot.setLineRenderer(data, null);
        AreaRenderer area = new LineAreaRenderer2D();
        area.setGap(3.0);
        area.setColor(color);
        plot.setAreaRenderer(data, area);
    }

    @Override
    public String getTitle() {
        return "Area plot";
    }

    @Override
    public String getDescription() {
        return "Area plot of three series with different styling";
    }

    public static void main(String[] args) {
        new AreaPlot().showInFrame();
    }
}
```

Index

110, 111, 112, 113

www.ingramcontent.com/pod-product-compliance
Lightning Source LLC
Chambersburg PA
CBHW062050050326
40690CB00016B/3040